DANDELIONS

Thea Lenarduzzi is a writer, editor and broadcaster, primarily for the *Times Literary Supplement*. *Dandelions*, winner of the 2020 Fitzcarraldo Editions Essay Prize, is her first book.

'This charmingly candid account of the tensions between an English present and an Italian past is also a fascinating family saga, teeming with idiosyncratic life and bringing with it a chunk of history that still conditions both countries today.'
— Tim Parks, author of *The Hero's Way*

'Local dialects, language and superstition, Mussolini, Red Brigades and the trials of immigration are woven through this captivating family memoir as it chases a home across three generations of movement between Italy and England and back again. Lenarduzzi transmutes conversations with a formidable grandmother into a prose of many textures and inflections, giving us a story that is as as rich as it is gripping.'
— Lisa Appignanesi, author of *Everyday Madness*

'Thea Lenarduzzi has written a profoundly evocative, lyrical meditation on family and kinship in their largest sense. A Natalia Ginzburg-inspired wandering through the life of her grandmother in pre-war Italy and post-war Manchester stimulates an exploration of home, homesickness, home truths, and homecomings. Lenarduzzi has an impressively patient capacity for acts of sustained attention: the dandelion will never be the same again!'
— Lara Feigel, author of *The Group*

'*Dandelions* is a book of hauntings, intensely experienced, pierced by occasional terrors, yet irradiated throughout by passionate attachment. Generations of family ghosts wander between Italy and England, their lives summoned from a beloved grandmother's long memories and the author's own wide-roaming, often poetic reflections on botany, history and language. Thea Lenarduzzi has spread out before us a feast of sensuous and sensitive, nuanced and deeply appealing testimony to migration, survival, and complicated identities at a time when such thoughtfulness is rare and desperately needed.'
— Marina Warner, author of *Inventory of a Life Mislaid*

Fitzcarraldo Editions

DANDELIONS

THEA LENARDUZZI

Per te, Nonna

I.

A woman with a soft brown perm walks slowly through tall grasses, between a Co-op distribution centre and an abandoned warehouse. She is far from Maniago, the small Italian town where she was born, where the plains pucker along the seam of the north-eastern Alps. Her dress – a simple, straight-skirted, below-the-knee affair in muted green polyester with, perhaps, some swirling pattern in a pale yellow – almost blends into the surroundings. You wouldn't spot her but for the occasional glint of a faux gold button on her cuff and the electric pink and blue of her half-apron, with its deep pockets designed to contain the multitudes of needles, threads, thimbles and safety-pins that are the seamstress's tools. She stops at irregular intervals and bends over, almost double, to pinch her fingers around clumps of leaves and delicately, decisively, pluck. As she straightens, she pushes handfuls of green into a bag before continuing on her way.

It's probably mid-morning on a Sunday, not long after Mass at St Robert's Roman Catholic Church on Hamilton Road, where the priest always stops her after the service to thank her for the cake, ask after the boys, or to see if she would like to help with a new family just settling into the area. Any other day, she'd be curved over the sewing machine. The shops are closed so there aren't many people about. Those who are tend to look over with furrowed brows and perhaps a shake of the head, before moving on. They're not sure what this woman is up to – has she lost something? – but they know they wouldn't be caught dead rooting around where stray cats and dogs and Godknowswhat do their business. Now she is alone, but often there is a boy, too – probably no older than twelve, the age at which he starts to think twice about

11

these family customs. His skin is darker than hers, which has its own subtle olive hue, and this causes him grief at school. They have many names for him.

The woman is my grandmother, *mia nonna* – sometimes with my father beside her, tugging awkwardly at the shorts she made him – and she is picking dandelions to go with the evening meal. She bobs and weaves between the flowers' perky heads, dotted like asterisks on a densely annotated page.

This is in Longsight, Manchester, sometime in the late 1950s, and it's one of my prevailing images of Nonna, who is now halfway through her nineties and living back in Maniago. I wasn't there, of course, so it's a kind of fiction implanted through decades of other people's talk. In the family, the story of Nonna collecting dandelions – *tarassaco*, in Italian; *pestonala*, *pissecian* or *radicèla* (derived from *radici*, roots) in the dialects of her native Friuli – has always carried more weight than fact alone. It's like a well-worn fable, a matter-of-fact fairy tale that doesn't accommodate requests for supplementary detail about dates and times, relationships or materials. *Che importa?*, she says, 'What does it matter?'; a question some would extend to whole lives and cultures.

All immigrants have narratives in which the mundane is ripe with symbolism, centred on moments in which the difference between them and us, the natives and the newcomers, are somehow distilled. We recycle abstruse parables, pass them down the generations, and find in them nourishment, confirmation of something never fully articulated. We keep the lines of the stories more or less straight, because embellishment, like questions, only complicates.

We Italians know how good gently wilted *tarassaco* tastes, once tossed with salt, perhaps a splash of vinegar or squeeze of lemon, and the essential olive oil, which, in England, you had to buy from the pharmacy back then (*t'immagini?* Can you imagine?). The British, on the other hand, do not. Dandelion and burdock is one thing, they'd say, picking weeds from a wasteland, something else entirely. So they think we're mad and we think they are – they're missing out. Free food! (That dandelion leaves were once a popular garnish among well-heeled Victorians doesn't quite fit this particular story.)

There isn't a family without such stories, in fact, whether they have travelled hundreds of miles from home or only down the road. They are a means by which outsiders and insiders are distinguished, often protracted in-jokes that acknowledge or test closeness, belonging, heredity. In *Family Lexicon*, Natalia Ginzburg's restrained and radical novel-memoir, published in 1963, the repeated tales and linguistic tics of her relatives trigger in her and her siblings an immediate falling back

> into our old relationships, our childhood, our youth, all inextricably linked to those words and phrases … It takes one word, one sentence, one of the old ones from our childhood, heard and repeated countless times… If my siblings and I were to find ourselves in a dark cave or among millions of people, just one of those phrases or words would immediately allow us to recognize each other.

Experience becomes language becomes story becomes identity, and everyone's place is settled. Each family has its own 'dictionary of our past'.

A couple of summers ago, imagining myself as an archivist of family lore, I sat down with Nonna, a thermos of coffee between us on the kitchen table to forestall our having to get up for more, the blinds pulled down against the late morning sun, and the rest of the family shooed. I had warned her it might take hours – I wanted to start 'at the beginning', meaning her birth, and proceed from there. But no sooner had I tapped the record button on my phone, its mic propped up against a packet of biscuits, than linear time deserted me. Nonna's memory was in full bloom and would not be tamed by anything like conventional narrative structures. Like an excited schoolgirl, her stories began and ended abruptly in mid flow; topics were conjoined indiscriminately, little and large weighted equally. Words and names were left hanging like loose threads, sometimes accompanied by a gesture, a shake or nod of the head, a shrug or sigh, 'Ma Pietro...', 'eh, si...', 'purtroppo...' But Pietro, oh yes, unfortunately.

Some stories, prompted by yellowed photographs released from ancient rubber bands as brittle as dried linguine, took shape in increments. 'He was a local boxer, a friend of a friend,' Nonna said, pointing at one man who towered above her uncles and cousins and their companions, excitedly arranged either side like a billowing cape. 'And,' she placed her finger on one smart, smiling man, 'my father, here.' He seemed Lilliputian by comparison. Nonna knew little more than that the shot was taken outside a nearby restaurant, probably sometime in the early 1930s. The local boxer, I later discovered with the help of the internet, was Primo Carnera, the Ambling Alp, the Vast Venetian, back home on a visit from America. At the time, he was the heavyweight champion of the world, the tallest anyone had seen. In 1931, he made the cover of *Time* magazine. Today he is remembered less for his skill than for his associations – with Benito Mussolini, who saw him as a model of Italian masculinity, and with American mobsters, who took control of his career, and probably his finances, bribed opponents and transformed

14

him into a professional 'monster'. For my family, though, Carnera is a footnote, asterisked in the main story. 'He died. I don't know when.'

*

The dandelion's ubiquity has made it many things to many people. In medieval Christian art, where flowers represent virtues and concepts (a violet for humility, a pansy for remembrance), the dandelion symbolizes Christ's Passion and, for reasons obvious to any tender of lawns, the Resurrection. Each seed, white and wandering, is a ghost of the flower that once was, and an apparition of the flower to come, looking for a place of rest. The leaves are often included in the Passover Seder as *maror*, the 'bitter herbs' mentioned in Exodus, to be eaten alongside lamb and unleavened bread; the acrid taste should recall the suffering of the Jews.

Online, a rich seam of blogs and articles extends the identification between the dandelion and the downtrodden or marginalized. In one case the weed provides a 'simple parable of purpose and self-worth'; elsewhere, its delicate white fuzz is an analogy for the mind transformed by Alzheimer's disease. In an article on *Psychology Today*, Greg O'Brien, a writer and psychologist diagnosed with Early Onset Alzheimer's, recognizes in himself the 'decay of a flowering brain, pollinating the world'. 'What is a weed?' he asks, quoting Ralph Waldo Emerson, but 'a plant whose virtues have not yet been discovered?'. In his late sixties, Emerson himself began to manifest symptoms we would probably now ascribe to the disease – scattered thoughts and forgotten words. Emerson, the man who once described memory as 'a primary and fundamental faculty, without which none other can work; the cement, the bitumen, the matrix in which the other faculties are embedded'.

In literature, too, the dandelion has provided a fertile metaphor. PhD theses may well have been written about garden imagery in *Lolita*, a novel introduced by its green-fingered narrator as a 'tangle of thorns'. The Haze family lives on Lawn Street, where there are 'pubertal surprises in the rose garden' and thwarted attempts to meet in the bushes at night. There's Lolita herself, first spied lolling in the grass, 'my brown flower'. Consider this passage, which comes immediately after Humbert Humbert compares his pure 'nymphet' with her 'coarse', 'ripe' older sister: 'I decided to busy myself with our unkempt lawn. *Une petite attention*. It was crowded with dandelions.' Here, dandelions are a reminder of time pressing on (most of the flowers 'had changed from suns to moons'), and of the inevitable contamination of purity – innocence overgrown with experience. By Humbert Humbert's hand, 'the dandelions perished', a short-lived victory in a futile struggle.

Some months ago, a friend, who had patiently listened to me unpack my newfound interest in the dandelion, sent me a link to a story about John H. Wilson, a criminal court judge in Brooklyn, New York, who in 2006 wrote a children's book in which illegal immigrants are cast as dandelions congregating around a greenhouse. Within the 'beautiful' greenhouse are 'beautiful flowers', 'natives', tended by a 'Master' who feeds them 'only the best food and water[s] them at least once a day with pure, clean, clear water'. The 'jealous' dandelions – who are 'not as healthy. And ... not as happy. And it showed' – seize the chance to project their spores into the greenhouse. They sap the resources, and the natives are divided as to how to deal with the problem: those who would defend their home are criticized by others preaching tolerance, no matter that they too are choking. Finally, the Master returns and cautions his Chosen Ones to fight back. The next wave of seeds are forced to the greenhouse floor where they can't grow. The dandelions are discouraged and desist. We know this rhetoric well. Wilson's impartiality as a judge presiding over immigration cases was called into question.

The judge was not wrong, though, to find sympathy between the dandelion – its head heavy with seeds waiting to catch a breeze, settle, take root – and the migrant. It's a gift of a motif, not least because dandelions, like migrants, 'get everywhere', thriving anywhere but the extremes of the poles. Migrant families tend to characterize themselves by a similar perseverance. In 2000, President Bill Clinton, in a speech at a National Italian American Foundation dinner, lauded Italians' vim and versatility of skill. But what he failed to acknowledge were historic shortcomings and instabilities in the motherland, which made vim and versatility – adaptability – essential. 'An Italian discovered America,' Clinton said, 'another named it.' Others, he might have added, mined it, built it, shaped its constitution, steered its policies, told its stories, sang its songs, made its clothes, played its sports, acted in its films, and ran its favourite restaurants, bars and cafés. (And some, yes, were mobsters and monsters.)

For immigrants, precariousness is always part of the arrangement; the threat of failure stalks them. Success – measured in terms of exceptional contributions – is generally only observed decades or centuries later, once the dust has settled and there is nobody left to remember whether these newcomers were welcomed, tolerated, or chased away. I think of the old childhood rhyme: 'Dandelion, dandelion, tell me pray / must I go

17

home or may I stay?' If all the seeds have been blown off your dandelion by a third puff, breathe easy and unpack your bags.

According to one theory, North America was free of dandelions until the mid-1600s, when the genus was introduced by European migrants who carried seeds in their trunks and pockets, knowing that these would take in whatever ground they encountered and soon grant a steady supply of leaves, for salads and stews as well as various medicines. Nonna, too, describes them as a 'cure', self-prescribed for almost any ailment. Another theory has Native Americans using and enjoying the plant long before the first European ships arrived.

Dandelions appear to thrive best in the Mediterranean climate but do very well on the fringes of the tropics and in Central America. Still, whatever the origin, rather than see the dandelion as a resilient golden wonder, people persist in considering it an invader of otherwise pure spaces. The definition of a weed: wild plants that grow where they are not wanted and compete with, and so threaten, the native or cultivated plants. It may seem paradoxical, but if a person is weedy, he or she is feeble, physically inferior, probably dependent on the strength or kindness of others.

The thing about dandelions is they take care of themselves. Once seeds have dropped – sometimes as far as 500 miles from where they began, thanks to a method of flight so complicated that it was only recently discovered – they self-fertilize through *apomixis*, a compound of the Greek for 'away from' and 'mixing'. This gives rise to hundreds of microspecies of dandelion, each varying slightly depending on the ground in which the seed finds itself. There are 229 microspecies in the British Isles alone, so any given patch of earth can contain dozens of identical-looking flowers, each one distinct but indistinguishable from its parent. This makes it all but impossible to determine matters such as which came first, and there's something rare and liberating in that.

The Italian *tarassaco* derives from *Taraxacum*, whose origins are thought to lie in the Persian *tarashqum*, meaning 'bitter herb'. From that comes the Greek *tarasso*: to agitate, trouble the mind, confound, disturb. After these come the countless common names of which dandelion is only the best known. In English: Irish daisy, blowball, milk-witch, cankerwort, yellow-gowan, monks-head, priest's-crown, swine's snout. For Oliver Sacks, in his *Oaxaca Journal*, they are 'DYCs': 'damn yellow composites'. The French, as well as offering the British words to mangle ('dandelion': *dent de lion*, lion's tooth, named for the jagged leaves), also gave us *pis-en-lit*, wet-the-bed. This does at least credit the plant's medicinal powers as a diuretic and laxative, albeit with effects that might catch one disastrously off-guard.

Against all evidence, we teach children that blowing on a moon-headed dandelion will reveal time's progress: each puff needed to dislodge the seeds denotes one hour. 'Dandelion, dandelion, tell me pray...' The same action is said to grant wishes, or to carry thoughts to loved ones who exist in memory alone, whether because they are distant or dead. Everywhere dandelions take root these myths come up with them. Lately, science has brought its heft to bear, with research in mice suggesting a link between increased levels of chicoric acid, present in dandelions and other bitter-leaf plants, and a reduction of memory impairment of the sort associated with Alzheimer's disease. Did those seed-carrying travellers sense something of this?

*

If words and stories bind, they can divide and isolate too. An immigrant can spend as much time as she likes memorizing basic vocabulary, but her first word is likely to betray her roots: for Italians, there is no getting around the difficult aspirated 'h' of *hello* – they drop it, unless they are Tuscan, in which case they might overdo it. The English 'r', being flat, or entirely silent, can be problematic too, for a people used to rolling it with brio. For Italians trying to settle in France and Belgium after the Second World War, the 'r' became an alarm bell (again, cruelly present from the first *bonjour*). In the native argot, Italian immigrants are *les ritals*, a pejorative that runs together *réfugié* and *italien* and hinges on the outsiders trilling their 'r' on the tip of the tongue rather than at the back, *à la française*. It's the ultimate in-joke: *les ritals* can't even pronounce what they are.

Pronunciation plays a crucial role in the taxonomy of people, and anomalies trouble the mind. Always you will be asked for your story: after (the accent twigged) 'Where are you from?' comes 'And what brings you here?' – because, so the thinking goes, this story defines the individual, for better or for worse. You are the embodiment of your story and if people don't know the beginning or middle, how can they predict the end? May you stay? Must you go? You will probably have a long version and a short version and both will, over time, be well rehearsed. The aim is, generally, to help your listener place you without too much difficulty.

Your name may present another obstacle. Nonna's is Dirce. It is not, and has never been, a common name. If we ignore the rolled 'r' for the moment, one might pronounce the first syllable roughly like the dir- of 'dirt', the second like the cha- of 'change'. It's too neat, maybe, but it's true. Sometimes the truth is neat; more often, it's not.

When Dirce arrived in Manchester in 1950, she told me as we sat in her kitchen, no one could pronounce her name; it's true that the sound doesn't seem to belong in the English mouth. (She might have fared better in Scotland, I suggested.) The well-educated could have taken a punt, drawing on the Greek enchantress and gardener Circe, which would at least have been correct etymologically speaking. And yet what kind of parents would name their child after Queen Dirce of Thebes, a figure famous for jealously mistreating a vulnerable pregnant woman?

Here's how that story goes: After she is impregnated by Zeus, the beautiful Amazonian Antiope, crippled with shame, seeks sanctuary from King Epopeus of Sicyon. But Lycus, King of Thebes, captures her and, on the road back to the city, she goes into labour. Twin boys, Amphion and Zethus, are born, and abandoned in a cave while their bereft mother is imprisoned at the whim of Lycus' wife Dirce, her aunt and a devotee of that celestial drunk, Dionysus. But Antiope eventually escapes and returns to the cave in search of her lost sons (who do not, at first, recognize her – *t'immagini?*). Amphion and Zethus, outraged at the Queen's treatment of their mother, take their revenge: Dirce is strapped to the horns of a rampant bull and gorged and tossed and traipsed to death. A spring is said to have bubbled up from the earth at the site where she drew her last breath, a gift of recognition from her god.

When I told Nonna about this Dirce, she was horrified.

There is another Dirce, a lesser-known twin, whose story speaks of Christian virtue, of persecution and martyrdom. I found her, quite by accident, a few weeks later, in an enormous and dramatic historical painting by the nineteenth-century Polish artist Henryk Siemiradzki. The scene captures the bloody aftermath of a Roman spectacle, a real-life recreation of the Greek myth commissioned by Emperor Nero, who stands in the foreground, tugging his robes away from the carnage he demanded. Tangled in ropes decorated with flowers lie a slain black bull and a beautiful young Dirce, her naked skin as white as marble – a Christian expended as a prop. From the gallery, Roman citizens peer down on the entertainment, their faces inscrutable. *Was this for us?*

If either of these references struck a chord with Nonna's parents, it seems more likely to have been the second, picked up from the priest, perhaps, who was a regular at their table. Or maybe her father, Angelo, a pale-skinned, fair-haired man whose physique showed the signs of childhood polio, discovered the name in one of the books from which he read to the family in the evenings.

When I asked Nonna over the phone some months after our first *intervista*, she was eager to confirm this theory, gushing about Angelo's love of books. 'Just like you', she said, 'you get it from us.' The notion flowered somewhere in my chest.

Angelo adored stories of adventure, passion and tragedy, and anything by the Risorgimento-era author Silvio Pellico, who was, in truth, a far better patriot than storyteller (though the skills are closely related). Another favourite, Nonna told me, was the story of Fabiola, the ascetic patron saint of the widowed. This last one Angelo told on an almost nightly basis, and, with hindsight, this could seem ominous.

Two other roots for Dirce are 'cleft' and 'dual', and – Nonna told me in the kitchen – she has lived two lives, the first of which ended when an early attempt to leave Maniago for England failed abruptly. It was 1935, the

Great Depression was dragging on and Mussolini's government had taken control of around 75 per cent of Italy's businesses, a light touch compared to the policies that would soon follow. Underway were various domestic *battaglie*, as the Fascists liked to call them – battles for births, grain, land, the lira – as well as brash international manoeuvres, which were leading, as Dirce and her mother Novella packed the family's bags, to the Second Italo-Ethiopian War. Angelo had dodged the draft because of his slightly bowed legs and weak chest, but this had only rearranged the stakes.

And so, she said, he played his *briscola*, his trump card: England. He had family in Sheffield and Manchester, an uncle, *zio* Gioacchino, who told him there were opportunities – his tile and terrazzo firm had secured contracts with department stores and churches up and down the country, there was almost too much work!

Angelo would have heard of other local men who stayed in Italy but took their families south, to grand new cities that Mussolini was raising from the mud. They said the land was so fertile it was unreal and that the malaria was under control. *They said.* I imagine Angelo looking at Dirce and her younger brother Pietro, and then remembering the first son, Manlio, born in between and lost to a quick, violent fever.

That autumn, as the Regia Aeronautica dropped propaganda leaflets over Ethiopia promising Italian colonizers that help was on its way, the family threw in their lot with the millions of others who had fled the motherland.

'Nonna, listen, did you know that something like a quarter of the national population had already gone by then? I read that –'

'Ci credo,' 'I believe it,' she said, apparently uninterested in the wider picture.

'Ascolta', listen: Two months after the family's arrival – and as suddenly as this kind of story always has it – Angelo 'dies of rheumatic fever'. Days before Christmas, Nonna recalled, 'he comes back from the shops with a headache, a train set for Pietro, and a promise that he'll go back to find something extra special for me, as soon as he feels better'. She told me this with a mixture of sadness and pride in her voice. The injustice pitches her into an eternal present tense.

When he died five days later, he was thirty-three years old, a rare detail in the family gospel, thick with Christian coincidence. ('Trente-tre, anni di Cristo!' as they say in *tombola*, the quintessential game of chance.) Dirce's mother Novella, who had not had time to acquire much English, managed only a few months before returning the family to the old house in Italy. A new beginning had turned into an end, and who knows if the story of the good widow Fabiola held any comfort for Novella then.

'After *papà*, there were no more books,' said Nonna, as we nursed the last of the coffee. '*Mia mamma* forbade reading – I should always be working, doing this or that, sewing, scrubbing, washing, gathering firewood or *tarassaco*.' She was staring at the tablecloth as she spoke, tracing a finger around its hectic floral design. 'No more reading...' – she looked up – 'except in secret.' Her eyes sparkled.

'And the second life?' I asked, knowing the answer already.

It began in 1950, Nonna said, when, aged twenty-four, she arrived in England, this time with her mother and a two-year-old son, Manlio, named for the brother she couldn't remember. Leonardo, her husband, followed them soon after. She had heard Angelo calling her back to Sheffield, she said, where he was buried. 'He wanted

24

me near him.'

On some level, she had always known she would try again to settle in England. It was only ever a matter of when, and if pre-Second World War Friuli had been tough, post-War Friuli was in some respects tougher. The local industry, based almost entirely on steel, had been decimated, and the knife factory where Leo ('nobody called him Leonardo') worked was withholding pay. Sheffield represented a kind of parallel universe, a promised land inhabited by Angelo, her guardian angel, in which a way of life moribund in Maniago flourished.

And so, she went. When I think of her making the journey, with cardboard suitcase and child in hand, I picture her how she is now, silvered and stooped by age. And I hear whispers from a poem by Alice Oswald, 'Head of a Dandelion', in which disdain for the obstinate weed is challenged by an image of unreasonable strength.

This is the dandelion with its thousand faculties

like an old woman taken by the neck
and shaken to pieces.

This is the dust-flower flitting away.

This is the flower of amnesia.
It has opened its head to the wind,
all havoc and weakness,

as if a wooden man should stroll through fire...

The dandelion-woman knows she will be blown apart by exposure, reduced to 'one recalcitrant element', but still she goes. What is that final element? Tenacity, maybe.

By the poem's end a transformation has taken place. A simile, slipped in with the casual certainty of someone explaining that night follows day, alerts us to the tremendous change: old dandelion-woman has risen to sit alongside the mighty Osiris, whose green-tinged skin speaks of fertility and the muddy banks of the Nile. Osiris, Lord of the dead and the living, who 'blows his scales and weighs the soul with a feather'. She has crossed over.

'I have so many stories from that life, *nina*, so many.' *Nina*, short for *bambina* – a diminutive of a diminutive, which to her I will always be.

I could feel the pressure of them that day. I remember that as she spoke she raised both hands as if in surrender, or blessing, before almost slapping them down on the table.

'That's what I'm here for,' I told her.

Weeks later, back in England, I read about the British Ministry for Labour's Official Italian Scheme, which started in 1949, aimed at boosting the workforce in foundries, mills and other industries. Skilled foreign workers like my *nonni* had been in demand, if not unreservedly welcome. In *Lovers and Strangers: An immigrant history of post-War Britain*, a well-thumbed copy of which has become a permanent fixture on my bedside table, Clair Wills describes how all migrant workers were deemed 'socially suspect' – particularly Italians. She quotes a Home Office official:

> I have been given to understand that the order of intake of foreign labour is approximately Poles, Balts, Ukrainians, other Dps, Volksdeutsche, Italians and finally Germans. I have never been at all happy about the proposal to take in male Italians in preference to Germans ... The Home Office experience suggests that Italian immigrants do not,

generally speaking, make any valuable contribution to the economy of the country.

There was also, Wills explains, some concern over their 'Latin' ways, their 'sex appeal', which they said corrupted British women and girls. There were plenty of stories doing the rounds.

I made notes, jotted down questions, and arranged to telephone Nonna every Friday until she had told me 'tutto', everything.

*

A few years ago, I began to notice the dandelion fountains – water features consisting in tens of stalks each spraying fine mist to form large hazy orbs – in city parks, outside office blocks or banks, sometimes in the lobbies of big businesses. Ubiquitous and unremarkable. The US has examples in abundance, in California, Texas and Minneapolis, Kentucky, Illinois and Pennsylvania – there are two at the base of the Alliance Bernstein building in New York City, a prime location on Avenue of the Americas. (Isn't it neat, that this country built by immigrants should be dotted with monumental dandelions, as though dropped from the pockets of new arrivals?) The fountains are, though, a global phenomenon – there's a dandelion in Christ Church, New Zealand, and Guangzhou Shi, China, and others in Romania and Ukraine and Poland. Closer to home, there's one on a roundabout in Nuneaton, Warwickshire. When, in 2016, another was unveiled in Windsor, it was compared to an outsized toilet brush.

The original designer is difficult to trace, and yet something about the apparent banality of the fountains made me want to try. Having plucked one in Houston, Texas, from a line-up, I sent William Cannady, a professor at Rice University School of Architecture and that fountain's designer, an email.

Cannady's version, in the middle of Buffalo Bayou Park, was, he explained, commissioned in 1978 by Mayor Fred Hofheinz on behalf of a Mrs Wortham, whose husband, Gus S. Wortham – a man of local if not national significance as the founder, in 1926, of the American General Life Insurance Company – had died two years earlier. (His obituary in the *New York Times* bears quoting: 'A native of Mexia, Tex.; Mr. Wortham left home in 1911 to punch cattle in the Texas Panhandle for $25 a month. He came to Houston in 1915 and retired 57 years later a multimillionaire.') Mrs Wortham was herself frail, so speed was crucial. The brief, Cannady told me, was concise: 'She had mentioned to the mayor that she and Gus had seen a fountain in Australia and gave him a photograph of the fountain.' The request was, then, to create a twin.

The Australian dandelion was the work of Robert Woodward, a Sydney-based architect who, in 1959, some twenty years before Cannady's commission, had won a design competition held by the City Council to construct a fountain in Fitzroy Gardens, Kings Cross, to commemorate the involvement of the 9th Division of the Australian Infantry Forces at El Alamein in 1942. When he won the project, the young Woodward was not long back from a tour of Europe and a spell working under Alvar Aalto, 'the architectural god of Finland', as Woodward put it in an interview in 1972.

In 'The Trout and the Stream' (1947), an essay on the role of intuition in architecture, with which Woodward was surely familiar, Aalto wrote:

28

> I simply draw by instinct, not architectural syntheses, but what are sometimes quite childlike compositions, and in this way, on an abstract basis, the main idea gradually takes shape, a kind of universal substance that helps me to bring the numerous contradictory components into harmony.

Woodward's vision of delicate bronze stems and water at the whim of the wind, revealed to the public on 18 November 1961, reflects his mentor's ideal of the man-made set in an ecosystem forever in flux. In another interview given in 1996, when Woodward was in his seventies, he recalled being inspired by 'an old photograph of a dandelion'. 'You don't draw from nature,' he says, 'so much as nature imposes itself upon you.'

Woodward was not the first to consider the humble dandelion worthy of attention – of art, even. I have printed out the sombre mid-eighteenth-century studies of Barbara Regina Dietzsch and pinned them on a corkboard beside Jean-François Millet's drooping specimens from a century later, Monet's plump orbs, and Van Gogh's snowy heads, bobbing in the overgrown gardens of the Saint-Paul Asylum. But it seems fair to credit the architect as the first to globalize the concept. An article in the *Australasian Post* boasted:

> It is probably one of the most beautiful man-made things in the land ... people from all parts of the world have asked, "Who dreamed it up?" And they're still asking. The designer is an Australian, Mr Robert Raymond Woodward, and the fountain has made him famous.

Not bad for a toilet brush. By the late 1970s, the Australian *Bulletin* could claim 'at last count 72 American companies were manufacturing it in seven different sizes and exporting it worldwide, making it probably the world's most copied fountain.' Indeed, Mr and Mrs Wortham were so struck by the late modernist creation that they captured it on film and carried it back to Texas, where, years later, it grew into something distinct and virtually indistinguishable.

There is, though, the matter of Harry Bertoia, the American sculptor perhaps best known for his Diamond chair – a now iconic example of mid-century design, with its gently scooped seat, a lattice of steel and air – produced while working for the design firm Knoll International in the early 1950s. (It was Bertoia rather than Woodward who sprang to Cannady's mind on seeing the Worthams' photograph.) So pleased was Knoll with Bertoia's work that the company awarded him $10,000 to – as his daughter Celia Bertoia put it to me – 'pursue art in any manner he desired'. So, in early spring 1957, Bertoia set off for Italy.

It was a homecoming of sorts. My heart fluttered when I learnt that Bertoia was born about 30 kilometres from Nonna's house, in 1915, and that the small *frazione* of San Lorenzo is still full of his relatives. Such coincidences seem to me to combine the solidity of fact with some higher, intangible meaning. ('Go on,' I hear them say, 'now you're getting somewhere.') Around the same time as Angelo started to wring his hands and plan the family's departure from Maniago, Bertoia, aged fifteen, left San Lorenzo to join his older brother in America. That's where this man's story cleaved in two, and Arri, as he was christened, was anglicized to Harry. 'Harry': of Proto-Germanic origin. *Harjon*: to ravage or overrun.

For Arri, dictatorship and drought had made Italy inhospitable, unworkable, barren; decades later, Harry found literal and figurative fields of gold. By the late

1950s, the *miracolo* or *boom economico* that Dirce and Leo couldn't possibly have seen coming, as they packed their bags at the start of the decade, was well underway. Whole industries had burst back to life. The forges were burning again, and the country, it seemed, had grown from darkness into light.

Like countless visitors, Bertoia was, his daughter says, 'inspired by sunny Italy with all its energy'. And immediately on his return to the US 'he began to do his first versions of dandelions'. He 'felt so much energy ... that he was compelled to make shapes of explosive spheres'. ('We refer to them as sunbursts.') Bertoia's first dandelion was commissioned for the US pavilion at the World's Fair in Brussels, in 1958. At first, Celia explains, they were 'rugged and brutal', becoming softer and 'more refined' in the 1960s, and by the time the World's Fair came to New York in 1964, Bertoia was integrating them with water.

Had Woodward seen Bertoia's earliest efforts before pitching his own design? Did Bertoia draw inspiration from Woodward's softer lines and use of water for his later work? Had the two men even heard of each other? *Che importa?* The story of the dandelion fountain is a fuzz of maybes and alsos that carry this way and that, the significance of each developed according to time and place, by a kind of *apomixis*. These memorials to mourned husbands, decisive battles or life-changing trips can mean something or nothing at all, depending on who you ask. They are studded into the fabric of towns and cities, where we pass them every day and might not notice them at all – except, perhaps, for a glint in the corner of the eye, as the sun turns the water gold. At the heart of each a recalcitrant element holds fast. Time may pass, it seems to say, but this much I know.

*

Stories teach us how to be, how to see each other, in the same way that memorials teach us who, what and how to remember. Everything rides on the telling, and there has always been a preference for smoothness, a progression from beginning to middle to end. Deviation and digression are discouraged, flashbacks and flash-forwards difficult to pull off. In my notebook I have written out a passage from E. M. Forster's essay 'Aspects of the Novel', in which he bemoans the novelist's need – but surely also the reader's – for an ending:

'Why is this necessary? Why is there not a convention which allows a novelist to stop as soon as he feels muddled or bored? Alas, he has to round things off, and usually the characters go dead while he is at work.'

I have surrounded the words with a constellation of asterisks, to draw the eye.

I am aware, in myself, of this desire to trim and tidy. I must be on guard.

Beneath Forster, I have Joan Didion's famous lines:

'We live entirely, especially if we are writers, by the imposition of a narrative line upon disparate images, by the "ideas" with which we have learned to freeze the shifting phantasmagoria which is our actual experience'.

This, I have asterisked and highlighted in fiery orange.

To trim and tidy experience – the job of memory – is especially risky. Details might be skipped, qualifications muted, connected stories overlooked in favour of a single thread. Behind the teller's choices, conscious or otherwise, lies some kind of motivation, whether to entertain, to store for posterity or to promote a particular image of herself. I wonder about Nonna's motivations, and my own. As with the dandelion, one may try to pull up the

32

entire plant – 'tell me your story, Nonna' – but roots remain, and continue to branch off into the fertile darkness. An individual is composed of these filaments, too, and a family is the sum of its stunted, subterranean stories.

In the kitchen in Maniago tens of these strays came to light all at once, vivid and without order: the time Leo serenaded Dirce without ever having seen her; a rainstorm followed by a crazy fever; a bike ride and all the young men with swastika armbands; the time she didn't kiss her father goodbye because 'he didn't look like himself'; his death ('once upon a time there was destiny and you died'); Christmas presents never unwrapped; the night the music played on and on because Leo knew the band; the time Nonna's paternal grandfather, 'il primo Pietro', the first Pietro, 'built like Hercules', died alone in Barrow-in-Furness, after being crushed by the central beam of a house he was building; the day, during the war, when Leo found a dead man in the road; the night he burrowed under the corn stacks to hide from SS officers in search of recruits. This was also when an earwig crawled into his ear and left him deaf – a story I believed for much longer than I will admit.

There were apparitions that shook the bed; recurring dreams in which three large black birds fell from the sky; an aunt who placed her dead baby in a basket strung up in the rafters, while she waited for its twin to die of the same pneumonia ('coffins were expensive'); a beautiful orange company car; and *zio* Gioacchino in Sheffield, who received a commendation in a national Italian newspaper for his services to Fascism. 'He was a kind man.'

The intensity of Nonna's talk was such that a part of me worried about what I had started. What could this great opening-up do to someone so advanced in her years? I thought again of the dandelion-woman, her head thrust out to the wind, all havoc and weakness and will.

'And let me tell you this one,' Nonna said: when she was 'quasi ma non donna' – nearly but not yet a woman – an older man, 'too old', came to see her every Sunday and gave her a large, round, gold brooch.

'Ascolta questa', listen to this one: there were two heart attacks hidden from the factory boss.

'And this one': an adopted daughter, 'a gift from God', who chooses not to hear the story of her own beginnings. That particular tale is written down and tucked inside an envelope, in a place I am not allowed to describe. ('You mustn't forget where. Keep it for her, for when I'm gone.')

'And, *ascolta*, this is what happened': Leo did night shifts in the McVitie's biscuit factory; there was a cousin who anglicized the family name and set up a flooring company with the motto 'We excel' ('because we did'); the time Nonna made £100 ('!') in three weeks doing piecework at the kitchen table; there were shifts at the Senior Service cigarette warehouse; a nervous breakdown, at the resonant age of thirty-three. The nurse's description of electric shock treatment was so matter-of-fact.

This was 'before... no, *after*' a difficult third pregnancy, when, in labour, Dirce shouted 'Basta' ('enough') and the English nurses heard 'Bastard'.

Nonna who now, with what little English she has left, says 'i'n't it' like a true Mancunian.

The baby, born dead, was called Anthony, the patron saint of lost things. He was buried in Sheffield City Road Cemetery, in the same grave as Angelo and Old Pietro. Lost by the living and found by the dead.

Sometimes Nonna began a line and petered off... 'Ah, no, no, non mi ricordo', she didn't remember. She got up and moved things around on the stove, walked over to the cupboard above the television, hesitated, came back to me. 'Ascolta, ascolta...' And so it went on, stories like countless seeds held in fragile tension, their potential fuzzy and utterly exposed.

I did not tell her that she had told me almost all these stores before, only I hadn't really listened the other times. Repetition had dulled my senses and curiosity had waned. This is how we make myths, both unverifiable and somehow truer than true. Like Ginzburg hearing a family tale for the umpteenth time, I had always allowed my focus to soften and carry me back to the warmth of known things. For my thirty-odd years, Nonna's stories had been a comforting background noise, like water steadily following its course outside the house in which I lived. Now, the house receded, and I felt a new freshness on my face. I lay in the long grass, with an ear to the stream.

*

There will be no end, nor even a moral. I could never promise such things. But in Nonna's narrative entropy, in the phantasmagoria of her memory as it played out across the kitchen table and, later, down the phone, and as I listen to recordings now, there is, for me, something glinting in the thicket.

If, for Alice Oswald, there is sympathy between the mind of an old woman, with its thousand scattered faculties, and the head of a dandelion in its lunar phase, there is something childlike there, too, reminiscent of Charles Baudelaire's description of the child's special way of absorbing the world all at once. I see it in Nonna's limpid eyes, in the way she interrupts me without apology, giggles or visibly sags at a memory, and feels everything all over again, apparently unselfconsciously.

'The child sees everything in a state of newness,'

Baudelaire said, 'he is always drunk.' And drunks, we know, see double. Theirs is a world of fragments and ambiguity, of maybes and alsos, highs and lows, and quick inversions, in which pain and comfort are two sides of the same coin.

Everything has the potential to become its opposite. Nonna has played cards for most of her life; she knows how things can turn, just like that. A winner can become a loser, or a nobody a somebody – it is possible, in fact, to be both at once. A dandelion is a golden priest's crown but also a damn yellow composite, a contaminant but also a tonic.

Remember Alvar Aalto, who in his childlike architectural compositions strove to tap into the curious harmony beneath such apparent contradictions. Why select from the phantasmagoria if wild simultaneity is our best chance of comprehending a life, a family, a country, a history? You don't draw from nature so much as nature imposes itself on you.

*

'Basta,' said Nonna. Hours had passed and everyone was ready to eat.

'Can I do anything?' I asked, knowing the answer.

'Tutto a posto' – everything is fine or, literally, everything is in its place, where it should be. Except for the people. My aunt, *zia* Lucia, was racing around because she only gets an hour's break from the factory, where she is a nurse, on hand for workers' aches and pains. My dad was checking the football results to see how his beloved Manchester City was doing. *Zio* Giuseppe was in the *cantina* re-touching photographs of the region's mountains. My cousins in their attic rooms were studying geometry or scrolling through other people's lives. Old *zio* Orfeo, my nonno's only surviving sibling, was chopping logs next door. My sister Helen, on the terrace, was marvelling at Nonna's tomato plants, while my mum read out headlines from the British news on her iPad and despaired.

'Tell everyone to take their places', said Nonna, waving a hand in the direction of the table outside on *zia* Lucia's veranda.

'A tavola!' To the table.

A scattering in reverse, like steel shavings drawn to a magnet.

Here, the pattern is the same every time. The men go to the far end, so they can talk in thick dialect about work, the economy, politics, the General State of Things. My cousins sit by the door, ready to make a quick getaway to meet friends as soon as the meal is over. *Zia* Lucia settles near them, getting her fill of her children. My own mum sits about halfway along, counting out colourful paper napkins no one will use. And Nonna takes her place at the head of the table, so that she can see us all set out before her, watch us picking up dishes and passing them around, reaching over, swapping, dipping, serving each other. My sister and I position ourselves to her left and right, as close as her shadow, ready to top up her glass or dash back to the kitchen for whatever tablet she has forgotten this time, for her head, heart, stomach, blood.

Everything in its place. A most exalted state, reached on the dot of noon. A minor miracle. The *tarassaco* will have been collected in the morning and passed over to *zia* Lucia, whose bright yellow house springs from the side of Nonna's. She wilts and dresses the leaves the way her mother taught her. And now the heavy dish can make its way from hand to hand, each of us automatically looking up to see who has yet to claim a share. Eventually it will reach the men, where one of them will do the final honours and wipe a crust around the sides thinly gilded with oil. This used to be Nonno's prerogative; now it goes, unspoken, to whichever of his sons is around to claim it. After them, who knows.

All the while more stories will bubble up, about us or about others, and sometimes you hear the beginning, sometimes the middle and other times the end, as they leap from multiple mouths and clamour for air. *Listen to this one. Wait, let me tell you. It was like this. Did I tell you about the time. T'immagini?*

And someone, perhaps me, will tell the one about Nonna stooping behind an abandoned warehouse in Manchester to gather dandelions.

The looks she got!

But aren't they good – bitter and delicious – once seasoned to taste?

II.

On 21 September 1926, sometime after five in the evening, a cherry-red seaplane travelling at great speed circled a few times over Lake Varese, a minor lake in Lombardy's lake district, rose up as if to spear the sun and then nose-dived into the water. The plane's twenty-six-year-old pilot, the Genovese aristocrat and renowned military airman Vittorio Centurione Scotto, was killed, presumably on impact. They say that when they retrieved his body two hours later, there was a single scratch on his chin.

Scotto had been training for a popular annual race for seaplanes, the Schneider Trophy, founded in 1913 to encourage and celebrate aviation innovation. Competing nations took it in turns to host the event and every year hundreds of thousands gathered to marvel at the latest flying machines. By 1926, however, the Schneider had a more serious undercurrent. National governments, in particular Mussolini's, were increasingly invested – financially, psychologically, spiritually – in the aviation industry, and the races were now implicitly a testing ground for machines that would meet again in war.

The 1926[1] Schneider was to be held in Norfolk, Virginia, with Britain, Italy and the United States as the leading contenders. Apparently, Il Duce, determined to win after three losses in a row and no wins at all during his reign, had himself selected Scotto for the team. As the pilot hit the water that September, just one month before the competition, Mussolini's heart sank with him.

On the same day, about 300 kilometres away in the

1   1926: the year of my nonna's birth; the year it officially became
    a crime against the Italian State to oppose Fascism; and the year
    Violet Gibson, a middle-aged Anglo-Irish aristocrat living in
    Rome, cloaked herself in black, slipped through crowds of loyal
    fascists, and fired two point-blank shots at Mussolini, one of which
    scratched his nose. 'Una sciocchezza,' he said. 'A trifle.'

Cinque Terre, south of Genoa, a woman slipped on the edge of a cliff and caught herself in the nick of time. So one story goes. The woman – Amalia Liana Negretti Odescalchi, born in 1897 to a family of faded aristocrats near Como – was in the area looking to persuade her estranged husband, the decorated Marine officer *marchese* Pompeo Cambiasi, almost twenty years her senior, to annul their marriage. She had not long had his child, but there was nothing else between them. For the past two years, in fact, Liana, as she was then known, had been in love with Scotto.

Scotto's death set this woman on an unexpected course: soon she would be adored by generations of Italian women as 'Liala', the author of lush and racy romances between vigorous patriotic men and perfectly poised young ladies. Liala remains one of the most successful writers Italy has known.

I saw Scotto's lake almost every day growing up. If it was dark in the morning as I set off for school, I'd catch a glimpse on the way home, through the smudgy window of the bus, or over my shoulder as I traipsed up the garden, too hungry and burdened by homework to stop. At weekends, my mum and I would take our Labrador, Amber – extravagantly golden, a canine Marilyn Monroe – for a walk around the water's edge. When Amber dunked her head and blew bubbles in the shallows, I don't remember worrying about pollution – algal toxins, phosphorus, a sewage system in disrepair – but in recent years the lake has come to be known almost as much for its seemingly irreversible toxicity as for its beauty. Not dissimilar to poor Amber, whose beauty turned out to be the result of incest.

Then, I had no idea of the drama that had taken place there. Nor did I imagine, as I do now, a subaqueous cemetery of Icarian contraptions in the lake's depths, with

Scotto's plane lying alongside tens of others, launched before and after from the modest airstrip on the north side of the lake. Romeo Sartori, the aerobat and First World War veteran who designed the machine Scotto was flying, repeated the fatal trajectory himself just seven years later.

From our house on the opposite side of the water, my family still watches planes take off from the private airstrip, small white acrobats, doing loops, screwdriver drops and rolling free-falls. In spite of my reasoning that historical wreckages must have been recovered in order for their final moments to be scrutinized, a ghostly image perseveres. It seems especially dramatic – humiliating, even – that something destined for the heavens should be condemned to such murky green lows.

You can see something almost every day without guessing how many stories it has to tell. Not secrets, necessarily, but things you never knew to look for.

*

'Who was your favourite writer when you were young?' I ask Nonna one day over the phone, fingers hovering on zombie arms over an open laptop, ready to take notes.

'The usual things,' she says, distracted. 'Fairy tales'. *Roba da bimbe*, little-girl stuff.

'I mean, when you were a bit older?' I can't believe I've never asked her the question.

'Liala,' she says, without missing a beat. 'Appassionatamente.' Passionately.

I pause, deciding how to proceed, which version of myself to be.

'Sai chi è?' 'You know who she is?' Nonna asks.

'Of course,' I say. 'I've never read any though.'

'You'd like her. Beautiful stories. About aviators.'

41

Not my sort of thing. *Appassionatamente* not. But I don't say this. Instead: 'Ah, si, forse...', maybe.

I type 'Liala libri più belli' – 'Liala best books' – into a search engine.

'What did you look for in a book?' I ask.

'Stories about families, about love and intimacy – never anything instructive, though, nothing difficult. There wasn't the time.'

We know this plot line well. Her mother Novella would not let her read when there were chores to be done. (There were always chores to be done.) Reading was for young Dirce a matter of fragments snatched, when her mother was out or asleep; in the stable, if the cow had been especially efficient during milking; or on the loo.

(*Non lo mettere questo*, 'don't put that in'; 'Why not? It's part of the story'; 'OK, fine, *metti, metti...*')

Dirce would hide a book up the front of her top, tucked into her waistband to stop it dancing around. She remembers how the cover felt cool against her skin, soon warming up and sticking to her stomach. At a moment's notice she would pull it out and then pages would go by in a frenzy. Always she would keep one ear tuned to the everyday frequency of gravel underfoot, door-hinge, loose floorboard.

'Did you read to escape, do you think?' I ask, clunkily, because that's what they say about romance novels. Pure escapism, simple diversions for frustrated *sartine*, 'little seamstresses'.

'Of course!'

I imagine Dirce, neither fully immersed in the fiction nor wholly grounded in the reality, bridging the divide between the spectacular dream logic of romance and that of a humdrum existence as a half-orphan in a backwater town.

By the time I put down the phone, I have bought a copy of Liala's first novel, *Signorsì*, published in 1931. It is set around my lake, 'a delicious little lake of lovers'.

*

When, around Easter 1936, the nine-year-old Dirce returned with her mother and younger brother Pietro to the old house in Maniago, her world had been rearranged, its horizons reduced, and her feelings numbed. Her father Angelo's unexpected death in England in December of the previous year had left the family all but penniless. Money may not have been abundant before Angelo's death, but what little actual capital they possessed had always been attached, it seems, to an inherited sense of social elevation.

I can find no documents – no land deeds or registers – to substantiate Nonna's repeated claims that her father came from one of the 'four great families of Maniago', with 'il nome alto' (a high name). It may be so. But on leaving for England, he was unemployed, having refused to take a job in a factory. Before that, he had kept the books at the local cooperative – badly, given his benevolent habit of letting people off the hook. Still, they called him *il controllore*, the controller. He was also, I am forever told, an insatiable reader, as well as an amateur photographer and horticulturalist.

Whatever the social 'height' of this man, it is undoubtable that his death had social implications: with Angelo's veneer of exceptionalism gone, the family was ordinary, and sinking like so many others.

Zio Gioacchino, who had rushed from Sheffield to Manchester as soon as Angelo died, made arrangements – 'such a kind man' – for Novella and the children to

43

spend that Christmas with relatives nearby while plans to return to Italy were discussed. He oversaw the release of the meagre deposit Angelo had placed on a house in Manchester and urged Novella to stay on a few months, while he saw to some paperwork: Angelo had died a British citizen, Gioacchino pointed out, so she was entitled to a widow's pension. It would not be much to help them rebuild their lives back in Italy, but better than nothing.

Nonna's descriptions of the house in Maniago are proud. This was her father's house, and 'no one else had a bell above the front door'; in the courtyard, there was an aviary full of canaries, and little avenues of flowers; 'we had a cement toilet, while others had to make do with shacks full of flies' (*ma non lo mettere questo*...). But she always refers to it as the 'old' house – a step back, an already-read chapter, compared to Manchester's 'new' house, with its tantalizing sense of bright things to come.

During the family's six-month absence, the flowers in Angelo's garden had given way to dandelions. The aviary was empty, the birds having been sold to raise funds for the new life, now lost. And the cement toilet was nothing in light of the white bowls and wooden seats Dirce had seen in England.

'And where did your dad's trunk full of books end up?', I ask one day. *Chi lo sa, nina*, who knows. In Novella's eyes, books were both expensive and worthless, which seems surprising given her husband's devotion to them. The teenage Dirce kept that particular flame alive. As the 1930s gave way to the 1940s, she became increasingly resourceful – *sempre piena di risorse* – and made the most of her friendships, borrowing novels or trading them for favours, such as pretty little hairclips – ribbons and scraps of fabric fashioned into plump roses – which she

44

quickly ran up on the sewing machine when Novella was out. One girl, Aurelia, whose father owned the best gelateria in the nearby city of Pordenone, used to buy all the latest romances, read them, then pass them on, first to her sister, then to her mother, before, finally, handing them over at the school gates to Dirce, who would pay half the original price. 'It was our little system.' A trickle-down as suspenseful and sweet as ice cream melting down a cone.

By this time, Liala had written a sequel to *Signorsì*, as well as several other novels, with titles like *Pilgrim of Heaven* and *The Placid Hour*, and these were passed excitedly down the line, from one reader to the next. Beyond Dirce's personal situation, the transactional nature of her reading speaks of a particular cultural climate. The 1920s had been an era of marked expansion in Italian publishing, fuelled, as in other countries, by advances in production – seemingly tiny shifts, such as the pasting of books' spines with quick-drying synthetic glue, rather than the slower, more expensive, animal-based variety – that helped books keep pace with a society on the brink of mass consumption. Books became cheaper, their distribution fuller, their advertising more pervasive and aware of distinct audiences. And literature became increasingly itemized, even colour-coded – a detective novel was 'a yellow', *un giallo*; a romance, *una rosa*, 'a pink', or, the word is the same, 'a rose'. Any given Aurelia, then, skipping along to her local provincial *edicola*, newsstand, could now expect to pick up the same hotly anticipated *rosa* as her peers in central Milan or Rome.

This was the extensive and efficient system that, through the second half of the 1920s, Mussolini's government had so thoroughly appropriated, as part of their programme of cultural renewal and control. By the late 1930s – Aurelia skipping, Dirce waiting – the Ministry

45

of Popular Culture was running all new books through a censor, discouraging the translation of foreign literature, especially Jewish authors, and pressuring publishers to tailor plots to suit Fascist views and ambitions. Famously, in 1937, a directive landed on the desk of Arnoldo Mondadori, whose publishing house was renowned for its *gialli*: 'The killer must at no costs be Italian and he must not be allowed, in any way, to escape justice.' (A few years later, the series was ordered to cease all publication anyway.) In short, the books that moved from Aurelia's hands to Dirce's were those deemed appropriate for Il Duce's 'piccole italiane'. These 'little Italian girls' also had to wear the clothes he wished them to: a white blouse with a demure, pleated black skirt.

In these preternaturally still waters glided Liana Negretti Odescalchi, smooth as a swan.

*

After the death of Scotto, Liana and the *marchese* had patched things up, to a degree. In 1929 a second daughter had arrived. All the while, Liana later told reporters, she had been writing to conjure lost days and love, 'so as not to go mad'. When Arnoldo Mondadori – a friend of a friend, intrigued by her story – published *Signorsì* in 1931, it sold out in twenty days. A series of reprints followed, each exhausted faster than the previous.

It was, in retrospect, a safe bet for Mondadori: *Signorsì* is steeped in the 'aeromania' that had gripped Italy since the early years of the twentieth century, when the futurists, drunk on the machines' power and potential, urged writers and artists to place them at the heart of their work. Airplanes were eroticized, alternately feminized and phallicized. They were symbols of creation – of the universal mother, Madonna Queen of Heaven – and of destruction, the fruitful ravaging of war.

By 1931, Fascism was drenched in this maximalist aesthetic. And all this Liana poured into the story of Furio, a dashing and supremely patriotic airman in search of adventure, and the tortured Renata, whose saintly beauty, epitomized by thick golden curls that tumble to her ankles, breeds all manner of sin. ('If the Madonna has stepped down from the altar, what need is there to go to Church?' comments one soldier to another.) There are illicit glances, lovers with a father's eyes or a mother's warm touch, passionate jealousies, family curses carried in the veins. Relations between the men (who are full-blooded and promiscuous unless there's something wrong with them) and the women (the good ones childlike and innocent, the bad ones old and slutty), are set against a backdrop of vague social degeneration and a drive to make everything new or, at least, neo-classically old.

Women who intentionally or otherwise come between a pilot and his duty to serve do not fare well in this world. 'The women of aviators need to learn to take command of their hearts and put the brakes on their senses,' Furio's friend Mino says, after boasting that his girl kisses the gold eagle pinned above his heart before she so much as looks at his lips. The men's patriotic duties must always come first. As Renata's beauty distracts Furio, his passion mutates into routine punishment. Renata is driven to the edge of sanity. 'Signorsì!' – 'Yes, Sir!' – is the answer Furio gives at the novel's end when asked by his commanding officer if he is ready to set off on a state mission of the utmost importance – colonial reconnaissance, we presume. As his bright red plane takes off, circling the lake in a final salute, we know that Renata's body lies undiscovered, somewhere in the water's depths, entombed in a plane she

47

had pushed to its limit. 'Baci e frustate,' she had wailed before taking off; 'This is my life, kisses and lashings.'

A finishing touch in Liana's story of literary genesis: shortly before *Signorsì*'s publication, Italy's foremost poet of sex and violence, Gabriele D'Annunzio, on hearing of a new sensation, 'this woman who writes so knowledgeably about airplanes!', summoned her to the Vittoriale, his villa on a hill above Lake Garda. There he offered the elegant young woman a photograph of himself (typical D'Annunzio), addressing it with verve to 'My companion of wings and insolence'. 'To Liala,' he wrote, replacing the *n* with an *l* – because one so passionate about planes should carry the word *ala*, wing, in her name.

I tell Nonna these stories enthusiastically over the phone – about Scotto ('nel lago di Varese!' *My* lake!), about the futurists' sexy airplanes and D'Annunzio's creepy involvement. She knew about Scotto, of course. *Tutti la sanno quella*, she says. Everyone knows that one. The whole story is reaffirmed, in fact, in the back of my second-hand reissue of *Signorsì*. ('He fell hopelessly in love with Liana... But their love is fleeting... Liana, despairs... she begins to write...')

'Did you know the one about D'Annunzio, though?' I ask.

'Maybe I did,' she says, nonplussed. 'Non mi ricordo.' I don't remember.

This next part I do not tell Nonna, though I'm not sure why: After decades of recycling the story of Liala and Scotto's doomed love, people started to suggest that, in reality, another pilot of more humble origins, Pietro Sordi – with whom Liala had been involved since 1930 – had provided the real impetus to write. When, in 1932, it was discovered that Sordi, one of Italian aviation's brightest stars, had been living with Liala – a married woman and a mother, no less – he was forced to renounce active service, a falling from grace from which he never recovered. The couple stayed together until 1948, though Liala's divorce from the *marchese* never did come through.

Sordi has been more or less wiped from the tale, unmentioned in Liala's interviews and book blurbs (funny that his name is the plural of 'deaf'). Scotto, comparatively, had been a dalliance, passionately felt – surely? – but also convenient for mythmaking (no?). After all, 'Il mio miglior romanzo è la mia vita' – my best novel is my life – was a stock phrase of Liala's, reminiscent of a line from D'Annunzio's own enigmatically autobiographical novel, *Il Piacere*: 'You must create your life, as you would create a work of art.'

Perhaps I did not repeat any of this to Nonna through fear that I would seem cynical, that my evident glee in unravelling the original romance, in questioning Liala's account of things, would appear mean-spirited. Probably Nonna knows the story, anyway.

I probably never will tell Nonna that Liala is not for me. That until I bought *Signorsì* I had never given this Italian Barbara Cartland a second thought. Not for me this writer of pulp and titillation, whom I had first encountered as the butt of a cheap joke: 'Liale', the label given in the 1960s to writers deemed socially and aesthetically 'neo-capitalistic', purveyors of idle entertainments for the reader-consumer. This was according to the radical literary movement known as the Gruppo 63, co-founded by Umberto Eco, and I took their word for it.

Nor will I tell Nonna that I read somewhere that Cesare Levi, Primo Levi's father, banned his daughter Anna Maria from reading Liala's 'trash and nonsense', presumably seeing in the ramped-up prose a reflection of the ideals and emotions that seemed increasingly treacherous, especially to a Jewish family living in Turin. Once you become aware of these things, to try to read Liala straight is like trying to suck the air out of a meringue.

'Do you think your papà would have let you read such raunchy books,' I ask one day.

'Chissà,' says Nonna.

Who knows, indeed. But I suspect Angelo would have disapproved.

We agree that, either way, he would certainly not have allowed Novella to forbid reading all together.

'*Ma vedi, nina, erano così le cose...*' That's just the way things were.

*

'Let me tell you the story of how I met Leo,' Nonna says the next time we talk.

Since I told her I want to write about her life, she has started to suggest chapters herself. I let this happen, and she reels through the years – '*Allora*, so, I was born on 24 October 1926, on a Sunday morning in time for Mass...' – shushing me when I interrupt with questions whose answers would require us to travel to another time and place than the one she has in mind. 'I can only do it chronologically!' she says, though we both know this is not true. When she finds a thread, it's best to leave her to it. And today, she has one – it's clear from the way she answers the phone for our *appuntamento* – and it's a deep, plush pink.

Allora. It was 1942 – no, '43 – no, '42. It was November 1942 and Dirce had just turned sixteen. The other man, the much older one who gave her the gold brooch ('and a gold pen', so she would write to him after he was called away), was still on the scene. (*Ma questo non lo mettere... OK, metti,*

metti.) Dirce had left school by then, two years earlier in fact, when she had started to experience stomach pains. Novella had taken her to the doctor and he – looking the girl up and down, hearing that she skipped breakfast, listening to Novella's struggles as a widow, reasoning that the patient was fourteen now, after all – decided that the pains were probably an ulcer brought on by the stress of study, and a sign from the Fates, those three intractable weavers of others' lives. Yes, Dirce would be better put to work, helping her poor mother.

'Were you sorry to leave school?' I ask.

'I didn't mind – I didn't see the point of it anymore.'

On returning from England, the teachers had put Dirce back a year, so she gave up trying. Since her father's death, there was no one to impress; no need to be top of the class. He used to give her sweets and kisses for every good mark.

Te l'ho detta questa? 'Have I told you this one?' she asks, not waiting for my response (which would have been 'yes'), before continuing: 'Mio papà once made me give 1,000 kisses for one sweetie. I was six and I kissed while he counted. At 500 I said "*Ecco*! I'm done!", and he said "No, this is only half a thousand", so I kept going for 500 more.'

Era dolce mio padre, a sweet, sweet man.

Another time, Dirce and little Pietro went with Novella to meet Angelo off the train – this would have been in spring 1935 when he had come back to ready them for the move to England. He kissed Novella first and then Dirce, a big one on the top of her head. 'And later, he hugged me and told me that really he'd wanted to kiss me first but didn't want to upset *mamma*.' *Che dolce, che dolce.*

'Didn't you miss school, though? The books?' I ask, trying to pull her back to me.

'I regretted that we were just about to start studying the Greek myths.'

All those tales of brave and weary travellers, threshold dwellers and transgressors.

'I would have enjoyed the lessons, but I went to work, and that was that.'

One moment there is romance, the next crude fact.

The factory where Dirce was employed made blades, mostly for knives of the old reliable sort, whether for slicing onions or the neck of a deer. And pencil sharpeners – 'It was my job to punch the hole through the top.' This was in Montereale, about twenty minutes' cycle, or one hour's walk from the old house, on the other side of the bright turquoise Cellina river. If she went on foot, she tells me, she would take a hunk of bread (doctor's orders) and, sometimes, the most recent letter sent by the man who was courting her from a distance (whose name she still refuses to tell me). She'd walk and read and walk and think and walk and chew, her eyes on the road before her.

'What did you think about?'

'Nothing really. That things were like this or like that' – *così o cosà* – 'and that I wasn't hungry.'

She noticed Leo – slim, fair-haired, eyes the colour of the water below – taking the same route, often in the opposite direction, and sometimes she would spot him hanging around outside the factory at the end of the day. When she was on foot he was, too, wheeling his bike alongside him, and she began to think that this was not coincidence. He seemed to jump off when he saw her in the distance. He always said 'buongiorno', but in Veneto (*bondì*), not Friulano (*mandi*). She offers me this with great meaning and seems frustrated by my failure to comprehend.

'But the Fascists had banned all regional languages...'

I say.

'And what? They could stop us talking to each other?' she scoffs. 'No,' she explains, 'because he knew that I spoke like *quelle di Maniago*' – he knew, that is, that she lived in the town, and not among the fields and the beasts like him. To say *bondì* instead of *mandi* was, then, to recognize this young woman's elevated status, and that he was 'troppo contadino' – too much of a farmer for her.

It seems strange to me that Nonna should tell this story of nascent love as one of class-transgression, rather than as one delicately unfurling against a backdrop of state oppression, midnight raids, killings and disappearances.

'His friends told him "don't go for her, she won't have you, you've got cows."'

A pause.

'But you had a cow,' I say.

'Yes, but *he* didn't know that.'

Months went by in this way, with Leo and Dirce seeing each other every few days, mostly passing by quickly on their bikes – he: 'bondì'; she: 'bondì' – but at some point, I imagine, he caught her out of the saddle and said something banal along the lines of 'Lovely weather we're having,' because slowly the pair began to feed each other crumbs of information about themselves. That Dirce lived with her mother and brother on the road out of town. The one on the corner? *Sì, sì...* With the big gate? *Sì, sì...* Leo cycled by there all the time. That Leo's best friend lived in Montereale, so he came up from Campagna, ten minutes out the other side of Maniago, to see him most days... He was on his way there now, in fact. Ah, well, Dirce had friends in Campagna, in the big house with the enormous tree in the garden... Near the *roja*? Enzo and Giovanni? *Sì*.

And then one day: 'Are you going to Marta's place this

Saturday?'

That was how it was then, Nonna says – they danced in people's houses. There weren't any clubs to speak of, except for the *casa del balilla*, a hall-cum-gymnasium that was intended, as part of a nationwide network of *case*, to *fascistizzare* – 'fascistify' – the youth through physical and moral education. But the plumbing had never been put in in Maniago's *casa*, and, more than a decade after its inauguration, the roof still wasn't finished. In 1942, with the war on the turn and Italy's new colonies and annexations looking increasingly precarious, the *balilla* probably wasn't Il Duce's priority.

'And so, did you go to Marta's?'

'Probably. *Non mi ricordo.*'

Whenever she went dancing, she would clip a ribbon-rose in her hair. She had one to match every outfit, and her friends would pester her to make more for them.

Something must have happened at one of these dances because when, in March 1943, Dirce went to the cinema to meet a friend she took a flower, a red rose cut from the garden. Her plan was to give it to Leo, whom she knew went to the cinema often. This seems quite forward to me, a grand gesture for a polite young woman to make, but I hold my tongue and imagine her waiting in line, twirling the stem in her fingers, shifting from one foot to the other, scanning the piazza. A friend came over, Nonna recalls, 'a male friend, and he goes "*oh che bella rosa*, give it to me."' She says she laughed and demurred, but he insisted and eventually, when it was evident that Leo wasn't coming, she snapped the stem and threw it down to the ground. I picture the petals spread about her feet like fat drops of blood.

'I don't understand,' I say. 'Had you arranged to meet Leo?'

54

'No, no, nina', as though I had, again, missed the point.
A pause.

'*Ah, che bei tempi, nina....*'. Such good times. She sighs.

It's the suspense, the long stretch of will-they-won't-they, that delights her still.

Suddenly it's May and everyone has gone to the Rosary, to mutter their way chapter by chapter through the Joyful and the Sorrowful and the Glorious mysteries that comprise the stories of Jesus and Mary. A crown of prayers like the crown of roses, one hundred and fifty-three red and sixteen white, which garland the Divine heads as they sit in Heaven listening. After the Rosary, Dirce and her friends would stand outside by the door, *chiacchierando*, chatting, and the boys would pass by and sometimes they'd come over to talk. And this one time, in May, Dirce's cousin from Milan was staying, having fled the Allies' bombing campaign which was steadily intensifying. (Lancasters were now flying over even in broad daylight, and the pilots had been told to aim their loads at the Duomo at the city's heart.) Perhaps Dirce was emboldened by her cousin's company, perhaps this guest told her 'carpe diem!', because this time, when Dirce said 'bondì', something in her manner told Leo that he should stop for more than a moment.

'We talked.'

'About what?'

'Non mi ricordo.'

He seemed serious, more mature, though he was only two years older than her.

'And so...'

They grew closer.

A week later he brought a punnet of cherries to the house ('or something... I don't remember – let's say cherries'), but Novella wouldn't let him in. Little Pietro was sent out to receive the gift and send Leo on his way. Another time, he swung by after dinner, on his cycle back from Montereale, and he must have been feeling brave – he had surely been drinking – because he rang that bell that was the family's pride. Dirce went down to meet him and after a few minutes Novella followed, waving the *mestolo per polenta* – a long wooden utensil, thick as the handle of a broom, with a paddle at one end, used to stir polenta. Then there was the famous *serenata*, when Leo came down from some party in the hills with a rowdy bunch of friends and stood in the street outside Dirce's window, belting out songs between fits of laughter. (Novella must have loved that, I say.)

Every love story needs its turning point, and this Nonna tells me – *attenta!* – is ours: in the summer, Novella sent Dirce to Venice for two weeks, to stay with an aunt, Clarina, who needed help with the housework. And when it was time to come home, Dirce called Aurelia – the call going to the public phone in Maniago's main piazza ('Oo, 'Relia, it's for you!') – to tell her what time the afternoon train was due in. They could walk home together and catch up, they decided; there was lots to discuss after a fortnight apart. And, while changing trains in Sacile, which was the only way (and still is), Dirce saw Leo get off the train that had just come from Maniago. She watched him help a woman and her child onto the platform and asked herself, 'But what's he doing here, this one?'

Before she knew it, he was touching her shoulder. 'Bondi.' She says she shivered but didn't shrug his hand away, and this point requires a brief explanation: 'No one could touch my shoulder,' Nonna had told me a couple of phone calls previously. I had noted it down, at the time unsure why. If someone did touch her, she said: *Io, gentilmente ridendo* – 'I, politely laughing' – *spostavo la mano*

– 'would move their hand'. At sixteen, she was *molto bambina*, very much a child. 'I bloomed all at once, let's say.'

When Leo touched Dirce's shoulder that day in Sacile, the flowering was already underway. He told her a lie – she knew it even then – pretending that he was on his way to Venice to collect his papers, something to do with the military; he'd go another day now. But, then, Dirce would have been lying, too, had she said, hand on heart, that she didn't know that Aurelia, on hearing the train times that morning, would pass on the message to Leo, who was usually hanging around the piazza at that time of day. ('Aurelia knew I wanted to see him,' Nonna tells me now. Aurelia, whose name means 'golden one'.)

And so Dirce and Leo boarded the train from Sacile together, and when they arrived in Maniago an hour or so later, *era tutto diverso*. Everything was different.

There are gaps in this version of the tale, though, as if Nonna were reading a book whose pages are warped and sporadically stuck together, having been dropped into water and dried in a fierce sun. Time and space have shrunk. Consequences have lost their causes. The order seems wrong. For one thing:

'I thought the *serenata* happened before he'd ever seen you?'

'Sì...'

'But you said you first saw each other on the way to Montereale.'

'Sì...'

And surely it would make sense for you to take Leo a rose *after* having got to know him a little outside the Church that day?

Era così nina. It's how it was.

And so that, I understand, is that.

Some weeks and several phone calls later, a couple of pages begin to peel apart. Before Dirce's trip to Venice, it transpires, Leo and Dirce were at a dance and she was wearing a skirt with an emerald-green trim, to match the ribbon-rose in her hair. Leo commented on the beautiful blue of it and this was how they found out that he was blue-green colourblind. 'He saw his own eyes every day in the mirror and thought they were green!'

At the end of the night, Leo asked Dirce to be his girl. 'Just like that he asked me.' She – *molto bambina* – hesitated, fiddled with her hair. He – *serio, maturo*, and scared she would say no – touched her shoulder and told her to take her time and give him an answer when she got back from her aunt's.

When she got home that night Dirce ate three bowlfuls of cold minestrone, standing up by the unlit stove, with her shoes off and her stockingless feet on the cool stone floor. She knew, with her temperamental stomach, that the minestrone's beans were *un veleno*, a poison, 'but I was so hungry I couldn't stop'. She felt wild with emotion, as if she were on the edge of something. The stew aggravated her ulcer. She hardly slept. Early the next day, she left for Venice.

Now, when I imagine the Venetian interlude, it represents the period of separation between the hero and the heroine, which I have learnt is an essential part of the structure of a classic romance narrative. Phase 7: 'The heroine and hero are physically and/or emotionally separated,' writes Janice Radway in *Reading the Romance*, a famous literary ethnography and deconstruction of the genre, published in 1984. Phase 7 comes halfway between '1: The heroine's social identity is destroyed' and

'13: The heroine's identity is restored' by the crucial happy ending.

I picture Dirce pacing along the canals and the *calli*, running errands for *zia* Clarina. Walking and thinking. I imagine her composing plot lines in her head, much as I am now. One moment she remembers the feeling of Leo's hand on her shoulder and the sharpness of his blue eyes; another moment, she thinks back to the older man, who gave her the brooch, and whose letters are piling up in the drawer of her bedside table, unopened. One evening, I imagine, Dirce stood halfway across a bridge over the *rio dei Miracoli* – the 'Rio of Miracles', why not? – and dropped the gold brooch into the cloudy water below.

And a few days later, on a train from Sacile to Maniago, she looked into Leo's eyes and said 'Sì, sì...'

'And did he... take you into his arms?' I ask her now, piecing together the scene, with her resting her cheek on his chest, perhaps peering around him to look out of the window, filmy-eyed.

'Non mi ricordo.'

It took him weeks – 'maybe months!' – to work up the courage to kiss her.

In the meantime: 'I was waiting, holding my breath.'

While Leo and Dirce's story played out, the Allies invaded Sicily. Italy capitulated and the Fascist government fell. The Nazis flooded the north of the country. Mussolini and a band of loyalists retreated to Salò, in the far west of Lombardy, where they established a puppet state. There was civil war. All of Europe held its breath.

*

'Il mio miglior romanzo è la mia vita,' said Liala. My best novel is my life. Or, D'Annunzio: 'You must create your life, as you would create a work of art.' There is something of this narrative self-awareness in the way Nonna composes things, especially now that she knows I am taking notes. I tell her I feel nervous about committing her story to the page, about making her the heroine and telling it right. 'You're a writer, it's your job to write, just do your job,' she says, in a matter-of-fact tone intended, I think, to be helpful.

I am also an editor, whose job is to trim and tweak and tease out other people's stories. Trim, tweak, tease – these are the words I use to explain to writers what I have done to their prose. Or I 'nip and tuck', as if altering a skirt. I am aware of certain impulses in this process, of the needs I have as a reader. For the sense of an ending, for example, which should never be a summing-up, but rather an opening-out – an invitation for more, from other sources in other minds. I like to leave a few teasing threads, to encourage readers to finger the words like I have. I think about the rhythm of the words as they build towards a full-stop. Or the placing of a comma, a hesitation, that could make everything different. I am only beginning to understand these impulses, and that sometimes the story I want to write or shape might not be one the teller wants to tell.

*

Four years after that fateful train ride from Sacile to Maniago, on the first Saturday after Dirce's twenty-first birthday, the couple married in the church near the old house. It was October 1947, 'the same year as Queen Elizabetta's wedding in Westminster Abbey'. Their friends tied a thick white ribbon across the entrance so that Leo had to cut it with a penknife. He was dressed in a slate grey suit with a red tie, and Dirce, in a simple white dress of her own devising, clasped a bunch of roses brought to her that morning from the garden of a cousin.

'What colour?' I ask.

'*O Dio, nina*, I don't remember – red maybe... Let's say red. After the service, I took them up to the Madonna and left them at her feet.'

The bells rang loud and long that day, Nonna recalls, and when Leo said 'I do', you could hear it out of the door and over on the other side of the piazza.

'And how did you feel?' I ask.

'Contenta, serena, tranquilla. Sicura di lui.'

'In what sense "Sure of him"?'

Sure that he would always be there.

After a meal of *lingua salmistrata*, a Venetian dish of tongue, pressed for two weeks and seasoned with salt, pepper and cinnamon – 'butchers probably don't know how to do it anymore' – the whole wedding party jumped into trucks, on bikes or set off on foot to reconvene at Leo's parents' house, out among the fields, where the couple would now live. They all came to gawp at the new marital bed and the embroidered sheets and the dresser and the bedside tables with their doilies. They marvelled at the bed's in-built electrics, with lights like flowers on curved stalks attached to the headboard. There was dancing, and small fires were set in the road. A cousin sang for them in a voice so fine she 'could have been someone, she could have been on the radio'.

'What did she sing?'

'Ave Maria, the one by Schubert', and as she sang the colours of the room seemed to grow darker for Dirce, who knew that her cousin had learnt the song during the war, in jail, where she was held in the place of her brother, a *partigiano* then hiding in the mountains. She couldn't sleep and so every night she would sing and people gathered outside to listen.

'The words won't come to me... hold on,' says Nonna.

(Some do, out of the blue, a week or so later: 'Non negar a questo straziato mio cuor... tregua al suo dolor... Sperduta l'alma mia ricorre a Te... e pien di speme si prostra ai Tuoi piè'; 'Do not deny this tormented heart of mine respite from pain. My lost soul appeals to You and full of hope prostrates itself at Your feet.')

'I can see her now,' Nonna says. 'I can see everyone.'

But never, in 10,000 renditions of this scene, have I glimpsed the mother of the bride. It's as if Novella simply wasn't there.

Shortly before midnight, the priest arrived to make his speech, to send the couple on their way. Everyone had seen the bed, so... They offered him *confetti* – the sugar-coated almonds that remain an Italian wedding tradition – and he compared them to a marriage: the almond's halves bound together by a white sheet; sweetness with a bitter note at its heart.

*

Incurable. Hopeless. Two words commonly attached to romance – or rather, to the romantics themselves, mocked for seeing the world through rose-tinted glass. (Let there be no doubt, the condition is not easily contained to bookshelves.) 'Incurable' puts us in the realm of medicine, of typical and atypical symptoms and the treatment plan. The irony is that these incurables, in a perfect cycle of addiction, self-medicate by consuming romance stories. The shared origin of the words 'heroine' and 'heroin' could hardly be more poignant.

Consider this, from *Reading the Romance*: 'When she

successfully imagines herself in the heroine's position, the typical romance reader can relax momentarily and permit herself to wallow in the rapture of being the center of a powerful and important individual's attention.' 'Rapture', the language of religion. It's hopeless, yes, but also divine.

In America, in the early 1980s, Janice Radway surveyed more than 100 women for her book, all romance obsessives, aware of, if not necessarily persuaded by, second-wave feminism. While the context was quite different to Italy in the 1930s – where rights had been suspended for everyone, not least women – much of what Radway observes seems to reach back to the *edicola* in Pordenone where Dirce and Aurelia's little system was born. She points out how the readers 'feel personally connected to their favourite authors because they are convinced that these writers know how to make them happy'. There is talk of books that 'relieve some of the pressure build-up', of 'escape' and 'release', of reading until 'my body is in the room but the rest of me is not'. One woman, at 'her doctor's instigation', implemented a regime of one hour's romance reading per day, a small gift 'for herself', to counter everything else – the cleaning, the cooking, the how-was-your-day? – which was always for other people. 'We read books so we won't cry', says another woman, for whom romances show her the world as 'I would like it to be, not as it really is'.

Visions of this world, dreamy but familiar, are remarkably consistent among the women Radway interviews: the hero must be 'strong but gentle', 'masculine but caring'; the heroine must be 'spirited' and ideally this will be expressed early by rebellion against parental authority. Her needs are similar to the reader's: she wants love, safety, and self-worth rather than self-renunciation. She wants to feel significant for who she is rather than for what she does. There must be a happy ending and it must feel chosen by the heroine, rather than required by other individuals or institutions. Self-knowledge and determination will carry her into the arms of the hero, 'who declares his intention to protect her forever because of his desperate love and need for her'. The need is reciprocal. In modern terms, we could say that these readers are, in the act of imagining, demanding more from the heterosexual union, and that, says Radway, 'is a minimal but nonetheless legitimate form of protest'. (Oh, and a little class-based frisson is good, too.)

Not many would admit to compulsively reading mass-market romance novels these days. As a form of protest, it would be dismissed. Even in the 1980s, many of Radway's readers felt a certain guilt and knew they would be treated with condescension for enjoying books that were 'regularly ridiculed by the media, their husbands, and their children'. And yet the books continue to be passed from hand to hand, and the genre evolves, so much spume on the surface of 'real' literature. Or perhaps it's the other way around by now and 'mainstream', full and fast-running, is a term more precise than I have appreciated.

For Radway's respondents, to accuse such novels of toxicity for the way they pretend a revolution in male–female relations, all the while planning to sugar-coat a betrayal at the story's end, would be to miss the point. The women 'vehemently maintain that their reading has transformed them' in positive and 'important' ways. Radway nods to Bruno Bettelheim's theory about the fairy tale, in some ways a stepping-stone to the romance novel, which plays a fundamental role for children in creating and sustaining hope; fantastic tales are, she says,

64

'emotional primers', reservoirs of feeling. Romances are 'compensatory literature'.

But the stuff of compensation – for what and for whom and to what end – grows murkier the longer you look. It may not be surprising that Radway's story turns oedipal. She notes 'a daughter's desire to escape her intense symbiotic union with her mother', and that a woman's 'first real attempt at individuation is thus often expressed as identification with and desire for the father and all that is male'. The heroes of the most beloved romances, she finds, have sweet, nurturing qualities, so that their masculine embrace is also somewhat maternal. The mother, first rejected, is finally regained in a different body.

So, then: 'Liala, *appassionatamente*.' It makes sense that the young Dirce should have become devoted to Liala. She may even have appreciated a sympathy between the lives of author and reader, both defined by extravagant and incontrovertible losses. That was how Dirce saw her formative years, and still does. She lost her father, and her country, twice: first when Angelo removed her from Italy to England and promptly died; then, when she went back to where she had come from. 'I felt England was really mine,' she says to me one day. 'Mia, mia, *mia*', and suddenly it was gone. Her once 'high' family name had been dragged down in the process. And, of course – taken out of school, put to work, made to consider marriage to that older man before she had even had her first period – she lost her childhood.

'Perhaps that is why I was so *bambina*,' she says, as though the idea has just struck her.

'Perhaps you were pretending to still be a child, you mean?'

'*Chissà*?' Who knows.

Liala was a half-orphan, too, her father having died

when she was young; her mother was distant, leaving the grandmother, a severe woman intent on returning the family to its once superior social standing, to raise the child. It was she who insisted on preserving the maternal Odescalchi name (remember it), the last link to the princely family of Como who had once produced a pope. Little did the old woman know that her ward would one day shed every one of her given names. At seventeen, Liana was married to a man twice her age, who had a habit of disappearing, leaving her alone much of the time. Father, childhood, mother, husband, freedom – all lost. By the time she was thirty, her life was characterized by subtraction, decline, disappointment – little wonder that she fell for Vittorio Centurione Scotto, two years her junior, full of passionate positivity and sky-high potential.

So when Scotto's plane precipitated into Lake Varese, had she been, on some level, expecting another great loss to carry on her life's pattern? Did she tie her lover's death into a crown of losses, each one as vivid and fragrant as a rose?

Loss suffuses *Signorsì*, in which tragic circumstances have left the heroine Renata parentless and in the care of a spinster aunt. When Renata meets Furio his golden eyes remind her of her father's. And loss breeds loss: if Renata's youth had already been claimed by the fates, a turbulent affair with Furio takes her freedom, the modest happiness she had found, her sanity and sense of self, and, later, her unborn child and future. A plane crash, the author knew, could be both real and metaphorical.

Sometimes when I think of the young Dirce reading, the story I want to tell has everything to do with consolation, grief and the past, so that to focus on the arrival on the scene of a potential suitor, Leo, who ends by singing and dancing the heroine into a brighter future, is to miss the point entirely. Sometimes, the most intense romances are about the people you see every day, to whom you are already close, or once were. The aim is to recover a time before you knew what disappointment was, when there was still hope.

Dirce told herself a tale for almost ten years, she tells me, from the age of nine. On her first day back in her old school in Maniago, before they decided to put her back a year and then remove her altogether, the teacher set that evening's homework: she was to write a short essay in response to the question, 'What would you do if you were rich?' Dirce's answer was simple and apparently instinctive: 'If I were rich I would go to see my father's grave in Sheffield, because I don't believe that it exists.' She had not actually seen him dead, after all – and the last time she had seen him, he was propped up in bed telling her '*Nina*, don't worry.'

He shed a fat tear, she remembers, which she understood as a sign of his regret that they should have to be separated for a time, to allow him to recover. (Neither Dirce nor Novella attended the funeral, presumably it was deemed too gruelling, or perhaps, with no money, there simply wasn't one to attend.) From that primary-school essay, the tone was set, and it spread quickly, like a disease or a warm glow. Dirce entered a perpetual Phase 7: 'the heroine and hero are physically and / or emotionally separated'.

'I told myself that my father was still alive and that he wasn't with us because he couldn't leave England because of work or something that was out of his hands,' she says.

She believed this so fervently that one day, when she was about twelve or thirteen, as the bell rang for the end of school, she bolted and ran all the way home, convinced that she would find Angelo waiting in the kitchen, 'to ask me for 1,000 kisses'.

'And what happened when he wasn't there?'

She put her head in her hands and cried and convinced herself that something must have kept him away. She mentioned nothing to her mother, of course. This kind of feverish behaviour was precisely what Novella expected would arise from reading novels. And in any case, it was 'una cosa mia', my thing; and Novella's pain was all hers, 'una cosa tutta sua'.

Reality was selectively plundered for these fantasies.

'When the war began, it became easier to pretend: now he couldn't come because it was too dangerous.'

'So, what happened when the war ended?'

'I finally accepted that he was gone, because I knew he would not have stayed away any longer than he had to.'

She was nineteen by this point, and in love with Leo.

We are sitting in Nonna's overheated kitchen for this conversation. I prefer not to ask her about her father over the phone, when I can't reach her hand if I need to. I have listened to the recording tens of times and each time I remember how she shook her head and looked through me, smiling, as if the past were playing out on a TV screen behind me. Her eyes were glistening.

*

My edition of *Signorsì* is a cheap resissue, the cheapest I could find, whose pages are yellowed, well-thumbed and sweet-smelling. The cover is wrapped with a red banner that proclaims '1931–2001: *Signorsì* celebrates its seventieth year but it's as though Liala had written it today'. The author's name is by far the most prominent element, written in towering capitals above a faded image of a seaplane brought low over a lake at sunset.

The last few pages of the book are given over to the reader's 'appunti', notes to be written on dotted lines as if in a school exercise book. A place to list observations, judgements, things she has learnt, the ways in which the novel has transformed her. I'm struck by the spirit of the thing.

Appunti:

· After Vittorio Centurione Scotto's death, the Schneider Trophy was delayed until November. The British didn't have an entry ready in time. Major Mario de Bernardi took Scotto's place and averaged 246.5 mph in a plane whose engine dangerously overheated. Soon after crossing the finish line, he sent Mussolini a cable: 'Your orders to win at all costs have been carried out.'

· Scotto's father, the politician and *marchese* Carlo Centurione Scotto, never recovered from the loss of his son. He became a spiritualist, holding much-publicized séances in the family's castle, during which he tried to breach their separation. Reports of teleportation drew international attention and praise from Arthur Conan Doyle.

· In 1980, Umberto Eco, in annotations to his novel *The Name of the Rose*, summed up how postmodernity – its irony, incredulity and self-awareness – had changed human relations: these days, a hypothetical man cannot say to a hypothetical woman, 'I love you desperately' without adding: 'as Liala would say'.

· In 1995, at the age of ninety-eight, Liala stepped out of the hairdresser's and died instantly of a stroke. As though to narrate her own denouement, she had left detailed instructions for her funeral: she was to be dressed in a gold lamé blouse by Valentino and a cream-coloured silk skirt. Ready to meet her maker, whoever that may be.

· Since Leo died in 1999, Dirce has not danced with anyone else, not even with her sons.

· In the garden of the old house in Maniago, Angelo grew a deciduous plant of emerald leaves and drooping white buds like strings of pearls, called Lacrime d'Italia – 'Italy's tears'; or 'tears of Italy', depending on which way you want to play it.

III.

In a private chapel in the grounds of Villa Raimondi, erst-
while Odescalchi, on the outskirts of Como, Giuseppe
Garibaldi, aged fifty-two, stands ready to marry his
second wife, the eighteen-year-old Giuseppina, an il-
legitimate daughter of the *marchese* Raimondi Mantica
Odescalchi. On her birth certificate, she is a 'daughter
of unknowns'; today, she is the bride of a living legend.
Picture her wearing a full-skirted, puff-sleeved gown of
lace and silk. Her dark hair is parted in the middle and
plaited into a thick crown.

Although not one for ceremony, General Garibaldi
has, probably, swapped his worn-in uniform of vivid pon-
cho and velvet smoking cap for something a little more
proper. He is riding high, but feels more bruised than he
would ever let on. It is 24 January 1860, and his army of
volunteers, known for their red shirts and unbridled ide-
alism, have not long pushed the Austrian occupiers back
to the mountains of the south Tyrol.

The priest asks the congregation to rise. Skirts rustle
and leather boots squeak on the stone floor. Someone
coughs – someone always coughs – and the groom's pale
blue eyes flit about the room, taking in dashes of red: a
silk foulard, a brooch of rubies, a posy of claret roses. His
influence is everywhere. A couple of years from now,
Abraham Lincoln will ask Garibaldi to lead the Union
army, and he will decide against it, citing the President's
weak stance on the abolition of slavery. History will remember Garibaldi as the 'Hero of Two Worlds' and,
alongside only a handful of others – Giuseppe Mazzini,
Vittorio Emanuele II and Camillo Cavour – as a 'father of
the fatherland', an architect of today's Italy.

But on this winter's day, he is nervous: a man standing

in front of others, wondering if he is making the right choice, as he takes this woman's hand and envisages a hushed domesticity he has never known. He has told everyone how much he craves it. (He has made marriage proposals to two other women in the past year alone.) He knows that Italy's unification is nowhere near achieved, but he will – perhaps – father another child and rest in the cool, fortifying air of Lombardy's lakes, before pushing on.

His path here has been arduous. In the name of independence Garibaldi has lost more friends than he allows himself to remember. In 1849, his first wife, the Brazilian freedom fighter Ana Maria de Jesus Ribeiro da Silva – beautiful, *brave* Anita – died of malaria and exhaustion after a disastrous attempt to liberate Rome. Pregnant with their fifth child, she was buried hastily in a shallow grave and soon found by a young girl who tripped up on a hand. Pointing skywards, Anita's fingers had broken through the sandy earth; the dogs had already been. Garibaldi presumably blames himself for this indignity, and perhaps even for the failures leading to it. And he is not ignorant of voices that insist, still, that he strangled Anita to put her out of her misery, or because she was jeopardizing his escape. For Italy's sake – anyone could see – his life must come first. At some stage, he took to wearing Anita's striped silk scarf under his own. Probably today he isn't.

Behind Giuseppina stands her father, the *marchese*, a devoted *garibaldino*. This is his day, too – after all, didn't he bring the pair together? Last summer, while hiding in Switzerland from Austrian police who suspected him of conspiracy, he had enlisted his daughter to run messages and weapons across the border to Garibaldi's Redshirts. (Or had she in fact volunteered? Who can remember. A detail. *Che importa.*) And that was how, near lake Varese, her path came to cross the General's. It was perfect. So, when, some months later, Garibaldi asked the *marchese* for Giuseppina's hand – after countless letters, none of which won the girl around – he had not accepted her protestations that she was in love with someone else, someone far closer to her own age. He shook his head, baffled, and raised his hands to the vaults, begging for an end to her nonsense. Did she not realize? No matter that the man is nearly three times your age. This is *Garibaldi*, Glory incarnate. Everyone should fall at his feet.

The *marchese* shakes his head at the mere memory and fixes his eyes on Giuseppina's profile, holding his breath until, finally: '*Sì, lo voglio,*' she says – 'I do,' I want it. I want him. He could swoon.

No sooner has the priest blessed the couple and let his arms drop to his sides in satisfaction, than someone steps up and whispers into Garibaldi's ear – some accounts mention a scrap of paper – informing him that Giuseppina has been unfaithful, with more than one man. Last night she was with Luigi Caroli, one of the General's soldiers; she is five months pregnant by him. A scuffle ensues in which, apparently, Garibaldi lashes out at Giuseppina, narrowly missing her head. He throws her against a chair, calls her a 'great whore' so that the packed chapel can hear, and makes for his horse. Giuseppina, who has grown up with shame at her shoulders, is incandescent: 'I believed I'd married a hero,' she says, 'yet you're nothing but a brutal soldier.' And maybe this is what Garibaldi's biographer and former lover Elpis Melena meant when she wrote, 'Garibaldi will always shine resplendent as a sun; but even the sun has its spots.'

Lasting less than an hour, they say the marriage between Giuseppina Raimondi and Giuseppe Garibaldi is the shortest in history. But that ignores the twenty years that it took the General to obtain an annulment. In the intervening years, he wrote vindictive letters to newspapers, accusing Giuseppina of being sex-crazed and incestuously involved with her own father, and although the editors did not publish these claims – perhaps to leave the young woman a scrap of dignity; more likely to prevent Italy's hero from embarrassing himself – Giuseppina refused to agree to the dissolution without a promise that Garibaldi cease the slanderous campaign.

The bond was definitively broken on 14 January 1880, at the Court of Appeal in Rome. Garibaldi and his lawyers made their case on the basis of Austrian laws, still officially in effect at the time of the marriage, which must have left the Italian patriot with an acrid taste. At seventy-two, and all but paralyzed by arthritis, he was desperate to remarry and, so, legitimize his three children, Rosita, Clelia and Manlio, by Francesca Armosino (then aged thirty-one). Two years later, the father of the fatherland was dead.

It remains a favourite among spinners of alternate history, this moment of collapse on the steps of the Raimondi-Odescalchi's chapel, when Garibaldi had to make a choice: to dismiss the sinful stories about his bride or believe them; to stay or to go. Had the ageing general hung up his rifle and given himself over to domestic bliss then, people wonder, would Italian Unification have been realized? Italy should thank Signorina Raimondi for messing things up! They do not entertain the idea that, had the marriage endured, this beautiful daughter of unknowns might have been the one to insist that he – or even, they – set off and finish what had been started.

*

74

I know the story of Garibaldi's wedding, or a version of it, because I grew up with it. The chapel sits across a court-yard from the apartment, converted from the *marchese*'s servants' quarters, which my parents and sister were living in when, in 1986, they brought me home for the first time.

I told Nonna this over the phone one day, when I called for our weekly *appuntamento*. She had started to ask me for stories about myself – 'I tell you everything and you tell me nothing!' – as though ours was ever going to be an even exchange.

When I shared the story of Giuseppe and Giuseppina, she went quiet for a moment, so that I wondered if she had left the phone sitting beside its cradle and nipped off to the loo (which she had done before).

Then: 'My father loved Garibaldi.'

It was hardly surprising.

'Him and every other Italian,' I said, because few figures have been so widely revered. Garibaldi is everybody's general. He was 'Il Duce' before Mussolini was, and the Fascist leader was only too keen to emphasize the association. And yet when, in April 1945, the defeated Mussolini and his lover Clara Petacci were caught and shot near Como, it was by one of many partisan *brigate* named for Garibaldi, whose members wore red neckerchiefs. He is a floating signifier of justice, freedom, hope, the best that Italy can be. He is a shapeshifter of the highest order.

A framed print of Garibaldi hung in the hall of the old house in Maniago, Nonna told me, alongside a map of the area and a few photographs taken by Angelo ('of other people, the family, aunts and uncles, no one special'). 'And he was forever telling me to read *Cuore*. It was his favourite.'

Cuore, 'Heart', a children's book, first published in 1886, by Edmondo de Amicis, an immediate bestseller, which probably no child in Italy has escaped since. Saturated in romantic notions about the newly formed Italy, *Cuore* conveyed in a straightforward style – in language precise and modern, stripped of regional variations – the duties owed by all citizens to friends, family, strangers, God and country. To read *Cuore* is to be immersed in a sweet and sticky kind of nationalism, sticky like honey or drying blood.

The book is presented as the diary of a fictional eleven-year-old boy – a good little bourgeois destined for a good bourgeois adulthood. Each entry contains a lesson on how to be, or not, in the new Italy. So full a primer of *italianità*, 'Italianness', was *Cuore* that the Fascist government included excerpts in the official elementary school textbooks. Passages such as this one, entitled 'Italia':

> 'I swear to serve you with my intelligence, with my arm, with my heart, humbly and boldly; and that if the day comes in which I must give my blood for you and my life, I will give my blood and die, screaming your sainted name at the sky and sending my final kiss to your blessed flag.'

Blood is everywhere in *Cuore*, hot and red as Garibaldi's shirt. A person is Italian, so the ideology insists, because the blood that runs in his veins is Italian. With that blood, a contract is signed. During Mussolini's reign, every young person in Italy was conscripted to a scholastic-cum-paramilitary organization, the 'Gioventù Italiana del Littorio', and issued with a two-page booklet. Small enough to fit in a breast pocket, close to the heart, it set out the mutual obligations of state and individual.

I have Dirce's booklet here: a vibrant clementine-coloured cover carries the benevolent face of Il Duce, throwing his head back in laughter, superimposed across the silhouette of the Fascist eagle. The year is 'Anno XVI', 1938 – because the Fascists had rewritten time itself – and inside, beneath the subject line 'La Piccola Italiana' ('The Little Italian Girl'), are basic administrative details: membership number (Nº. 1655374), name (S––utto), date of birth (24 October 1926), the name of the man of the house (since the death of Angelo, this was young Pietro). On the facing page are the 'Terms and Conditions of Italianness': in the case of temporary invalidity, the individual will receive 2 lire per day, beginning on the eleventh day of invalidity, up to a maximum of seventy days. In the case of death, the family will receive a one-off payment of 5,000 lire (roughly €5,000 today). In exchange, *la piccola italiana* 'swears, in the name of God and Italy, to execute the orders of Il Duce and to serve with all my might and if necessary with my blood the cause of the Fascist Revolution'. Prose of such simple, righteous violence would have seemed natural and right to one raised on *Cuore*.

Angelo preferred Dirce to read from his own childhood copy of the book. It was scarlet, she remembers, its cloth binding worn and fraying at the edges. (There is a volume that fits the description, published by Fratelli Trevis in Milan in 1913, when Angelo would have been eleven. It was probably given to him for his birthday.) Often, while he busied himself with some chore or other, he would ask his daughter to read aloud to him, and the chapter on Garibaldi was a favourite. The page was dog-eared for ease of finding:

> At the age of eight he saved the life of a woman, at thirteen he saved a boatful of companions who had been

shipwrecked, at twenty-seven he saved a boy from drowning off the coast of Marseille, at forty-one he stopped a ship catching fire at sea. He fought in America for ten years for the liberty of a foreign people, he fought three wars against the Austrians, for the liberation of Lombardy and the Trentino, defended Rome from the French in 1849, freed Naples and Palermo in 1860, he fought for Rome again in '67, and, in 1870, against the Germans in defence of France... He took part in forty battles and won thirty-seven of them.

I picture Angelo, pausing at his task, looking into Dirce's eyes: 'Thirty-seven out of forty!' The sum, and the lack of punctuation, left them both breathless. '*Eccezionale*!' Truly exceptional.

After the family's move to England in the autumn of 1935, Angelo was especially insistent on Dirce's reading, and the recitation of Garibaldi's successes took on a deeper significance. I imagine the repetition of passages, the comfort found, the devotion, the marvel. Stories known off by heart, muttered, half-consciously, almost in song. *At the age of eight ... saved ... woman ... thirteen ... boatful ... shipwreck ... twenty-seven ... boy ... drowning ... forty-one ... fire ... liberty .... defended ... won.* A secular rosary. Smooth beads of Italy.

'Voleva che tenessi l'Italia nel cuore', says Nonna. Angelo didn't want his daughter to forget Italy; literally, he wanted her to keep the homeland in her heart. Perhaps he thought the ancients were on to something when they said that that's where memory resides. We get the word 'record' from the Latin *cor*, heart, and, in Italian, the verb *ricordare*, to remember.

And then there's the fact that home – we have it on the authority of Pliny the Elder and a legion of scatter cushions, doormats and novelty mugs – is where the heart is. No matter how many times I turn the proverb over in my mind I can't work it out. Is it intended as a consolation or as a bald statement of fact? Is it: *Wherever you may go, don't worry, you carry your home in your heart.* Or is it: *Your heart stays at home. You'll have to return there if you want it back.*

This, I think, has something to do with a feeling I've had since September 2004, when I left Italy for England: a more or less constant sense of having forgotten something important, like the housekeys or my own name.

I wonder if 'home is where the heart is' is also why, when you sing the national anthem, you're supposed to put a hand to your heart, to shield it or prevent it from escaping.

*

Patriotism and romance, ideally, tragic, were the main elements that Angelo looked for in a tale. We know this from his daughter, the only person who remembers him, his legendary trunk of books and the stories he told over and over. From her we also know that, at the old house off via G. Mazzini – how he must have loved the revolutionary ring of the address – he kept canaries and other small birds. And exotic plants, which he sought out, read up on and preened.

'Plants you'll have never seen, obviously. Peanuts! Chinotto trees! *Rabarbaro*! When no one in Italy grew rhubarb!'

At one point, he had several angora rabbits, bought at exorbitant cost from a man in Genoa.

'Did he sell the fur?' I ask, puzzled.

'Ah, non mi ricordo... I think we probably ate them.'

He developed his own photographs. In a toy chest in Nonna's basement, among the debris of several generations, is a shabby old camera with long bellows. 'Always, he was taking photographs, always... Two minutes I'd been born and he was taking my photograph. *T'immagini*? My *mamma*, the poor tired thing.'

In the late 1920s, before Angelo took his family to England, he did the accounts at the cooperative, keeping sums of what people paid and what they owed. Surname after surname in his neat italic hand, each followed by an address and columns of figures that kept track, week after week, of the precarious balance of a family's existence. When people didn't pay – couldn't pay – he would make a note. More often than not, he wouldn't.

'Everyone had too many debts. Where would you start? For what?' Sometimes, Nonna says, he got 'creative'. One day, she tells me on the phone, when she was in her seventies, running errands in Maniago, a woman about ten years older than her, tapped her on the arm. 'She told me a story about my father. That when she was about seven, this woman, she went to the coop to buy some vinegar. Her mother sent her. If you had debts sometimes it was better to send a child. And so she took the bottle to him but she had no money. He said it was a present and he gave her some mints, too. She told me she would never forget his kindness.' I have heard this one before. Sometimes the encounter happened 'just the other day', sometimes in the supermarket, sometimes at Church.

For the rest of that day's *appuntamento*, Nonna and I re-tread familiar ground. I let her tell me about the 1,000 kisses, about the sweets Angelo always had in his jacket pocket, about generous presents, charitable acts and impressive home improvements, including a quite elaborate compost system. Angelo liked to be liked, I think. And he liked to be talked about.

Beyond Nonna's memories, there is little to help us piece together Angelo's story, let alone to understand what he made of it as it unfolded. When he took his young family to England in 1935, did he feel like things were opening up, getting better, or did he feel cornered, as if the choice to go were only an illusion? Did he tell his wife Novella that everything was going to be fine – *you'll see* – and did he believe it himself? Did he tell himself that he, like Garibaldi, could – *should* – achieve great things, or did he satisfy himself with the knowledge that – *thank God* – he had his health, his family, and a bit of money, which was, after all, more than many could say? Did he feel in control of his own situation? And when, later, on his deathbed, he shed that single tear, what life, what vision of the future was he mourning?

Few documents survive, if they ever existed. A birth certificate tells us that the move to England was in fact more of a homecoming than a fresh start. Angelo was born in Holborn in London, on 2 April 1902, down a lane that no longer exists, off City Road, in what appears to be now the bureau de change of a Marks & Spencer's department store. From the birthdates of two older sisters, one of whom was born in Italy and the other in Holborn, we infer that the parents, Pietro and Romana, moved to London sometime between 1894 and 1900.

In the working-class district of Holborn, among other Italians, they will have found a small community of Friulian migrants, some of them perhaps relatives, the first of whom had arrived about twenty years earlier. A report on London's 'Italian colony' published in 1895 by the Italian Embassy paints a picture of the family's new home: 'organ grinders in the public streets, ice-cream vendors, artists' models, street peddlers... fruit sellers, grocers,

81

cobblers, upholsterers, cabinet-makers, opticians, and makers of musical instruments'.

In the 1901 census Old Pietro is listed as a 'worker in mosaic manufactory'. His wage will have been low, supplemented by whatever odd construction jobs were going. The address given here is different to that on Angelo's birth certificate the following year, but all that tells us is that they moved to a new house before the third child was born. We don't know if this was for better or for worse.

Between Angelo's appearance in 1902 and the next census, in 1911, there is no sign of the boy's whereabouts. Nonna says it's likely that, being a weak-chested child in run-down lodgings, he was sent back to Maniago, where the pre-Alpine air was pure and would surely help him 'grow strong'. The 1911 census seems to confirm this notion: Pietro, age forty-six, is the only one left behind, now living in a poor area of Sheffield in a two-up two-down terraced house with six other men, ranging in age from fifty-four to seventeen, none of them apparently related, all Italians, all 'mosaic workers'. The census date is 2 April, Angelo's ninth birthday. He is figured by his absence. It's probable that father and son didn't see each other for years at a time.

Our next glimpse of Angelo comes in a reference letter dated 14 May 1917. Just turned fifteen, he is three years too young to fight in the First World War. He would have failed the physical anyway. Instead, he is working in Bologna, about 150 miles south of Maniago, in a hardware store at n.4 via Zamboni, one of the city's main arteries, running through the university area and the Jewish quarter. His employer – the elaborate signature is difficult to make out, but I think he is a Signor Fossardi – describes him in quasi military terms as having spent the preceding six months in 'active and honest service'.

The letter suggests that Angelo's school days are already behind him.

I see a scrawny teenage Angelo sitting on the step of n.4 via Zamboni at noon, tearing absent-mindedly at a hunk of bread. Perhaps he is remembering his history lessons and thinking of Luigi Zamboni, an early martyr for Italian Unification. According to one apocryphal tale, Zamboni is the originator of the green, white and red *tricolore* flag. More likely Angelo is just watching students rush to their lessons. What books did they hug to their chests? Would he have had the confidence to ask? And to tell them in exchange what he was reading? Did he envy them or was he glad to be working? Then Signor Fossardi calls him back inside to serve a customer. He briskly smooths his apron and throws the bread crust to the pigeons. Or stuffs it in his trouser pocket; he has known hunger.

A few years later, probably around 1920, we find active, honest Angelo wearing a chef's toque and white coat, over a pristine shirt and tie. His hands are on his hips, resting above a holster carrying three impressive knives of the sort his daughter would one day make. He looks like a stock character. Nonna says this was in Malta. Nobody can account for it.

Click, wind the camera on.

By 1925, Angelo was back in Maniago, nursing a broken heart. The young woman 'didn't want him,' says Nonna, 'maybe because he was short. And he limped.' A family friend quickly set him up with Novella. 'It made sense. They were both from high families.' By the end of the year, they were married.

A photograph from 1926 shows the couple sitting side by side in their Sunday best: Angelo wears a dark suit with a white shirt, bow tie, pocket square and felt trilby;

Novella is more understated, in a shapeless white dress. Based on the dress's light fabric, I think it must be springtime, and, from the way it bunches around her middle, that she is already pregnant.

You can tell that Angelo has been photographed many times before, that he has studied the art of the pose. He knows to sit up straight and turn his face slightly to the side, to tilt his chin down to accentuate the chiaroscuro and strengthen his feminine features. Novella slouches and stares straight into the camera, like a surly teen.

Later that year, their first child, Dirce, was born. Another photograph: Novella in a nightcap, propped up in bed, cradling the new arrival. ('Two minutes I'd been born...') Mother and child are dead centre, with a crucifix nailed to the wall above them, slightly askew. Novella's face is inscrutability incarnate. One moment, I convince myself that the start of a smile tightens the corners of her mouth; the next, it's vanished, and her brow is as heavy and grey as wet cement.

'Were they in love?' I ask Nonna one day.

'They fought like anything.'

A pause.

I think of Novella and Angelo's bed, now relegated to the cellar of *zia* Lucia's house, to a room with no windows, whose only source of natural light is a few glass tiles set into the terrace above, where we eat in the summer. When there are too many visitors for the beds in the rest of the house, we grandchildren flip a coin and hope not to lose. We think the mattress is stuffed with horsehair, which seems to have preserved the shape of other bodies in other times.

'But they loved each other.'

Click; and wind on.

*

I have just two other photographs of Angelo, both se-
pia-tinted and faded. My copies are copies of copies,
and I point out to Nonna that it's impossible to tell that
Angelo's eyes were blue.

'They were brown!'

I have the temerity to ask if she's sure.

(Later that day, I ask my sister what colour she imagines Angelo's eyes to have been: 'blue,' she says, without
hesitation.)

The original photographs were taken in Maniago. In
the one dated 1933, Angelo strikes a dandyish pose: a
louche intellectual, leaning back on a high stool, his hands
in his pockets. He is thirty or thirty-one. Above two-tone
brogues are pale wide-legged trousers, neatly creased
down the front. His slightly crumpled blazer is open and
his shirt collar unbuttoned. This carefree arrangement
is undone by his frown. He is visiting from Manchester,
probably for the summer, and I don't think he wants to go
back, to leave his wife and children behind again. By now
there is little Pietro, too.

An entry from that year in Kelly's Directory lists
Angelo as a 'terrazzo specialist' in Manchester. This
sounds far superior to 'mosaic worker'. Could Angelo,
with his hands on his hips, have insisted on that wording?
It sets him at a remove from his neighbours: poulter, shop-
keeper, greengrocer, bricksetter. His is the only Italian
name among Kennedys and Cohens, on Johnson Street
in Collyhurst, a down-at-heel inner-city neighbourhood.

Another directory from the same year has him at a
different address and I imagine that 1933 was a time of
flux and anxiety for him. It was for many, after all. I'm
sure he read the newspapers – perhaps, like me, one

English and one Italian. Adolf Hitler had become the German Chancellor and talk of war was building; there were reports on the Nazi Party's persecution of political opponents and the use of concentration camps for those deemed 'dangerous'. Italians in Britain, whether newly arrived or British-born like him, were viewed with increasing suspicion and hostility. Had Angelo lived a few years longer, he would have read about anti-Italian riots in some parts of Britain. He would have been grateful that Manchester was not one of those places, but then he would have worried whether this might change, and when. Later came Winston Churchill's order to 'collar the lot!'; the mass internments, the displacements. In that sense, Angelo was lucky.

Bound up in the changes of the early 1930s was the knowledge that a particular way of life – the easy movement between two countries, which Angelo had always taken for granted – was hanging in the balance. He would have to choose. It was around this time, Nonna tells me, that he started to plan the whole family's departure from Italy. She was seven and Pietro was two, and this, she thinks, is when her parents began to argue.

Behind every question I pose about Angelo's state of mind in this period is a host of others that gather, unspoken, at the margins. How did my great-grandfather feel as Italy fell in line with Germany, as the two countries between which his life was split became enemies? Did he believe war to be necessary? Just? Was the move to England a denunciation of the Fascist regime, or was it a simple matter of pragmatism, of making money to live on while waiting for order to be restored, or imposed? Who did he think was in the right? Was his Italian patriotism, his nationalist enthusiasm, of a nineteenth- or twentieth-century sort? That is, was it spurred by a

Mazzinian belief in liberty and each nation's right to self-determination, or by a destructive quest for domin- ion? I can go in circles picking at the edges of the picture, delaying the inevitable question: was Angelo – like his dear *zio* Gioacchino – a fascist? Might he one day have been praised in the *Gazzetta Ufficiale del Regno d'Italia* for 'services to fascism abroad', as *zio* was in December 1935, a few days before Angelo's death? Had Angelo been alive in 1938 when the 'Manifesto del razzismo Italiano' brought into effect laws banning Jews from publishing, education and the workforce, would he have thought back on his time in Bologna and said to himself, 'Well, yes, that seems right, all things considered.' And if he was a fascist, how would that change things for us now? Would I still want to tell his story and bind it so closely with my own?

The second of the Maniago photographs is undated but was, we think, taken in 1935, not long before the family set off for England. There is something decisive about it. Angelo stands with his arms folded, his hands tucked out of sight and his feet apart, as though challenging someone to try to knock him down. He wears a dark suit, buttoned up, with a pocket square and tie, and round tortoiseshell glasses. His hair is swept back from his forehead and slick with pommade. To his right stands his cousin Luigi, and in front of them are two other cousins, Aldo and Osvaldo. All are impeccably dressed. I shouldn't say it – it's what other people say, people who have seen too many films – but they look like mobsters. Everyone but Angelo appears smiling and relaxed. The background is one of those mottled photographer's screens, like an artist's ren- dition of fog, or a haze of other memories, untamed by the lens.

The only documents left to mention speak of abrupt

endings: in 1929, Angelo and Novella's first son Manlio died shortly before his first birthday. (Was he named for Garibaldi's last-born son?)

In October 1931, at sixty-six, Old Pietro, the family's Hercules, still taking whatever jobs were going, died alone in an infirmary in Barrow-in-Furness, after an accident on a building site. Pietro had not long returned to England after a brief retirement back in Italy: it was so much easier building houses than mucking out the cowshed, he had said.

Four years later, at precisely half his father's age, Angelo caught rheumatic fever. His heart gave out.

The burial record for the grave that father and son share in City Road Cemetery in Sheffield tells us that Angelo was a 'stone mason' – nothing special about it – who died at '123 Crescent Road, Crumpsall, Manchester', a workhouse that was transitioning in pre-NHS England into a general hospital. We know that there was no money, and that his burial, like that of his father, was paid for by *zio* Gioacchino. *Zio*, it seems, took care of a great deal.

There is a neat circularity to Angelo's life, which began on one City Road and ended on another. But this belies the unrest of his thirty-three years. There is a suggestion of disorder in the register's misspelling of the family surname: at birth Angelo was S--utti; at death, S--utte. In the same grave, his father is S--ite. Elsewhere, I have found –uti, –utto, –ute and –uto. Ashes to ashes, dust to dust, and in between scraps, mislabelled boxes, and questions.

One afternoon in Nonna's kitchen, I ask her what his voice was like.

'Calma, raffinata'; calm and refined. (Could a nine-year-old have appreciated the second quality?)

I ask her to try to remember more details. Did he speak

English with an Italian accent?

'Non mi ricordo.'

Or Italian with an English accent?

'No, no...'

Was he different when you were in England?

'Non mi ricordo.'

What did he smell like?

'Non mi ricordo. Tobacco, maybe.'

And his hands?

'Non mi –', she catches herself.

'He had nice hands, elegant, you know? Refined.'

That word again.

'His hands were not like mine.'

She holds hers up to show me. Her fingers are long and bent by arthritis, and her palms are large, disproportionately so.

'I have my mother's hands.'

She pulls at a particularly crooked finger, tuts, and puts her hands back down in her lap, out of sight under the table.

'My hands worked hard.'

As a child I used to press my fingers into the tips of hers, or gently pinch them, and count how long the imprint remained in her flesh. 'The elastic has gone,' she would say, as though talking about an old pair of gloves she hadn't got around to replacing. 'It will come to you, too.' But Angelo's hands are eternally youthful, frozen at the age of thirty-three. Mine are older now than his will ever be.

The things Angelo's daughter remembers about him point to an exceptionalism that the scant documents don't support. But I see something of it in the photographs. The self-conscious stance and the careful dress. These things he chose. Much like he chose to be photographed in Maniago rather than in Manchester, as though to commemorate one version of himself over another, the Italian over the English. In Maniago, he was Angelo, from a good family with nice things – not a member of the gentry, but better off than most. His hobbies were rarefied, at times extravagant; he did not – *would not* – work in a factory, and had the authority to waive the cost of a bottle of vinegar on a kind whim. To be another little girl's hero. In England, he was a manual labourer and a foreigner, no matter the country given on his birth certificate. His choice was, then, whether to photograph a somebody or a nobody.

The anxiety of choice is, I think, Angelo's most enduring legacy, and perhaps this is why photography appealed to him. It was for him to decide what moment and who deserved to be captured for posterity, for him to arrange and frame. If we have only a handful of photographs of Angelo himself, we have hundreds taken by him. Nonna discovers them still in envelopes and drawers and between the pages of old books, where she must have put them years ago for safekeeping. Now, she saves them up for my visits, so many fragments of the story he wanted to tell, in which photographs are like paragraphs, words written in light and dark. His eye discerned, his finger hovered, and he held his breath until everything was steady, just as he wanted it. Click.

*

We tell ourselves stories to live, Didion said, they reassure and guide. A cherished one is that people care about the past, and that they learn from it. In May 2014, an article by Gregory Rodriguez in *Time* magazine reported that genealogy is the second most popular hobby in the U.S. after gardening ... and the second most visited category of websites, after pornography. It's a billion-dollar industry that has spawned profitable websites, television shows, scores of books and — with the advent of over-the-counter genetic test kits — a cottage industry in DNA ancestry testing.

Phrases such as 'identity crisis' and 'finding oneself' became common from the 1960s, part of a 'newfound need to locate oneself in uncertain cultural terrain'. Rodriguez repeats the psychologist Roy F. Baumeister's suggestion that genealogy is popular because it is the only 'quest for self-knowledge' whose techniques are 'clear cut, a matter of definite questions with definite answers'. You are this because your ancestors were that. You have always felt different, somehow. Now you know. There must be something in the blood. Here's the proof. You are the great-great-grandson of a queen. Or a scullery maid. One minute you're a weed, the next you're made of gold. Or vice versa.

Stories are currency, too. You can run a country on stories. In Italy, a narrative reminiscent of Judge Wilson's greenhouse tale of invasive dandelions and noble roses has long been prominent. 'Migrants are a social bomb that risks exploding,' said Silvio Berlusconi, the country's longest-serving post-war prime minister, in 2018. Infamous from the 1970s for his monopolization of the media, Berlusconi has done more than anyone to shape the nation's appetite for tales. Generations, mine included, have been brought up on the soap operas he commissioned or bought-in from abroad, with dating and talent shows providing a steady diet of happy-ever-afters and rags-to-riches.

The longest-running talent show, *La Corrida: Dilettanti allo sbaraglio* (roughly, 'Amateurs under pressure'), saw contestants demonstrate their unique capabilities on stage, to be voted 'in' or 'out' by the public at home. I remember an ageing businessman singing Pavarotti, a housewife dressed as a child performing a song in some Alpine dialect, a male volleyball coach dancing on roller skates to a backing track of Aqua's hit song 'Barbie Girl'. The studio audience made their feelings known through a mixture of clapping and whistling and by beating wooden spoons on pots and pans. The host's beautiful assistant sang a ditty to the tune of Domenico Modugno's 'Volare': *Sei tu, il pubblico tu, decidi chi vale di più* ('It's you, the public is you, to decide who has most value'). At stake was a new television set, and the chance to be somebody, however briefly.

Where once there were only television and newspapers, now there is social media, with its many conduits to the public imagination. The rise of Matteo Salvini, the head of the right-wing Lega party and, between June 2018 and September 2019, Deputy Prime Minister of Italy, was fuelled by the dissemination of sensational stories in which intimidating immigrants victimize natives, preventing them from reaching their true, stellar potential.

For Salvini, immigrants have always been slackers, thieves and rapists, and as the country's economy continued to falter and the winds of populism gathered force, these views found increasingly fertile ground. As early as 2009, he had called for the two front carriages of every train in Milan's underground to be reserved for women, 'so that they can feel safe from the intrusion and rudeness of non-EU citizens'. Because their ways are different to ours. In 2016, he promised that, under his control, the government and the police would have a free hand to 'clean up the cities'. 'Ours,' he explained, 'will be a managed and funded ethnic cleansing' – he used that term precisely – 'the same as that the Italians are suffering, oppressed by illegal immigrants.' He quotes Mussolini freely. Casting himself as 'the last of the good Christians', he has called on all Italians to assist him in a 'battaglia di civiltà e legalità per salvare vite', a battle of civility and legality to save lives. Certain lives.

In government, Salvini focused his ire on the Roma population, Italy's largest ethnic minority, as well as on closing the country's ports to aid ships and shutting down centres that assist migrants. In 2019 he refused to allow a ship containing refugees to dock in Sicily, imposing a kind of quarantine in which the people themselves were the disease. Never mind that the number of arrivals on Italian soil had been dropping steadily for years. The number perishing at sea, on the other hand, has risen. Still, his narrative remains the same: they are a threat to us. They are invading, holding us back, crushing us underfoot. Other politicians have followed Salvini in appealing to our darkest impulses, most recently and successfully Giorgia Meloni, leader of the nationalist party Fratelli d'Italia, and her acolyte Rachele Mussolini, granddaughter of Benito. Mussolini was elected to Rome's council in 2021, with an emphatic share of the public vote.

Sei tu, il pubblico tu, decidi chi vale di più.

Who remembers the Italians deemed 'socially suspect', pulled out of their homes and rounded up, whose contribution to the British economy was deemed weak, and whose sexual appetites gave cause for fear. As Emerson said, 'Time dissipates to shining ether the solid angularity of facts.'

*

My uncle Manlio, named for his grandfather's lost son, says that emigration divides families, and not only physically. The unvisited graves of the S––utti, –utte, –ite, –uti, –utto, –ute and –uto are a testament to this. Emigration splits the individual, too. I am a different version of myself in Italy to the one I am in England. I'm not sure how discernible it is to others, but I feel it in my bones, in my skin, in the way I hold myself and speak to people. In Italy, I am quieter, more timid and awkward. I start sentences and halfway through lose my way. I have been told I tilt my chin down and talk into my chest. I mumble. This was not always so – that used to be the English me.

When you move between countries or cultures you might, like me, imagine it as a process of splitting, of parcelling out; a protracted negotiation in which belonging is measured in terms of years served or documents amassed – certificates to prove birth, education, marriage, death. I used to say I was fifty–fifty Italian–English, making an automatic gesture with my hand, slicing the air somewhere around my middle. As though heritage were biometric, certifiable, something you could capture and frame.

Now I see it more as a process of draining, as though the Italianness is running out of me with every year spent abroad. I need to go back periodically to top up my levels. When I attempt to explain this to Nonna, she is dismissive.

'You'll always have Italian blood,' she says.

And though I know this is a ridiculous, and dangerous, notion, I can't say I don't find some comfort in it.

'But you should read more Italian books,' she says. 'To keep it up.'

I wonder whether Angelo made these kinds of

calculations too, where he drew the line, and what images and metaphors served him. The two spools of a camera's film, perhaps: one taut with rolled-up potential; the other, a series of realities exposed and already fading. And you only get so many shots.

In each of the photographs we have of Angelo, he appears to be trying out a different version of himself: aesthete, newlywed, master chef, boss. Like a jobbing actor's showreel. The identities drift free of any convincing scene I can set. I can't put him in motion and struggle to imagine him outside of the photographer's studio – in a train carriage, say, or at a bar or walking with friends in the street – because my mind can't determine where he belongs. Will I set him in industrialized, inner-city Manchester, one among many men in workman's overalls; or, in agrarian Maniago, strolling down via Mazzini on market day? Is it sunny where he is, or overcast? Is he a butterfly on a stable door or a moth on a factory wall? His body, the way he carries himself, the tension in his muscles, the texture of his skin, the tone of his voice – everything changes depending on the answers.

It is possible that there was something over the top about Angelo's Italianness, something performative, as though to compensate for his having been born on foreign soil. You've heard of the zeal of the religious convert, but there's also the zeal of the immigrant or mixed-heritage individual, who acts out his belonging for all to see. This usually goes in one of two opposing directions.

In the first, he assimilates in every way possible, often shedding whichever culture supposedly holds him back or doesn't fit anymore. He is playing a figure in the crowd and does not want to stand out. In the second, he enters the new country screaming at the sky and blowing kisses over his shoulder, knowing that, even though he is relieved to have arrived – and, in Angelo's case, found work – the place he has left behind is far superior. That place is home. His heart is there. The displacement, in other words, is begrudged but necessary, and he wants you to know that he is not like you. Or not entirely. He has something you don't, something special.

This is, I know, a simplistic opposition, when in fact most people find themselves – like me – somewhere in the middle, oscillating between cultures. A friend of mine, a psychotherapist, talks of the process of cultural integration, both into a society and within the individual, in terms borrowed from travel, marriage counselling and grief therapy. Nostalgia, romance about where you no longer are, she says, can prevent you ever truly 'arriving and unpacking' anywhere else. But you can't go back, either. *Nostalgia* joins together the Greek words *nóstos* (νόστος) and *álgos* (ἄλγος), 'homecoming' and 'pain'. It's painful because you intuit that return is impossible. You need to find a way of 'mediating', my friend says, of 'reconciling' the different aspects of yourself. You must allow yourself to 'mourn the loss' of the old culture. A part of you – in fact, a version of you that could have been – has died; or, at least, is being kept alive by artificial measures, by imagination alone. Perhaps you need to let it go and be happy with the memory. (But it is precisely the memory that smarts, reproaching you for not reading enough books, for taking a culture for granted and letting it slip through your fingers.)

Where there is disappointment and insecurity, as there was for Angelo in England, one might use one country or culture as a stick with which to beat the other, which has, you feel, let you down or abused you in some way. 'You think this country is so good, you think *I* need it?' And the more tenuous your claims to that other place and its other you become, the more extravagantly you will perform the role. It consoles you.

I do it myself. In England, asked for identification, I proffer my Italian ID card rather than my British driver's licence. I tut at the recklessness of people who drink on an empty stomach (though I am not exactly innocent of the charge), swim on a full one or sit in a draft. And often, when I can't sleep, I wonder what kind of life I would be leading if I were in Italy now or if I had never come to England at all: What job would I be doing? Would I be successful? Better off than I am? What kind of house would I live in? Where would I shop? What would I do at the weekends? These musings are the luxury of someone raised in a peaceful Europe with the free movement of people enshrined – until recently – in law.

The more you depend on a place for survival, for practical reasons (employment, say), and the more unreasonable a return to the other place becomes, the more you feel trapped, wrenched apart by circumstances beyond your control. Bitterness might build as reason (the head) loses to resentment (the heart). I imagine Angelo measuring himself out, slicing his hand through the air in front of his body, perhaps near his neck, to cleave himself in two. The head: England. The heart and the rest of him: Italy. The gesture has another, more macabre, meaning.

In an English hospital bed in December 1935, Angelo realized he would never again set foot in Italy. He had run out of time. The stories he adored and the men he admired all placed the gravest importance on homecoming, as though Italianness itself were defined by the moment of return. 'You will know what it means to be Italian,' the father tells his son in *Cuore*, 'when returning from a long trip, after a long absence ... you'll see the great blue mountains of your country; you'll feel it then in the impulsive

97

wave of tenderness that will fill your eyes with tears and rip a cry from your heart.' Instead, Angelo died worrying about the future of his family, and, perhaps, that his children would forget Italy, that their Italianness would escape them. And before he departed, he shed that single tear, *una lacrima d'Italia.*

I tried to visit Angelo's grave in Sheffield about fifteen years ago, taking a small bunch of white roses with me. Unprepared for the sheer size of the cemetery, I failed to find him and was left to imagine his gravestone written in a language he did not consider his own, in a country whose inhabitants might puzzle over his name. Like Angela, a girl's name and common enough in England, too. Or, like 'angel', but not quite. *Angel-oh.*

I left the roses at the cemetery entrance, hoping that counted for something, and touched the iron gate on my way out – *tocca ferro* – as Italians do, for luck.

*

Nonna, on the phone, is trying to convince me that she is more English than Italian. She is ninety-three at this point. Only about twenty of her years were spent in England; the rest were in Italy. She barely speaks English anymore. It just doesn't add up, I tell her.

'It could only ever be this way,' she says. 'Too much of me is in England.'

By this, she means: 'My father, his father, my child' – the triple-decker grave that had escaped me.

I tell her that I have been reading *Cuore*, because I think it will please her, and ask if she remembers the tract on Garibaldi?

'Ma no, nina – how could I remember after all these years?'

A pause.

'How many battles,' she says, half question, half exclamation. 'Many, many... And thirty-three won.'

Later that day, I read a passage in which the boy is asked in an exam, 'Why do you love Italy?' When his father learns that he was unable to answer, he wants to know (and takes over the writing of the diary, in fact): 'Didn't a hundred answers spring to mind?'

> I love Italy because my mother is Italian, because the blood
> that runs in my veins is Italian, because the ground in which
> are buried the dead my mother laments and my father
> venerates is Italian, because the city in which I was born,
> the language I speak, the books that teach me, because my
> brother, my sister, my friends, and the great people among
> which I live, and the beautiful nature that surrounds me,
> and everything that I see, that I love, that I study, that I
> admire, is Italian.

When Edmondo de Amicis wrote this passage in the mid-1880s, Garibaldi was dead and for many his dream had become a nightmare. Thousands of Italians, my own among them, were fleeing the chaos of post-Unification Italy in search of better lives abroad. I suppose that de Amicis could not have appreciated that he was building unrealistic expectations for the fragmented families of the twentieth- and twenty-first centuries; that he was setting up generations for a sense of failure, nostalgia and neuroses.

No doubt he was trying to dissuade his compatriots from leaving. Or perhaps he genuinely thought that, given the chance, we would all return to those great blue mountains, no matter the cost.

My parents moved away from the apartment opposite the Raimondi-Odescalchi's chapel about six weeks after I was born. My sister was due to start nursery in a European School about an hour away, in Varese. (Strange that the Italian word for 'nursery' is *asilo*, 'asylum', as if the children are fleeing their homes.) She, and later I, would be in the school's English-language section because English was our mother's tongue; there were also German, French, Dutch, and Italian sections. Apparently, for some time after I started at the *asilo* I refused to speak anything but English to anyone and this came as a surprise because until that point I had spoken Italian almost exclusively. My father used to call me his *piccola italiana*, ignoring the historical echo, and still laments how much Italian I lost through this early internal schism.

We left our tenuous connection to revolutionary history behind in Como, pocketing the story of Garibaldi's wedding as we did the special bits of flint we sometimes found on the banks of the Cellina. But for some years after, almost two decades, in fact, when we went over that way, we would often take the long route home, meandering down via Vittorio Veneto and pulling in by the tall gate for a moment to check that, yes, our name was still on the buzzer, my father's handwriting faded but decipherable. And for the next hour or so as we drove back to Varese, a question hung silently between us: Who would we be had we stayed living on that other lake, whose waters are cleaner, colder and deeper?

We all play these games of make-believe, but some of us do so more frequently, and with greater intensity. We put our heart into it, and sometimes, I think, we leave it there. I count this as part of my inheritance.

100

'It is what it is,' says my dad, his motto for life, recently adopted. Born in England and now living in Italy, he seems at the age of sixty-six to have learnt to quieten the what-ifs.

It strikes me one afternoon, talking to him on the phone, that Old Pietro died at his current age, and Angelo died at mine. Just one more coincidence to be alert to, as if it's part of some underlying mathematical pattern that – like years spent here versus years spent there; a tally of documents; this fiction of blood – helps us to keep track of where we are in the family saga.

'Let's hope we get to our next birthdays,' my dad says breezily before hanging up.

Click; and wind on.

*

I imagine that, if Angelo were around to read this account of his brief life, he would not object to the sorrowful wash of it all. What parts would make him nod as he recognizes something true? What parts would he censure or correct? Have I got the balance right between the light and dark? He could, once and for all, tidy up this story about the 'high' name – if there was money, where did it come from and where did it go? – and clarify his politics.

We might find ourselves talking about Garibaldi and how, a few months after that fiasco in Como, the General led his band of 1,000 patriots – ragged, half-starved and ill-equipped – to overwhelming victory in the south. How, in Sicily, where he pronounced himself dictator, he was viewed as a demi-God by the peasants he freed from slavery. What a guy. *Eccezzionale*.

And Giuseppina? I'd tell him what little I have managed to find out. That she was bundled into hiding by her father, in a house on the western shore of Lake Como. That she lost the baby, a boy, at full term. (That I can't stop wondering where he is buried. There's nothing to go on.) That sometimes the locals spotted her out walking – thinking, maybe playing make-believe – always dressed in the finest silk dresses. That the rest of her life appears to have been uneventful. There was another child and, after the annulment, a second marriage. She died in 1918, at the age of seventy-seven, almost four decades after Garibaldi. She never attacked him in public, and never told her side of the story. An inscription on her tomb reads: *Amò l'Italia più di se stessa*. 'She loved Italy more than herself.'

I think it would please Angelo to point out the mistakes in my stories. *It wasn't like that at all; I never had my heart broken by a woman; no, no, you've got de Amicis all wrong, you're missing the point, read the book again, you'll see.*

Specifically, though, he would catch me out on the colour of Garibaldi's eyes.

'His eyes were brown!'

It's true. The blueness of the General's eyes is a myth hatched in his own lifetime and rehearsed so many times by so many as to become more real than reality itself. Still it goes on. Until recently I had believed in their rare blueness, too, and even now that I know the truth I can't undo the fiction. We see what we want to see and what we want to see is the exceptional. Our stories seem to depend on it. But Garibaldi's eyes were probably brown. Like Angelo's, like Dirce's, like my father's and mine. And it is what it is: the most common eye colour of all, shared by more than half of the world's population. So not very special at all.

IV.

It is summer 2019 and the mercury is pushing 40° Celsius outside. Nonna and I slouch at the kitchen table with our shoes off to make the most of the cool tiles. 'We need rain,' Nonna says, squinting out of the open window towards the mountains, as if they might hear her and oblige. She scans for the iron cross that stands at the top of a pilgrim route. You can only see it if you know it's there – a fine black outline grazing indigo trees.

We sit side by side in front of my laptop's screen. Scattered around us on the floor are the inanimate bodies of flies, dozens of them. Dirce's Christianity recognizes all creatures great and small but these she cannot abide. With her trusty red swat, a cheap marriage of plastic and wire, patched together with decades' worth of sticky tape, she shows no mercy. A thwack on the table and then a flick to the floor. When I wince, she laughs. 'Tell me, what is the point of them?'

I have found a short film online, *Ritratto di un paese*, 'Portrait of a Land', shot in Maniago in 1949 by Romolo Marcellini, the second in a series called 'Tempo in cammino', 'Time on the March'. It was commissioned by the Italian wing of the Economic Cooperation Administration, a US government agency founded the previous year to administer the Marshall Plan. Until the mid-1950s, the Plan pumped the equivalent of about $130 billion into a ravaged Europe, and the ECA produced hundreds of films like *Ritratto*. The aim was to convince viewers that the Plan was achieving dazzling results, and that Italy, now under the banner of democratic neo-liberalism, was back on track after the misadventures of fascism and war.

Another kind of war was underway and cinema had

been enlisted. In 1951, a few years after the establishment of the United Nations Educational Scientific and Cultural Organization (UNESCO), Ross McLean, head of the Films and Visual Information Division, summed up the spirit: 'The frontiers which divide mankind are not only, and not even mainly, the national or political frontiers,' he wrote in the organization's monthly magazine. 'They are frontiers of the mind and the spirit which spring from limitations of training and experience, differences of memory and tradition and belief and taste, and the wilful or accidental exploitation of these limitations and differences for sinister ends.' *Differences of memory.* Such a hard-working phrase to slip in so lightly.

I spent last night propped up in Novella and Angelo's old bed reading a print-out of a study of the Marshall Plan films by Regina M. Longo, in which she quotes McLean. Even in the *cantina* it was too hot to sleep. But it was also too hot to concentrate much, so by 2 a.m., more of Longo's text was underlined in red biro than not. Everything is important when you're not sure what you're looking for. I underlined the titles of Marcellini's films twice: *Talking to the Italians, The Struggle for Men's Minds, Italy and the World.*

When I was a child, an indeterminate fear kept me awake in that bed. I used to be petrified of being pos-sessed by a spirit and forced to relinquish control to its diabolical plans. I kept my jaw clenched because sleeping with an open mouth allowed them an easy way in. I'm not sure I ever narrowed down who 'they' were, beyond an idea, borrowed from films I was too young for, that those wronged in life would return to settle the score. And, probably because I was in her bed, I imagined Novella's presence, too. Once, I convinced myself that her face had surfaced in the rough stone of the *cantina*'s wall, like people who see Jesus in the skin of a potato. I remember reasoning that she, at least, would mean me no harm – if anything, she might be curious to meet me – and that, in any case, it was unfair to be scared of someone purely because they are dead. She might even be here to protect me from the others. That settled, I would transfer my anxieties to the earwigs that lived in the mattress (they didn't), fearing that one might crawl into my ear and make me deaf, as had happened to Nonno in the corn stacks. Eventually I would fall asleep with my hands clutching the sides of my head and my pyjama bottoms tucked into my socks.

In her essay, Longo describes Italy's Marshall Plan films as falling somewhere between documentary and neo-realist fiction, a patchwork of newsreel footage and orchestrated scenes. Italy produced far more films than any other country in receipt of the aid, Longo says, and this speaks to the strategic position that it held for the US during the Cold War. In America, a number of the films were broadcast at prime-time slots, in a series entitled 'A Report to America Via ABC Television': 'A timely, instructive and entertaining series – showing how the Marshall Plan is aiding Europe to build strength against internal subversion and external Communist aggression' (said the trailer).

For Longo, these American–Italian collaborations represent an understudied body of work in which she finds 'multiple narratives of history, civic discourse and cultural identity that challenge the familiar narrative of economic productivity and progress' that the countries' governments sought mutually to promote. Her story speaks of dependence, cultural amnesia, and a shallow post-war Italianness styled by Americans with their own agenda. 'Are the Marshall Plan films ... to be considered

Italian films or American films?' she asks.

For Italian filmmakers, the films were a case of same work, different master. Longo cites Mussolini's view of cinema as the 'strongest arm of the state' and his creation of the Cinecittà studios in Rome in 1937. *Cinema è l'arma più forte* became a familiar phrase, she reminds us, 'emblazoned on banners and cinema caravans that travelled the length of the Italian peninsula'. It was during this period that Marcellini made his name, directing films for the regime, including the docufictional *La conquista dell'aria*, a sweeping history of aviation beginning with Icarus and ending with air acrobats like Centurione Scotto. But after Mussolini, the country needed new stories – powerful enough to reshape memories and experiences at home and abroad – and generous American funds provided the means.

Ritratto di un paese, rather depreciatively renamed *Handicraft Town* for anglophone audiences, begins on a sombre note with a funereal bell ringing from the clock tower of Maniago's late Gothic chiesa di San Mauro. ('That's the main church of Maniago,' Nonna nudges me excitedly, as if I'd never seen it.) The camera cuts to a cemetery – ordered, full, nothing living in sight – and then to a tree-lined avenue, empty but for two hobbling old women, in long dark clothes, with their heads covered.

But this is a tale of rebirth, set at the foot of the Carnic Alps – 'a few steps', the narrator emphasizes, 'from Yugoslavia and the Iron Curtain' – and as the camera returns us to the main piazza, virtually unchanged to this day, a postman walks towards us, sorting through envelopes and newspapers. He stops and turns back to look up at the clock tower. He, we understand, will be our guide, state-sponsored no less, to a typical day here.

Il postino, the narrator explains, plays an essential role in this place that lives off exports, where commissions for 'precious sharpeners, hunting knives, machetes, navajas, in steel and deer horn' are destined to 'sparkle' in the windows of shops in Copenhagen, Marseille, Madrid, Brazil and America. 'In this way, Maniago is a part of the world. A hard-working and vital little cell.' (Nonna dabs a small piece of bread around an almost empty bowl of minestrone and nods vigorously. 'È proprio così' – it's just like that – 'we're known all around the world.')

In Maniago, 'Almost everyone is master of his own house, with a little plot of land,' says the narrator. We see one *maniaghese* and his wife digging up an allotment; in another frame, a man tends to modest vines with the help-hindrance of his toddler.

'Do you know that guy?' I ask, half-seriously.

'I don't think so, no... but I know the house. It was just like that.' She smiles as if she had caught sight of her own front door after years away. 'We all had everything we needed.'

Maniago, we learn, is a town of *artigiani*, whose skills stretch back more than seven centuries. The first works were weapons, swords and daggers of all styles, created for *la Serenissima*, the nearby Republic of Venice. And still, the narrator emphasizes, 'the man of Maniago works', constantly renewed, like the Cellina, whose fast-running waters gave life to the first machines. Every house is a little factory, where the craft is passed from father to son and to grandson. A woman approaches shouldering what appear to be colossal, shimmering wings. Only once she has moved on behind the camera do you realize that the feathers are infinite assorted blades, polished and lethal.

Next, we are in the workshop of the oldest *artigiano* in the town, who, still loyal to 'primordial' instruments and techniques, makes eight delicate pencil sharpeners per month, with sides coated in mother of pearl; each is a jewel, beautiful and razor-sharp. On the wall behind his spinning grinder are postcards of New York's skyscrapers, the Empire State Building, the Eldorado – another gentle reference to foreign money and the wider world with which Maniago is bound. 'Beyond the work of man,' the narrator says, 'are needed steel and coal,' and for both (he does not add) the *maniaghesi* were dependent on the Americans.

'I always wanted to go to New York,' says Nonna. 'I had a cousin there. You don't know how many times I went to New York in my dreams.'

'But Nonno wanted to go to Africa to see the lions,' I say, knowing my lines well.

'So we went to neither,' she concludes.

The film moves on to talk of *modernizzazione*, for which the credit is given to the *maniaghesi* themselves, especially the young, who have built new factories, 'modern, airy and sound, for an ever-better product'. There is, too, a vast programme of European 'reconstruction and collaboration' that '*also* works for the man of Maniago, and the man of Maniago makes his contribution to a new Europe and a new world and' – here the narrator's voice becomes extravagantly emotional – 'millions of knives, of blades, and millions and *millions* of scissors depart for the housewives of all nations'. The music has turned oddly ominous and remains so as our attention is directed to an impressive new hospital being built – 'the pride of the village' – commissioned with international aid but maintained by the voluntary contributions of every single worker. Maniago is 'un paese prospero', a prosperous land, with a quality of life 'to be envied, not only in Italy'. It is 'un paese eccezzionale', where the future of each *artigiano* and his family depends on him, his ability and desire to work. He is, to borrow a phrase from another story, a self-made man.

Trombones and trumpets are pushed to their limits as the camera zooms in on glowing blades, sweating coal-streaked faces, the mouths of forges with tongues of flame. It's an inferno, but the workers are serene.

(This, Nonna says as we watch the men move strips of white-hot metal back and forth across anvils, beating them with hammers, is the job that Nonno did.)

'Each blade will carry the personal imprint of its creator,' we hear. 'There cannot be two identical knives.'

('Si, si, esattamente,' she beams. 'It's impossible to make the same twice.')

Now, a short sequence shows the *maniaghesi* at leisure, playing football, hunting, fishing in the pools of the Cellina, and drinking in a crowded bar. There is Alpine music, a woman laughs, a dog barks, the grappa flows. Old men play cards – *briscola*, perhaps Italy's favourite card game, similar to bridge. It was the first game Nonna taught me. A man signals to his partner, flicking his eyes up to an imaginary crown. He has the king!

'The wine is good, and the people drink it with cheer.'

('Esattamente,' Nonna smiles, still conversing with the screen.)

And then the scene abruptly cuts, to the sound of those church bells again, back to the chiesa di San Mauro, back to the *postino* and his bundle of international lifelines. A new day begins.

I have not seen Nonna so happy since we arrived three days earlier, bearing gifts from England to replenish her stocks of tea, McVitie's ginger nuts and Boots own-brand paracetamol.

'Maniago in 1949 looked like the place to be,' I say, closing the laptop. Apart from the peaceful cemetery, there had been no acknowledgement of the cataclysmic destruction of recent years, no bombed-out buildings, no sign of the mass upheaval of lives or of families and bodies torn apart, traumatized and in mourning. That apparently went on elsewhere.

'It was, yes, just like in the film.'

Prosperous, exceptional, enviable. Platitudes tumble from Nonna's lips: we *maniaghesi* get on with it; our work is known the world over; life was hard but good; no one is as diligent, or as tough, as us; we always bounce back, just like in 1976... She is on the brink now of the Great Earthquake story, about how the region recovered because of the back-breaking determination of the *friulani* themselves, about how they all slept outside on the ground for a week because of the aftershocks, toiled every hour of the day to rebuild crumbled edifices, and never complained once.

I draw her back to 1949.

'But you said you hated the factory?'

I remind her that when her job was to punch the holes in pencil sharpeners, she used to sit in a dark corner, virtually alone. Positioning each one beneath an enormous hammer, she would turn the thing so quickly between her fingers that the friction scorched her skin. They called this part of the factory 'il posto dei sospiri' – the place of sighs – because the clank of the hammer was so loud 'no one could hear you even if you cried your heart out'. This is the story as she has always told it. But she seems to have changed her mind now.

'It wasn't so bad. And we had everything we needed – like the film said.'

Marcellini shot the film the year before she and Leo left for Manchester, I point out. 'If things were good, why did you leave?'

I have always understood that my *nonni* left for England because the industry had not yet returned to Maniago after the war, that the factory where Leo was employed refused to pay wages for what little work was done, and that the whole town had fallen in on itself like a push-puppet. Everyone struggled and squabbled. England, meanwhile, was crying out for immigrants of 'good stock' to fill countless jobs. I have this precise line from a recording of Nonna made some years ago: 'Leo said, "Enough, let's go, we can do better, much better," and so that's what we did.'

Nonna looks at me for a moment, and then beyond me to the cupboard above the TV, where she has recently stashed the paracetamol, alongside a little bottle of holy water in the shape of the Virgin Mary and innumerable knickknacks. I wait as she recomposes the story from various sources, perhaps herself unsure now what was truth and what fabrication, whether her own or someone else's.

'No,' she said. 'That's another tale, a unique misfortune.'

The factory where Leo worked was, she says, owned by two brothers, who had overstretched themselves to build grand new premises, like the airy ones of Marcellini's film. When they couldn't make the money back quickly enough, they withheld workers' pay. 'If he had been in another factory, we would never have left.'

'They were in a difficult situation,' she says. 'One of the brothers had had two daughters already. He was desperate for a son to hand things over to one day. When his wife gave him a third daughter, he beat her.' Nonna seems understanding of this, being intimately familiar with the underlying logic.

'Which reminds me,' she says, manoeuvring her contorted feet back into her sandals and slowly standing. 'I must give you my book to read.'

She rifles in the cupboard above the television and eventually produces a battered exercise book. On its cover is a cartoon of two girls with mohawks and safety-pin piercings and the word 'Rebels' written in graffiti style.

'I haven't written in it in years,' she says, handing it to me. 'But you'll find ... things.'

She puts a full packet of tissues on the table next to me and walks out of the room.

*

Fifty-six pages of neat, cursive handwriting, in the distinctly slanted Italian style. Born in the Renaissance, enshrined in the first calligraphy manuals, and still taught in most Italian primary schools, the italic script transcends gender, class and age, so that the lines in Nonna's book could have been written by a nine-year-old or a ninety-year-old. They used to say that the measured loop-the-loops harmonized the brain, uniting both sides, the artistic and the scientific.

The opening page is dated 22 February 2003. She would have been seventy-six and beginning her fourth year as a widow. She begins: 'Irene' – Nonna's daughter-in-law, my mother –

always said she wanted to make a book of my life. Last night in bed I couldn't sleep, so I set about thinking of my past... It's sad, because until now this has never happened, I have always thought about the future. Now there is more past than future. This got me thinking and so, also to please Irene, I want to write something about my past, not to make a book of it, but because mine is a life lived, real and without fiction.

112

The next two dozen pages are given over to Dirce's youth, taking in the family's first flight to England with Angelo, his abrupt death, and the painful return to Maniago, in 1936, 'a year of misery for the farmers because the previous year had seen a drought and there was no grain'. She is prone – I knew this already – to streams of consciousness. One sentence can span ten lines or more. Punctuation is erratic. There are strangely placed parentheses and insistent underlining, often added later, with a different pen. Many passages are instantly familiar, word-for-word repetitions of lines spoken during our conversations, as though Nonna has been quoting herself all along.

'I was born on 24 October 1926, a Sunday, in time for Mass, and my mother wasn't happy because she wanted a boy.'

'My father made me feel important and he spoke to me like an adult.'

'My father didn't want me to forget my Italian so he made me read from the book *Cuore* and I had to explain the meaning and the themes to him and he would give me a sweet and lots of praise so I worked very hard.'

'One Friday I was playing with my cousins and I heard a scream from the other room. (My father was dead: from that day my life split in two.)'

'I always felt my father was with me – my Guardian Angel.'

There's the story about Angelo kissing Novella first ('so she wouldn't be jealous'); about Angelo, the poor girl and the vinegar ('A little girl never forgets moments like this'); and a heartfelt confession about the time Nonna, aged nine, mistook salt for sugar and put a pinch in little Pietro's mouth to stop him from wailing. He started coughing and spluttering 'and papà, running in and seeing everything, slapped me across the face'. 'In my defence,' she writes, seventy years after the event, 'I was used to Italian salt, which is much coarser.' Squeezed between these lines, black ink in a river of blue, she writes: '(Apart from this, I never had any trouble with my father.)'

There is no mention here of the war, nor of her first encounters with Leo.

Suddenly we are in 1949: 'Though I had wanted a girl and got a boy, I was a happy mother, but Leo drank and this annoyed me – he liked company and he couldn't stop.'

This is the alternative version of my grandparents' emigration story, withheld until now.

It seems that Leo had fallen in with a bad crowd with bad habits. *Brutti giri.* Straight after work, on an empty stomach ('or with just polenta or bread and milk from lunch'), he'd go to the bar to drink and play cards, often for money. His friends would wind him up 'in the usual way: "Oh he's married now, he's under the thumb."' There were accidents when cycling home. On 'Christmas eve' 1948, getting back even later than usual he failed to put his feet down in time and fell sideways against the rough wall of the stable. He ripped a good shirt, which Dirce had made. 'The next day, we didn't speak a word to each other.'

I thought Nonno was the family's leader, a romantic hero of the old sort. That's the way Nonna has always told it. And so we all have too. Now I see, in Nonna's own words, that, at this point at least, he was more of a liability. I wonder if this is why she gave me the tissues. She thought I'd take it too hard, this sudden loss of the fiction.

*

In 1950, Dirce, with her mother Novella and little Manlio,

went ahead to England. With the help of *zio* Gioacchino and a cousin in Manchester, they found lodgings in Longsight, where all the buildings were made of red brick, 'un rosso forte, come il sangue' (a strong red, like blood). The three of them shared a single bed in the attic, beneath a small, leaky skylight. 'When it rained the house cried.' Having received British citizenship from her father – and, thanks to the British Nationality Act of 1948, having been allowed to keep it in spite of marrying an Italian – Dirce would find it easy to get set up. That's what *zio* Gioacchino said. And the idea was that then, after a few months, she would be able to apply for permission to have Leo join her as a legal resident. She would be allowed to work straight away – she had brought her heavy sewing machine with her – but Leo would have to wait. In the meantime, *zio* said he would help them in whatever way he could. If they needed anything, Sheffield wasn't so far away.

Though she did not know it at the time, Dirce's lodgings were about five miles south of streets she had strolled hand in hand with Angelo. 'When I got to Manchester,' she once told me over the phone, 'I was consumed by a desire to see the church he used to take me to. There was a little grotto of the Madonna, like at Lourdes, and as a child, I thought it *was* Lourdes. I dreamt about it frequently, sometimes many nights in a row.'

Dreams mean something to Nonna. She would not disagree with scientists who say that sleep is when our minds process the past, ours and others we have heard about, looking for patterns by which to understand the present and so prepare for the future. But dreams are more to her, more than preparations: they are predictions, divine interventions, with a language of their own, sometimes direct, other times oblique. Often, they feature animals.

Fat black vultures, gentle doves with unusual markings (*'stains?'*), snakes with human mouths, cats, sheep, once a hare with purple eyes who stood up on his hind legs and spoke. A bestiary of omens, not to be ignored. Only try to dismiss one of Nonna's dreams and she will set out her record: the night of my first asthma attack, at the age of four, she dreamt that a rabbit was hanging in the mouth of a snake ('And the next morning your father told me'); a few nights before Leo died, she dreamt that three big black birds were flying towards her and suddenly one dropped to the ground like a stone; a week before her niece ended her own life, a grey-blue cat looked her square in the face, then slinked away. 'She was saying goodbye.'

Not speaking any English but remembering the name 'Ciii–Tam', Dirce asked her landlady if she could help her find the church of the beautiful Madonna. She, a garrulous Genovese woman who kept the shared bathroom (but not much else) spotless, seemed to know it immediately. The next day, Dirce set off on an empty stomach, too nervous to eat, and walked along the city's thoroughfares. I imagine her now, passing the haberdashery where she'd bought everything to make Leo a smart new shirt, past the Marks & Spencer Penny Bazaar that her cousin had taken her to not long after her arrival to admire the *terrazzo* flooring he had laid, past countless newsagents who shouted so loudly that she flinched – 'Better Pay For the Forces!', 'UNA Chief Says, War If We Fail In Korea!', 'Distressing Accident at Torrisholme!'.

'Ciii–Tam?' she asked strangers every few minutes, to make sure she hadn't strayed from the landlady's directions. And almost two hours later, she saw beside Cheetham Hill Road a familiar honey-coloured church. But inside there was no grotto and no one to ask, had she even known the words.

116

'I never felt so lonely,' she told me, 'I don't remember getting home. Years later I realized that the scene I remembered must have been the nativity crib, which my father took me to see some days before he got sick.'

Slowly, though, things got better.

'Better': one of the first English words Dirce learnt, at the clothing sweatshop where her landlady's husband, a Ukrainian who used to bow whenever Dirce entered a room, had found her a job. 'You're doing better,' the manager told her, resting one hand on the machine, at the end of the first week. Not knowing what this meant Dirce smiled and replied with a non-committal, 'Yes, yes.'

'You're doing better, *understand*?'

'Yes, yes.'

She kept repeating the word to herself – 'betta' like the Queen, 'la regina Elisabetta' – until the evening, when she could ask the landlady what it meant.

Better, she soon learnt, also meant more money. Because she was so fast on the machines – 'sveltissima', she says, as though the word itself were flying through her fingers – she moved into piecework. The best scenario was when the components had already been cut so it was simply a case of stitching them together. She could run up items at ten times the normal speed (it is possible that this is an exaggeration), and before long the owner's wife had commissioned clothes for herself on the side. 'My only fault the *padrona* told me was that I left too many hanging threads.'

I know that piecework is where pay is granted per item produced, but I can't retrain my mind not to think of it as a work in which an item is pieced together from constituent parts. The definitions are not mutually exclusive, I suppose. But in the first I imagine a finished 'piece', entire and, ideally, indistinguishable among others, whose value lies in quantity. In the second, I picture a process in which fragments are integrated into a whole, each with its own quirks – there cannot be two identical – shaped by the worker's skill, choices, mood, surroundings. In the first, I see a pile of inanimate things; in the second, the creator herself, absorbed in the act.

As Dirce worked, she studied the expressions of the women around her, in whose chatter she could not yet participate, trying to match the word to the tone to the gesture to the outcome. She gathered everything together in a personal dictionary. She learnt *dumb* and *goody-goody* and *eejit* and *bitch* and *filthy*. But also, *never mind* and *int'it* and *starvin'* and *help* and *cake*. *Help* signalled an opportunity, when she would jump to her feet and run over to whomever had said the word, ready to intervene in whatever mess they had got their needle into. *Cake* was what one of the women, 'una Africana', probably Caribbean, brought her in gratitude. *Thank you*, was what she said. *Wop*. That was one of Edna's. Edna who studiously ignored Dirce's 'good mornin'' and scoffed every time Dirce went up for more cloth. *Goody-goody. Show-off.* Then a chorus of directionless tuts and *never mind*s would ensue from the other women.

Pauline, who lived next door and who had started inviting Dirce around so that their sons could play together, became an unofficial teacher, soon adding *biscuits*, *chips* and *friend* to the list. Afraid of going to Pauline's empty-handed, Dirce would buy bottles of dandelion and burdock to share, and when the habit became too expensive, she simply stopped going. Pauline berated her when she found out why. *Don't be daft.* And that was that.

'I learnt English quickly from there,' says Nonna. The pair used to take the bus to visit Pauline's mother, or just to get them out of the house, and Dirce's friend paid both fares. Pauline was desperate to get away from her fuss-pot husband, a real *pignolo* (now they were swapping words). 'I know a joke about Italy,' he said to Dirce one evening when she had stopped by for tea and biscuits. 'What's the shortest book in an Italian library? The book of Italian war heroes.'

Leo came earlier than planned, on a tourist visa, with one flimsy cardboard suitcase of belongings, like a shoddy theatre prop. 'He didn't listen when I told him to wait.' Perhaps, after his *brutti giri*, he had convinced himself that Dirce was walking out on him. When she had been gone just a few weeks he had sent her a postcard from Maniago with a carefully staged ring of red wine across one corner. Would she have seen the funny side then as she does now?

'Things got better,' Nonna writes in her diary, 'because we were together and we were in love,' but also worse, 'because I was the only one earning and everyone was eating.' As a tourist, Leo was not eligible for a work permit. By this time, Dirce was making about £6 per week, equivalent to around £200 per week today and somewhat below the national average. Half of this went to Novella, 'to look after Manlio while I worked,' with the rest going on rent and feeding the family. Anything left over was split between two envelopes – the first, to be sent back to Italy, to Leo's parents; the second, stashed in the attic, wedged behind the bed. At night, she took on more work, producing cushion covers for another factory, and with the scrap bits of fabric, she made her rose hairclips, which she sold for a few extra pennies to colleagues and their friends.

To save money, Dirce walked to work rather than taking the bus and skipped breakfast, dropping a hard-boiled egg into her pocket for lunch. 'All morning I'd think about the egg and tell myself it was as heavy as metal so that when I ate it, I felt full.' At dinnertime, she served everyone else first and ran a bit of bread around the pan. Sometimes she pretended she had a headache and excused herself. 'I lost a lot of weight. I didn't look after myself.'

Starvin'. One Sunday, she fainted in Church and everyone turned around to stare at her. She was upset, concerned about having disrupted Mass. *Never mind.* Someone helped her into a car and drove her home. *Thank you.* Tea and biscuits. Everyone was kind. She was out of action for weeks.

'What was wrong with you when you couldn't work all that time, after fainting?' I ask her, looking up from the book.

'Ah, nina, non mi ricordo. But during this time,' she starts – 'well, I'll let you read it yourself.'

And she retreats behind the orange faux-satin curtain that separates the table area, where I am, from the working part of the kitchen, where she is.

'During this time,' the book continues, they received notice that Leo, whom Dirce had registered as her spouse, would not be allowed to stay in the country. 'He had come too soon he was always hasty he should have waited. Now what will we do?' I appreciate the switch to the present, the dramatic flourish, and imagine her writing it so many decades after the moment in question, up in the middle of the night, when the past, present and future lose their definition.

'As usual,' she continues, 'I kept everything to myself, like my mother had taught me, so that anyone who met me thought I was full of sunshine.' Pauline knew, though – 'by now, we were like sisters' – and she would come over to take Manlio out of the way, to give the couple a few hours of peace. One day, turning to speak to her, Dirce knocked a cup off the table and it smashed into a hundred pieces, and in that instant, 'something inside me broke too'. She went to bed for a week and couldn't get up. There was a lesson in this, a dream omen slipped into the waking world for all to see, but somehow, she missed it.

After that, for a time, things did get better again. They visited *zio* in Sheffield and he told them to apply again for Leo's permit. It was the first day that Dirce had left the house in weeks and the first time she'd left Manchester since arriving. *Zio* met them at the station and took them straight to the cemetery, to Angelo and Old Pietro's grave. 'What would they say,' he asked Dirce, 'if you gave up so easily?'

He took them to his house and showed them the allotment, a whole section of which was given over to red *radicchio*.

'"Zio," I asked, "please can I eat one?", and when I did it was a pure taste of home. Bitter, fresh. It was a medicine for me.'

And before they set off back to Manchester, Gioacchino's wife gave Dirce a necklace. 'I still have it in a box by the bed: silver, too heavy to wear.' I know the one she is describing because she has tried to give it to me several times. It looks like blackened steel, with irregular shapes hanging from a thick chain, like a machine's innards.

A month or so later, Dirce had a dream. 'I saw a tower of files, each with someone's name written on it, and a pair of hands sorting through them. And then I saw Leo's name and the hands disappeared and two other hands came in and picked up the file and put it to one side. And I woke up and I knew what it meant.'

'I'm reading about your dream and Nonno's work

permit,' I call through to her. I hear her tap a wooden spoon on the rim of the pot she has been stirring for hours, and she appears by the curtain.

'The second pair of hands I instantly recognized,' she says, giving me the next line.

They were her father's hands. 'I have to believe that. It's the only thing that makes sense.'

Leo's permit came through. Of course it did. For all of Nonna's suspense, I knew it all along; otherwise we'd be telling very different stories today. He set to work as a *terrazziere* in Dirce's cousin's firm. Their slogan: *We excel.* 'Because we did.'

*

Terrazzo: a fifteenth-century Venetian craft in which broken bits of tile, glass and stone are set in cement and buffed until the surface is smooth and gleaming. Otherwise known as poor man's mosaic; a most functional art. The craft of generations of my family, of Angelos and Pietros long before the ones I have recently started to get to know, stretching back who knows how far. Pietro: the name itself comes from *pietra*, stone.

It's difficult to think of a process better suited to the rebuilding of post-war Britain, where bombs had splintered edifices, producing an abundance of materials to be reused. The silver lining of destruction was creation; the detritus of war poured into the bejewelled floors of new department stores, office blocks, train stations and airports, universities and hotel lobbies. Terrazzo's resilience makes it perfect for sites of transience and exchange. But did anyone stop to wonder how many stories they were mixing up, levelling, treading on?

Leo's first post was to Cardiff, where he stayed for

three months so as not to spend the wage on train trips home. After that came Glasgow and Reading and Gloucester and London and, according to Nonna's diary, 'everywhere in between'. He would be gone for weeks at a time and when he did come back, he tended to spend the whole weekend sleeping. With more money coming in, Dirce moved the family to different lodgings: first, briefly, to a place just around the corner, where the landlord, a British woman, accused Leo (wrongly) of using her husband's toothbrush and chased them from the house (*thief, filthy*); then, to a house a few streets away, with a bigger room in the basement. Two single beds at opposite ends, one for Novella and Manlio, now nearly four years old, and the other for the young couple. At the midway point, the women tied a length of string between two nails and draped their clothes along it. Over this, they hung a wide sheet, to keep the dust off. 'It was the only privacy we had – the first wall I ever owned.'

Things soured. Nonna relays the events of the house with the heated enthusiasm and emotional investment of a TV soap addict. The landladies were two sisters from Tuscany, one married to a British man but with a *child* secretly fathered by his *friend*, a Pole who was married to the *sister*, but the first sister loved the *Pole*, too, and had only married the *British* guy so she could stay in the country – '*see?*' The sisters fawned over the Pole, cooking him *this* and *that* and bickering, *always* bickering. With Leo away, he started to pay attention to Dirce. She ignored him but the sisters began to treat her harshly, as if it were her fault. One of them, who offered to take Dirce's kitty and procure some weekly staples from the shops, 'because she knew the good places', lied about the price of tinned tomatoes (*thief*). Then the wife of the Pole got TB and disappeared for a month or two. And then *all of a sudden,* she's back from hospital and feeding pieces of pear straight from her hand to little Manlio. 'I almost *died;* my heart was in my mouth. I prayed: O, *Signore,* help me.'

'And so?'

'And so what do you think? When Leo next got back, we moved again.'

'What year is this?'

'Well, let's see, where was I working? What was I making?'

She thinks for a moment, measuring the years in terms of companies and commissions. There are the quick-fire cushion-cover years; the bed-sheet years, when the whole house stank of the glue used for the hems; the *dull* menswear years; and, much later, the little-goes-a-long-way hot pants years.

'The dresses with the wrong sleeves,' she says defin-itively. 'I had to correct them all myself.' Then, piecing things together: 'Elisabetta had the crown. Your father was just born. He had the blackest hair anyone had ever seen. There was a man who used to stop by after visiting his own wife in the maternity ward, just to marvel at it... Exceptionally black, it was.'

*

127 Palm Street, an address we all recognize, even those of us who never knew it. It was the first house in England from which the family could not be evicted. Dirce and her brother Pietro, then twenty-two and, like Leo, working for the cousin's company, had taken out a joint mortgage, so everyone lived together again. There were four floors and a cellar full of junk left behind by the previous ten-ants. They had three lodgers at a time, always *friulani,* brought over by the firm. Dirce cooked and cleaned for

them, worked in various sweatshops, and took on extra commissions, working until the early hours, when the neighbours thumped on the wall and the machine had to fall silent. Leo worked long hours, too. Weekends paid more so he worked those as well, and if he did take a day off, he spent it sleeping or watching the boxing or wrestling. A photograph taken outside the house shows Leo and Pietro, wearing identical wide, double-breasted suits made by Dirce, squaring up for a play-fight.

Dirce's stomach started to trouble her again – dull pains at first, which gave way to a deep and constant burning. Food was 'poison'. She had more fainting spells. Her hands throbbed. Her weight plummeted. The doctors put her on a strict diet of boiled potatoes, white fish and milk. An operation was inevitable, and Leo decided it would be better for him and the boys to go back to Italy so that they could be looked after by his mother. Nonna writes in her book: 'Leo was, I must say, very worried, and more depressed than me, so I needed to give him courage and I told him stories and jokes and the same for my mother. I kept everything to myself – my anxieties (<u>because I had many</u>).'

A photograph from the period, taken at 127 Palm Street just before the trip to Italy, captures a jovial scene: it's New Year's Eve, a particularly major event in the Italian calendar, and about twenty people are gathered around a table strewn with bottles of wine, grappa and vermouth. Leo is waving at the camera with one hand and, with the other, lifts an enormous demijohn in a wicker-basket, pouring out its contents for the guests. He's biting down on his pipe and smiling. Behind him, in an apron, is Dirce, looking wizened and drawn. Everyone is celebrating but her.

Beyond the occasional photograph, it's difficult to imagine the happiness in this period, although everyone assures me there was plenty. There's something Cratchit-like about the whole thing. At the back of the drawer in Nonna's kitchen table, we found a letter written at Christmas by my father, when he was about six years old: 'As I am too young to buy presents I will offer my prayers to God thanking him for having given me such good parents and placing me in a good home and a good brother and relations. Your Loving Son John. P. S. : I am sure Manlio agrees.'

Manlio, five years older than John, remembers the same doting mother but a mostly absent father, and a society stacked against them. He remembers a rough school, with sixty-odd pupils to a class, where every afternoon, when the bell rang, everyone rushed to a bombed-out house down the road to see who was taking on whom, hoping it wasn't their turn. His name was a beacon for ridicule – 'Why do you think they called your dad good old English "John"?' – and the children's favourite game was 'Second World War': 'We're the English, you're the enemy, get over there.' Dirce told him to hold it together, keep his head down, keep it in; Leo, had he been around to give advice, would have told him to be like Primo Carnera.

Dirce was herself suffering from her own advice. Living with Novella was taking its toll; her mother was getting under her skin and seeping into her blood like lead. Novella did not like people, especially not women. She was angry at the world and she did not make a secret of it. Every morning she would come into the bedroom as Dirce got ready for work and rail and pick and pull everything apart. No one was *good*, everyone was *corrupt*, thieving, two-faced, out to get her, to take her things and leave her with nothing. She fought with the neighbours and insulted Dirce's friends. Pauline was frightened of her; Emmy, a German woman who Dirce met when Mario Lanza played the Belle Vue music hall, called Novella 'la gatta nera', the black cat. When young Pietro met Anna, a factory girl from Apuglia, and looked set for marriage, things got worse. 'Novella was jealous,' Nonna writes. 'She said she was powerless, but she had so much power over us.'

On Dirce's thirty-third birthday, Emmy sent her a card – 'Happy birthday for a devoted young mother from sunny Italy!' – with a poem she had composed specially:

Birthday cards will often say,
That this should be a perfect day,
From hence: happiness all the way!
But on this earth is <u>no</u> perfection,
So is the will of Great Perception;
If all were faultless and we too,
There could not be achievement true;
Life would become a constant bore,
Could none of us improve it more.
So let's be glad if all are well,
And nothing untoward befell!

The sanguinity is touching. In the bottom left-hand corner, a cat is inked in black biro, mid-pounce or running away, and beneath the sign-off – 'from your friend for life Emmy' – is a single line of newly learnt Italian, couched in quotation marks, an in-joke with gravitas: 'Battere della carne calmerà il cuore', 'Pounding meat will calm the heart', and a doodle of a kitchen mace.

'I couldn't eat. I couldn't digest anything.' Dirce went from 79 kilos to 52 and was hospitalized. 'One day,' she writes, '5 or 6 doctors were doing the rounds and one said to the other that I was only 33 and I thought my time had come because my papà died at 33 and clearly things didn't look good for me.' And while she was lying in the hospital – she does not know which, but it is likely it was the same one Angelo had died in twenty-four years earlier – her thoughts drifted back to what had brought her to this point. She notes in the diary: 'I didn't want to see anyone and when my boys came back from school I didn't want them I didn't want weights or responsibilities – having to clean them care for them cook for them was for me a sacrifice too heavy, I would not have killed myself, but if a bus had come towards me I would not have moved.'

After a few weeks – maybe more, no one remembers – Dirce was told she would go home. 'I was very sad because I knew I would have to do everything and show myself to be serene, while in hospital I didn't need to pretend.' A psychiatrist was assigned to her. She was given a three-month course of injections and put on the waiting list for 'electric shocks'.

'Did you know what this meant – the "electric shocks"?', I ask, a finger pinning down the words. 'Did the doctor explain it to you?'

'I remember that he was kind. He told me it was normal for a case like mine. I would maybe have some problems with remembering things afterwards, some headaches, but that this would pass, and then I'd feel better.' She pauses, taps her spoon on the side of the pot. 'But, anyway: I had another idea.'

I took a breath, poised to ask a question.

'Read, read and you'll see,' she says. 'I'm busy now.'

She is chopping parsley, which the ancient Greeks believed grew out of the blood of the infant Archemoros, after he was mortally wounded by a snake. They used to scatter it over tombs, to encourage the work of memory.

Dirce's idea, it turns out, was to go to Italy. I would say

128

she went 'back home', in the way that I always frame my own returns. Or, sometimes, now that I've built another home in England, I say 'I'm going *home* home', the original home. But 'home' is not a word that Nonna often uses. For her, by the late 1950s, it was a concept adrift, neither here nor there, constantly being remade wherever the family found itself. 127 Palm Street was home, for a time.

I suspect it troubled her, too – made her feel ambivalent or wary – this word that was so often spoken in anger, thrown at her like a rotten vegetable. 'Go *home*.' At the very least, it was a word that made a mark, that divided you from others. Even if through benign curiosity: 'So, where do you call home, then?' In a factory tale Nonna tells me one day, a woman tells her to 'cheer up luv, feeling homesick are you?' Nonna does an impression of her, smirking.

'Was this Edna?' I ask.

'No. Another.'

Home was something you had to wipe off your face, then, or at least a card to keep close to your chest. It certainly wasn't anything to be proud of.

Dirce was accompanied to Italy by Checca, a young Friulian woman who had been lodging with the family for some time. They stayed in Maniago for three months in early 1960. There is no mention in Nonna's book of how Leo and the boys coped while she was gone. Neither of her sons remember the absence. Novella must have stepped into the breach and held things together; she does not seem to have weighed on them as she did on her daughter. The book describes another course of injections and a self-prescribed 'cure' according to which, every day, Dirce and Checca would sit at a table in the courtyard of the old house in Maniago – it was early April, 'the sun was not too strong, Easter was coming' – and pour a

129

half-glass of wine. 'We would not leave the table until I had drunk it, even though ½ a glass of wine made me *brilla* at that time.' *Brilla* – tipsy, though a better translation might stick closer to *brillante*: the wine made her brilliant, she sparkled again. 'We increased the dose until I could drink 2 full glasses. I was not allowed to move until all the wine was gone.'

Whether through injections, friendship, sunshine, Italy, wine, or divine intervention, when Dirce returned to Manchester, the psychiatrist said, 'I was no longer the person he had first met. But he also said I should not live with my mother – we needed our own house – I needed to be careful not to fall <u>down</u> again'.

The rest of her life has been lived in the light of his warning. These days, she eats little but well. She grows most of the vegetables herself and eats lean meat only once or twice a week, generally as *cotolette*, beaten until thin and tender, fried and patted down with kitchen paper to remove excess oil ('a poison for me'). She takes lots of medicines, never goes out without a thick shawl, and tries to sleep at night. She also tries not to get 'in the middle of other people's business', although 'everyone is always trying to put me there'. She drinks wine with every meal except breakfast, when it's a shot of brandy in strong coffee, and a single piece of toast.

'I almost died at thirty-three': another line she repeats frequently, pouring each word into a glass that, miraculously, always ends up half full. 'I always see the glass half full, you know' – a favourite expression. 'And sometimes two-thirds.'

*

The story of the years leading up to 1971, when Dirce

and Leo moved back to Maniago, is best told through snatched scenes, brief flashes of something solid in a fog of dates (rare) and random details I dwell on (though I'm often not sure why). The combined memories of three people who were there and are still living.

A special day out with Leo, home for the weekend. Belle Vue Zoological Gardens. Manlio and John taking it in turns to sit on their father's shoulders to see the African elephants.

Urine-soaked school trousers. 'Too scared to go to the toilets because the older boys were there.'

Pietro – who likes to go by Peter because it makes things that much easier – brings home a television with a screen about as big as a postage stamp and the longest back end you can imagine. Novella pretends not to be impressed.

Pauline's diet of brown bread and lettuce. She's put on so much weight all of a sudden. (It turned out she was pregnant.)

A biscuit box made of mottled metal, which Novella stashes under the sofa and shows only to the boys. Money curling and glinting among the biscuits.

A scar the length of Manlio's stomach, from a case of appendicitis that developed into near fatal peritonitis.

Wrestling on the carpet with *zio* Pietro, after watching Tommy Mann's match on TV.

Leo buying toothpaste and squirting it onto his brush only to discover it is shaving cream. (He couldn't read the label.)

A beautiful new Friulian lodger called Antonietta.

Dirce starting a snowball fight in the street on New Year's Eve and 'the English looking at us like we were wild animals'. But then they joined in.

The first day at a new school, Manlio putting up his

hand to ask the teacher: 'When do we go home?' She, elderly, points to a fake clock made of cardboard: 'When that points to 12.' ('So, *never?*')

A Christmas tree – artificial – in flames. The candles have caught. Baubles crashing to the floor; two land on the carpet and roll to safety.

Singing lessons in the school canteen with a small German woman on the piano. Belting out 'Rule Britannia' and 'Men of Harlech'. *Hark I hear the foe advancing, barbed steeds are proudly prancing, helmets in the sunbeams glancing...*

A thirteenth birthday and a favourite meal of rabbit and mashed potato. Manlio so excited that his nose bleeds all over the plate so he can't eat it.

Whit Walks, when the churches paraded through Manchester city centre for hours, with banners and bands. Monday was for the Protestants, Friday for the Catholics. Everyone cheering like it was the football.

Holidays in Italy every two years. Changing trains in Milan where cousin Angelino always met them with wine. 'You're home now,' Leo would say, flushed and *brillo*. Getting to Maniago, in the middle of the night, looking for Sebastiano in his taxi to drive them to the old house where Leo's mother excitedly waits. A family of four sharing one bed, topping and tailing. The smell of Leo's feet. And oh God, the snoring.

Things you didn't get in Manchester: Cows! Rabbits! Mountains! No running water! Leo teaching the boys to scythe, and the women arriving at lunchtime with huge enamel containers of pasta. Drinking wine from the bottle and sleeping in freshly stacked hay. The next day, a cart drawn by two cows, its wooden wheels crunching the gravel. Piling on the hay and driving off. John sitting on top with the cousins, looking at a cloudless sky. Drinking wine from the bottle.

Denison Road, Hazel Grove, a new address. Leo has built a greenhouse. Tomato plants tickle the roof.

Woolworths' Classics series; books bound in red leather (fake). Manlio reading the story of King Arthur to John in bed. Both in tears at the end.

John coming downstairs to find a bucket with a dead mouse in it. How did it get in there? A mystery to this day.

Manlio's birthday. His mother has made him invite his classmates. She has baked her *torta alle mele*, an apple cake in a ring mould with a missing centre. A volcano cake. The next day at school, the other children, in hysterics: 'Couldn't your mum afford the full cake?'

Another trip to Italy. Giovanin, Leo's father, is in charge of the house and nobody doubts it. At every meal, the salad bowl starts with him and does the rounds before returning to him for the bread-dunk. He doesn't talk to children. During the First World War, he was buried under snow for three days and then found his way home. (This must be when Orfeo, Leo's surprise brother, twenty-one years his junior, was made.) Giovanin has so many stories, but he doesn't tell them to anyone.

In the *tabaccaio*, Manlio buying ticket after ticket for the *tombola*. One day the kind owner, wafting his hand over a particular corner of the tray of individually rolled-up tickets: 'You need to be lucky somewhere around *here*... right *here*.' Then: Winning, 'I don't remember what, but winning.'

Driving back to England in Leo's red Fiat 1100. Hiding grappa under the seats, so as not to have to pay duty at the border. Dirce hasn't told Leo. He would only have worried. 'He didn't know what to do with worry.'

Leo taking a job at a rival terrazzo firm. He is made supervisor. There will be more responsibility, more travel, longer shifts. And a bright orange company car. Dirce counselled against it, but he wouldn't listen.

A new house on Clitheroe Road for just Dirce, Leo and the boys. It's springtime 1965 and Dirce is pregnant, about halfway along. There is new linoleum in the kitchen, and a moss-green three-piece suite bought second-hand and stuffed with rags to make it better. Every night she goes to bed early, to be alone with the baby inside her.

John getting into grammar school. *Eccezzionale!*

Dirce makes new curtains for the house. It's early July, about four weeks before her due date. As she hoists herself up a stepladder Leo looks up and tells her to be careful. 'Don't worry,' she says, 'I'm so close now even if I fall, she'll be fine.' (She.)

Manlio painting the rooms upstairs with Leo, a thick custardy colour. Beniamino Gigli playing in the background. *Mamma, sarai con me, tu non sarai più sola!* Dirce comes in, ashen, tears rolling down her cheeks. The baby will be born dead. *Sei tu la vita e per la vita non ti lascio mai più!*

Leo's new bosses are unreasonable. They ask too much and make him botch jobs to cut costs. The workers are being exploited. Leo is never at home.

27 August 1965 – a funeral at Sheffield City Road Cemetery. Manlio, aged seventeen, and John, a few days into his thirteenth year, standing on the grass looking at the single headstone and reading the names and dates of their grandfather and great-grandfather. Leo approaches the open grave carrying a white coffin the size of a shoe-box. Dirce is at home. The baby, a boy called Anthony, is placed 'in my father's arms'.

Not long back from a spell in Maniago, Dirce is at Mass when the priest tells a story about adoption. Later she asks the family what they make of the idea. Manlio and

134

John say 'yes'. Leo asks for time to think it over. By now Manlio has moved out. John rides buses for hours to get to and from school, and doesn't really want to go home, where his mother will be working every hour of the day and his father will be on a job, or asleep.

Manlio works summers on site with his father. They are laying terrazzo in Marks & Spencer on ('I think') Scunthorpe High Street. When the cement arrives, Leo says the real man is the man who can lift not one bag but two at a time.

September 1968. Leo has a heart attack while driving back from a job in Wales and is signed off work to recover. He goes to Italy alone. Dirce knows that she mustn't bring up adoption until he is better. She makes secret enquiries. Leo's Italian nationality may be a problem.

Manlio has finished university, History, and is engaged to Rosalind, who wears brightly coloured hot pants. Dirce, inspired, makes seventy pairs – *sveltissima* – to sell.

Orange metal upside down and battered out of shape in a field beyond a smashed fence, in the middle of the night. John, the driver, barely seventeen and not wearing a seat belt, thrown into the back seat. He notes shards of glass glinting in the weeds, feels cold, hears voices approaching and a siren growing louder. 'Bloody lucky to be alive.'

A friend, a Friulian with a funny, tittering laugh like a bird, comes over with news: a teenager from somewhere further North is lodging with her, sent away from home to give birth. She does not want the child. The father is an Italian. Dirce and Leo go to meet her. It's April 1969.

Dirce receives a call from the priest to say that the baby has been born and is hers, if she wants her. Leo drives them over in the red Fiat and Dirce worries that the girl will change her mind, or that they'll all be arrested. Leo:

'We are not *stealing* this baby.'

It takes months for the paperwork to go through. Leo has applied for British nationality because it's the only way. Dirce doesn't tell anyone. Not even Pauline. Only the priest knows. If she takes things for granted, they will fall through. One day a neighbour sees nappies hanging on the line and Dirce panics that it will jinx everything. Every night, she whispers the baby's name into her crown – Lucia Angela, Lucia Angela – and goes to sleep wishing for a reassuring dream that does not come.

Leo leaves the terrazzo firm and takes the first job he can find, in a cigarette warehouse. Architectural plans start to appear on the kitchen table every night after dinner. They are building a house among the fields where Leo grew up, and they will design it so it is exactly as they want it. Orfeo has begun the work already. Soon Leo and Dirce will leave Manchester, although only one of them wants to.

A party to celebrate the adoption's approval. Dirce spends hours deciding which dress to put Lucia in. She has made so many she is almost embarrassed (but not really). She chooses the one with two fat ripe cherries on the collar.

A new job at the McVitie's biscuit factory just down the road. Leo takes the night shift and it suits him. Workers can buy the biscuits cheap and for a time it seems as though the family lives off Jaffa Cakes and ginger nuts. He does not let on to the bosses about his heart trouble.

Dirce doubled over her machine, thrumming away at a big order for heavy winter coats. The weight of the cloth, as she rearranges it across the table, pulls at her shoulder. She needs to make as much money as possible. Lucia, tucked up in the pram in the garden, sleeping, oblivious to the journey that is coming.

Leo's heart again. He keels over on the production line. They do not sack him – 'a miracle!' – but send him home to rest. He takes Lucia out in the pram while Dirce works and works.

Mid-August 1971, Manlio and Ros marry. Two weeks later, John leaves for university and Leo and Dirce set off for Italy. The family scatters. As they pass the biscuit factory, Leo turns to Dirce: 'Had I gone to that factory first, we wouldn't be leaving now.' Another tale of misfortune.

A detour to Sheffield where Dirce places flowers on the grave and says goodbye to baby Anthony and Angelo and Old Pietro, and to England and the lives they have lived. *Addio*. To God. She makes the sign of the cross, as she does before every journey, and ducks back into the large green van they have rented. She sits in the passenger seat, her eyes brimming with tears and her hands clasped around Lucia's waist to hold her still. All the belongings they can carry are packed in behind them. She says nothing and Leo looks straight ahead. The road to Maniago is long and when they arrive there will be building yet to do. They are starting from scratch but also continuing something left in suspension, twenty-odd years earlier. Bricks and mortar are only part of it. Waiting for them now is a different kind of piecework. We might call it peace work.

*

There is no such thing as new, only old parts put together differently, and never the same way twice. I can't remember who said that – it may well have been Nonna – but as I study the fragments of this family, it's difficult to see it otherwise. In roughly two decades in England, the same things occurred over and over: acts of love, fun, charity, cruelty, hope, desperation, fear. There is trust, secrecy, faith, superstition, disappointment, prejudice, surprise, happiness, loss and anxiety – lots of anxiety. Only the intensity varies, and if you look closely, setting one story beside another, this piece next to that, you see how they relate. Break your gaze and it's a blur again, a vast composite worked so rigorously by so many hands as to appear as one integral work. A poor man's mosaic.

*

'I wonder what happened to Edna?' I ask Nonna a few days after reading her book. We're back in the kitchen, and it's cooler now. The rain came. Nonna is clattering about behind the curtain.

'Did I not write it?'

She peers around at me and I shake my head, my mouth full of volcano apple cake.

'Ah, well, let me tell you: one day when I was working I said to her, "Oh, Edna, I dreamt of you last night" and she was all' – Nonna makes her eyes wide and purses her lips – '"*Did* you...?" and I said, "Oh, *yes*..."'

'Had you?'

'Of course not, but I made up a whole elaborate dream with her in it.'

'And so?'

'And so we became good friends. She cried when I left the factory.'

All it took was a story.

*

I have not reproduced passages from Nonna's book lightly. How could I? She does not tell her stories lightly; she is always asking you to acknowledge some implicit

138

significance, to rub a story's stuff between your fingers and confirm the quality by saying something like 'because you worked so much harder', 'because you knew better', 'because of your past, of course, yes, it's clear'.

As I tucked the book back in the cupboard above the TV, it struck me that, when Nonna tells me what she tells me, when she instructs me to read on and assures me that I'll find 'things' in her account of a life lived, 'real and without fiction', she is handing me pieces to assemble. Not because she is tired or burdened by the responsibility of holding them all herself and recycling them for us whenever we show interest. But because she wants to see what my hands can do; to appreciate the nature of my craft. What, she wonders, will my personal imprint be? What will it add to the work of her family, to the labours of more than a century?

V.

Miles before arriving at Nonna's we would spot the *aquedotto*, like a red-and-white striped lighthouse in a flat green sea. This water tower marks the junction where the main road meets a dead-end track, at the end of which lies the house. When I was about ten years old, the track's uneven white gravel, full of deep milky puddles whenever it rained, was overlayed with thick tarmac. One day, expecting the familiar crunch of rubber tyres on loose stone, we were greeted instead by silent smoothness, and it was exciting because it was new.

On the right-hand side, running parallel to the track, was the *roja*, the narrow canal that carried water across the plain. In the early 1960s the *roja* was lined with concrete, and the fat brown trout and crayfish that used to nibble at the banks soon vanished. The crays were so clean and sweet, Nonna said, that you could rip their heads off and eat them then and there.

On the left-hand side was the corn, the tallest in the world, I assumed, which seemed to curve over the top of the moving car like the wall of a tunnel and concealed the house until the final bend. The anticipation was immense, as though we had been travelling for days, rather than only a few hours, from Varese. My father would sound the horn and Nonna emerged like a cuckoo from a clock, beaming and wiping her enormous hands on her apron.

I write in the past tense, but most things remain true. In fact, apart from the tarmac, and a brief period in the early 2000s when the corn was replaced by soya (supposedly more reliable and lucrative: in reality, neither), little has changed here in all the years I have known it. To the north-west, it is still flat for field after field, until

140

the sudden wall of blue mountains behind Maniago. To the south, you look back down the track towards the *acquedotto* and, from this angle, when the corn is low, it looks like an outsized carnation gaping at the sky; when it's high, the corn obscures the tower's stalk so the basin appears suspended, a spaceship skimming the land.

Scattered about on roads with names like via dell'Industria and via la Mola, Grinding Wheel Street, are the forges; there for as long as anyone can remember and still churning out knives, scissors and sharpeners. Straight across from the house is the one Nonno found a job in as soon as he and Nonna arrived back from Manchester late in the summer of 1971, when the corn would have been as tall as could be, waving for the men to come with their scythes and sickles. Every weekday until I was about four, when he reached pensionable age, Nonno would cut across the cornfield on his way to and from the factory, entering at the end of one row and emerging at the opposite end. In the summer months, he was like a swimmer, diving into the blue-green and not coming up for air until the other side, blinking at the sky. We watched from the kitchen window.

In the other direction, behind the house, there was, for most of my childhood, Nonno's small farmyard with hutches and a hayloft, and behind these, a modest vineyard – still there – about half the size of a football field, where thick vines twist sideways and slip sinuous arms around each other, like drunks holding each other upright. Between the vines' trunks, at regular intervals, are red roses, the winemaker's early warning system for mildew and rot; and everywhere you look, dandelions.

Cross the *roja* on your right and you're in a clump of trees, all that remains of the ancient forest that apparently gave our track its name, from the Latin *fagetum*, beech forest, which became *faêt* in Friulano. This sounds to my English ear a bit like *fate*, or even *faith*, said in an Italian accent. Finally, beyond the trees is a long straight road called via dei Radici, Roots Street, the furthest limit of my youthful roaming. I could not cross this white road, though I don't remember whether this was a rule I had been set or one I imposed myself, for fear of getting lost, or worse.

When Nonno was alive, the sounding of the car horn on arrival was a source of emotional conflict for me and my sister. On one hand, we wanted nothing more than for Nonna to appear and make a fuss of us. She kept sweets in the pocket of her apron, and a silver thimble which we treasured as a fairy cup, and her lips gave soft and profuse kisses. On the other hand, Nonno might be sleeping, as he did every day after lunch for an hour, sometimes two, when the bedroom door was closed, perhaps even locked, and the blinds were rolled all the way down so that not a speck of light could penetrate.

Nonno's sleeps were regimented, renowned and fabulous; they seemed essential to his very being, so that while we didn't know what the consequences of disturbing him might be, we knew we didn't want to find out. As the car approached the bend, our eyes would dart nervously to the clock on the dashboard and if it was before three in the afternoon, we'd beg our father not to beep. He always did. Our deference to Nonno irritated him, perhaps. I think he may have enjoyed the prospect of waking his *papà*.

As far back as I can remember my *nonni* slept in separate rooms, which struck me as odd for a married couple, especially one so famously in love. The story of their courtship was the first love story I ever heard – it was to me the definition of the genre, full of spectacle and obstacles and intuition and danger. I remember asking Nonna about their sleeping arrangements when I was about seven (clearly, it was a concern) and her patiently explaining that it was because of Nonno's snoring and because it was so important that he sleep soundly. The first part made sense – Nonno's snoring shook the walls – but the second was mysterious. (I did not know, then, about his heart.) Nonno's sleep is not normal sleep, I reasoned; something extraordinary must be happening when this old man closes his eyes.

My sister and I became fascinated by this private activity that seemed to involve us all by ending the ceremony of lunch and casting a spell over the entire household – especially Nonna who became slow and silent, like an underwater version of herself. Perhaps there was a seed of resentment in our feeling: when Nonno was asleep, Nonna hushed us, told us to play quietly, and at all costs to stay away – this was a warning – from Nonno's bedroom window. This imperative electrified our games. We would take it in turns to creep up on tiptoe, holding our breath, alert to minor disturbances in the rhythm of Nonno's breathing, to touch the windowsill with one finger before retreating, with barely supressed giggles, to the starting line, which was policed by the Madonna in her grotto.

Sometimes we heard him mumble, and one time I remember him shouting out – not words, or not ones we recognized, and not at us, I don't think. We ran away petrified. Other times, instead of touching the blinds, we would deposit daisy chains or palmfuls of purple beads pulled from the stalks of grape hyacinths, like offerings at a shrine. We had seen such things on television. We did it for the little Madonna too.

When, eventually, Nonno emerged from his bedroom, we expected him to look different – fortified by his important sleep, physically larger, maybe – but he looked exactly the same as always. Medium height and build, bright white hair, eyes like snowmelt. His mood, though, was often softer. Then, he would take us with him to the bar at the end of the track, at the foot of the *acquedotto*, where he would play *briscola* with friends and give us a few coins with which to buy whatever ice creams we wanted from the freezer.

The bar's blinds were never up, no matter the time of day, and the air was thick with smoke and the scent of old things put away years ago. I remember the total absence of women or anyone who might pay attention to me and my sister, and we wandered around as we pleased, letting ourselves behind the bar, sticking our fingers in the sugar and stroking the labels on tall bottles that looked like powerful potions: *Strega* – 'Witch' – its neon colour utterly unreal, the pungent herby smell reminiscent of the elixirs of eternal youth we made out of soapy bathwater and cuttings from the garden, and gifted to our mother. In my memory the men are all dressed in thick cotton and wool in shades of brown, like the wood of the tables and chairs and blinds – the air itself was sepia – and their skin is like the trunks of old trees. I was acutely aware of how neat and new my own clothes were, how garish and girly.

The old men all spoke a strange tongue, lilting yet harsh, often ferocious, as they thumped a fist on the table or threw their cards down. This was Nonno's language, Friulano, *furlan*, so different to our own – it seemed to us – proper Italian. Friulano is a *dialetto* – or a *lingua minoritaria*; the line between the two is difficult to plot with certainty – and though there are some common words, islands of understanding are few and far between. When my sister and I were spoken to, we were adrift, unable to gain purchase let alone respond. For as long as they could

144

the old men resorted to the international language of cheek-pinching and nose-stealing. After that, they mostly ignored us. And as we got older, more self-conscious, this began to feel loaded. We were *le varesotte* now – from a city well known for its wealth – or, worse, *le inglesine*, little English girls. Foreigners in both cases, just visiting this place.

*

Nonno was bilingual, as were most Italians of his age, for whom a regional language had always coexisted with *Italiano standard*. In fact, he was trilingual, speaking Friulano with his wife, Veneto with his children and Italian with his grandchildren, who spoke that alone. No one is sure why he came to use different tongues for wife and children – 'era così, nina...' says Nonna – but there seems to be an element of compromise. I think of Veneto as a kind of halfway house between Italian and Friulano, less strange to the non-speaker's ear; I can understand most Veneto, while Friulano flummoxes me. The rationale in Nonno's case may have been more personal, though: Veneto is the language that Dirce grew up speaking, the language of her father's 'high' family, and the language Leo knew to use to first get her attention. It is a tongue of airs and graces compared to the Friulano of the fieldhands. It was, his wife insisted, *better*. But this does not explain why the couple came to speak Friulano between themselves. Perhaps it was tit for tat.

Moving down the Italian peninsula, thirty-one tongues apart from Italian have been counted by UNESCO, from the *Francoprovenzale* of the far Northwest to the Hellenic *griko*, spoken in some parts of Apulia, and mostly they are mutually unintelligible. There's an old story about Italian

145

troops in the First World War: a platoon of Piedmontese soldiers meets a platoon of Sicilians and, each side assuming the other to be German, it almost ends in a blood bath.

That in the early twentieth century the Italian Army was not speaking Italian shows how little progress the idea of a national identity had made since Garibaldi's day, when the writer Alessandro Manzoni supposedly dipped his own Milanese in the waters of Dante's River Arno to create a plainer, modern Italian for all. Then, language was a flexing of muscles between rivals, who reached a truce: a single tongue to bind a divided people, to make them speak and write a new nation – an idea, really – into being. But when, on Unification, Manzoni's Italian was made the official language of the Kingdom of Italy, only about two per cent of the population spoke it. Because an Italian speaks Italian, sure; but what if he sees himself, foremost, as *Friulano* or *Piemontese* or *Emiliano* or *Sardo*? If you have more than one language in you, you will favour the one that rises to your throat most naturally.

Language is the flower of identity, and like the rambling rose it can be trained this way or that, to serve a purpose beyond its own desire to thrive. From the mid 1920s, when Nonno was born, Mussolini intensified the nineteenth-century drive to standardize the nation's language. He announced a war to 'defend' Italian from other tongues, regional as well as foreign, which sought, in his eyes, to poison noble Latin roots. Patriots spoke Italian only. Like his *bonifa delle paludi* – the vast Fascist project of swamp drainage, which sought to make marshland buildable, farmable and capable of attracting citizens who would otherwise emigrate – Mussolini called for a *bonifica linguistica*, a great linguistic reclamation. 'Dictator' is, after all, rooted in the act of speech. Notices appeared in

146

town squares:

> Once and for all, even in shops of any sort, <u>ONLY THE ITALIAN LANGUAGE</u> must be used. We Squadristi, with persuasive methods, will enforce this order.

(Think back to 1942, to the eighteen-year-old Leo approaching Dirce halfway across the Cellina river one bright afternoon. Did Leo look about himself, scan the area for soldiers or potential informers, or spot such a flier fluttering on the bridge's railings, before choosing his opening gambit? Not Italian's *buongiorno*, nor Friulano's *mandi*, but the Venetian *bondì*. Nonna was right; the word – a calculated choice – does carry more weight than a simple 'good day'. You could read it – could you? – as a daily act of self-definition, of resistance even.)

Expressions of regional identity were a direct threat to Italianità, which for the Fascists was really Romanità, founded on the myth of an ancient Roman essence, common to all Italians. And as Il Duce concentrated on building a neo-Roman empire, the promulgation of a standard language became increasingly necessary. Foreign words – *forestierismi*, from the Latin *foris* meaning 'out'; literally, outsiderisms – were banished. *Dialetti* were excluded from public spaces. He demanded that the Accademia della Crusca 'clean up' the language by finding Italian words to replace any corruptions or *esoticismi*.

In 1938, the word 'lei', as a polite version of 'you', was outlawed and replaced by the more imperious-sounding 'voi'. (According to one theory, Il Duce found 'lei', which also means 'she', dangerously emasculating.) Schools and public offices were put on guard.

The *bonifica linguistica* was ultimately about as successful as the war against water. By spring 1945, among

147

the ruins of the Fascist regime, self-expression was beginning, tentatively, to bloom again: on 18 February 1945, about half an hour south of Maniago, in the small town of Casarsa della Delizia, a young Pier Paolo Pasolini, enfant terrible in the making, founded the Academiuta di lenga furlana, dedicated to the study of Friulian language and poetry. Such a thing would have seemed unimaginable when Il Duce was at the height of his powers.

By now, though, Mussolini was effectively redundant, barely propped up by German forces. Since Mussolini's defected generals had signed an armistice with the Allies in September 1943, the Friuli and other northern regions had been overrun by the German army, which had no interest in the old *battaglie* and *bonifiche*. And when, in the last days of April 1945, Mussolini was captured by the *brigate* Garibaldi on the shore of Lake Como and made to stand against a wall while his executioner took aim, Walter Audisio, the man believed to have fired the shot, found that the dictator had nothing at all to say. 'Not a single word: not the name of a son, nor of his mother or wife, not even a cry, nothing.' Language, too, had turned its back on him.

A few relics of the time remain in modern Italian – *calcio* instead of football; *autista* instead of *chauffeur* – but by the war's end, Rome's Accademia, which had been going about its task alphabetically, slowly, in some cases recalcitrantly, had officially got as far as the letter 'C'.

*

'C' for *casa*, 'house' or 'home', the latter more a feeling than a material thing. 'Home', the place where we are most ourselves, perennial insiders. While English has two words to signal the difference between the fact of

148

bricks and mortar and the subjective sense of belonging, Italian has only *casa*. In Friulano: *cjase*.

Until the mid-1970s, more than half the population spoke *dialetto* at home and with friends, Italian being reserved for the workplace and when travelling. Fifty or so years later, this had been turned on its head, with the majority speaking Italian at home and with friends, and only 14 per cent expressing themselves most readily in their *dialetto*. Unsurprisingly, it was the older members of society that kept the *dialetti* alive: as late as 2015, 32 per cent of those aged over seventy-five – that is, those born, like Nonno, before the Second World War – spoke exclusively or mostly in a *dialetto*. Still now, *zio* Orfeo speaks only Friulano and, if necessary, because of out-of-towners like me, the more Italianate Veneto. After the obligatory school years, Orfeo simply let *Italiano standard* drop. It didn't fit him. As the poet Paul Celan said of the Romanian he grew up with, it was 'no more than a light coat one can take off easily'; how could it compare with Celan's mother's tongue, German, which was a 'domain', 'my fate', full-body immersion.

In the second half of the twentieth century, a certain stigma was attached to the *dialetti*, as social status, politics and language, twisted and turned back on each other. Nonno's kind of multilingualism was of a turbulent, un-celebrated sort, not at all like my own, which, I am always told, is *wonderful, so lucky, wow*. As the Italian economy boomed and the country strove to modernize and find its place in a global picture, local languages were increasingly seen as retrograde, nostalgic, embarrassingly provincial – far better to learn English. When I was younger, only able to look forward and in the most uncomplicated way, I would have framed it like that too. I was Italian and so I spoke Italian. (Except when I was English and spoke

English.)

A survey conducted by the Istituto Nazionale di Statistica in 2017 pointed to the preponderance of *dialetti* among those with lower levels of education. About a quarter of those whose studies ended with secondary school exclusively spoke a *dialetto* at home, compared to about 3 per cent of those who pursued higher education. In recent years we have become familiar with such surveys, conducted in various countries, that suggest an association between reactionary, or nostalgic, politics and lower levels of education. Stigma sticks, spreads, mutates. And it can make an easy kind of sense. I remember *snobbando* (the anglo-italianism so apt) the *lombardo* boys who hung around in the park behind the shopping mall, talking in their low yodelling vowels and clipped nasalities. They seemed to live on a different plain to me and my international group of friends. To them, who heard us talking among ourselves in English, we were foreign, *inglesi*, although most of us had been born and raised right there, probably beginning in the same hospital as them. To us, they were the foreign ones, speaking a language that didn't have a place in the modern world. And yet there was the uneasy sense that they belonged here more than us because of it. On some level I think we felt threatened, and so we generalized and mocked them as *leghisti*, supporters of the thuggish, far-right Northern League, a party then campaigning for the country to be broken up into pre-Unification regions. Could they *be* more backwards?

Once, regional tongues were seen as a threat to national unity. Now the risk lies in denying their place in people's lives and histories. From 1999, the year of Nonno's death, successive amendments to the Constitution have emphasized the historical value of a handful of regional cultures

150

and languages, among them Friulano. Nonno missed it by six months and I wonder if it would have thrilled him – *recognition, at last!* – or meant nothing at all, just politicians doing what politicians do, while we get on with the living and working. Friulano is now protected, granted special legal status that allows it to be used alongside Italian in schools and other public spaces. But the matter remains controversial, misunderstood and highly politicized. At school, as well as Italian and English, my cousins, ten and more years younger than me, were taught Friulano. They read the poems of Pier Paolo Pasolini, and grew up code-switching, the word itself an import that Mussolini could never have tolerated.

That a regional language should be taught in schools, rather than *imparato sul campo*, 'picked up in the field', recasts things somewhat. Legitimacy, identity, control, compromise, heritage, ours, theirs, foreign, local – look at how these concepts are somehow held together, the union tense, fragile and forever shifting. A change in the weather and everything is different.

For Nonno, the choice between Friulano and Italian was, I think, something like that between a favourite shirt, its cuffs and collar soft from years of use, and an over-starched Church shirt, hung out for him by someone else. The one gently hugged his form and movement, warmed by years of skin contact; the other never felt quite right, was restrictive, unnatural, and so reserved for official matters – births, deaths, marriages and visitors.

I didn't appreciate it when he was alive, but to hear Nonno speak was to fall through time, back to around 180 BC when the Carni, a mountain-dwelling Celtic tribe, came down to the Friuli's fertile plains seeking respite from the Alpine winters and the chance of a gentler life. The Romans arrived soon after, chased them back into

151

the mountains, and replaced their simple settlements with their own grander affairs. Only once the Carni agreed to submit to Roman rule were they allowed back down to farm the land, to mix with the powerful new landowners (as long as they did not forget their place). The Friulian language tells the story of this coexistence of unequals in its heavily latinized Celtic, supplemented over the centuries by the Germanic of the invading Lombards, the Slavic and Venetian of the neighbouring territories, and, for modern concepts, standard Italian. With wines we speak of *terroir*. A truer expression of place could not be found.

If this seems romantic, no doubt it is. I am Dirce's granddaughter, after all. But there is self-interest, too. I suppose there always is with romance. In both my languages I am difficult to pin down – in English, there's the odd Liverpudlian twang from my mother; in Italian, the closed vowels of the Milanese I grew up around – but mostly I sound as rootless as I often feel. And so, I twist back through my family. I cling to Nonno for support. My mind moves around his land like a ghost haunting a house it considers its own. Or a vampire, hovering on the threshold, hoping to be invited in.

*

The front door of the house that Nonno built is thick mottled glass framed by dark wood. Bodies seen through it are fluid, abstracted, identifiable only if you know them well already. We recognize them by colours: the bright red of Nonna's cardigan beneath a pale bluey-grey crown; the yellow of Lucia's hair and the rosiness of her cheeks. When they open the door, the first thing we see, beyond welcoming faces, is the long corridor, tiled in mossy green, as though the vegetation that surrounds the house has come up through the floor. We walk automatically into the kitchen and sit down. Even in the summer months the wood burner will be on, with various pots bubbling away for later. Nonna will have us guess what's for dinner and if it's Friday we'll know it is fish – probably the local *baccalà mantecato*, white and creamy, with polenta – and I'll widen my eyes and make all the ritual noises. She'll tell my mum and sister that there's mashed potato for them, and my dad and I will rub our hands together because that leaves more polenta for us. She'll ask about our health and then she'll talk about hers, and depending on how generous we're feeling, this will go on for one hour or two. And then she'll say that she has left towels on ours beds – the same thin, rough one I have used my whole life – and that's the cue to go and unpack, so that she can get back to the pots.

Except sometimes I don't go to the bedroom. I turn right out of the kitchen door into the mossy green hall, and immediately right again, my hand finding the familiar spring-and-creak of the door handle. The steps that lead down to the *cantina* are washed cement the colour of chestnut mushrooms. Their cold comes through the soles of my shoes, and I notice as I descend how the *cantina*'s familiar smell builds, layer on layer, until its mixture seems thick enough to cup in my hand and lift to my lips: the sour and soily plastic of a lifetime's cheap flowerpots; mouldering leather shoes in damp cardboard boxes; the sweetness of stacks and stacks of yellowed dusty papers.

The swing door that used to frighten me because I saw too many horror films too young – *imagine if it just started swinging on its own!* – leads through to a network of rooms in perpetual darkness; not a glimmer of light, the kind of absence that has weight. I can never remember

153

where the light switches are, so I continue blind, hands in front of me, instinctively reaching to open the fridge, as much for the light source as to see what's in there. Usually, at this point in the visit, it's more or less empty, waiting for us to fill it with our bottled water and shop-bought wines. Perhaps there are a few dishes prepared in advance. *Sarde in saor*, a sweet-sour Venetian dish of fried sardines, onion, raisins and pine nuts; *polpette*, with their secret cheese heart, waiting to be reheated; a hunk of boar brought down from the mountains by the son of an old friend.

By now you can smell the mustiness of the wine room, a little further along, where, lining the walls, are countless recycled bottles and *damigiane* (the word so much more elegant than 'demijohn'), ready to be filled with Nonno's wine, syphoned from the mother vessel that squats in the corner. They have been waiting many years now.

Nonno's wine was the first wine I ever tasted. And his, the first grappa, too. Nonna tells me that she used to dip my dummy in it, to help me off to sleep. My parents say this is nonsense, but I know who to believe. The wine was a bright, translucent magenta, served in tumblers gone cloudy through decades of daily use, and its taste was sweet but not remotely syrupy. There was, in fact, no aftertaste that I can recall – no spice or flavour of wood. It was young and untamed, alive in your mouth and then gone.

And so, you would take another sip and try to catch something that lasts: strawberry and... strawberry. Because I knew it contained two types of *fragolino* – 'little strawberry' – a cheap grape imported from America in the 1860s, after Europe's vines were decimated by pests. Fragolino, or *uva Americana*, took particularly well here in fact. It is disparaged by oenophiles for its unsophisticated taste, and the commercial production of it was banned by Mussolini's government in 1931, because, so the story goes, its methanol levels were so unpredictable that a drinker might be blinded. An alternative explanation points to un-Italian origins – the vine is an invasive species, a *forestierismo* of sorts. The government and the European Union uphold the ban still, but the law has never dared to meddle with private consumption. ('*Beef e vjood mjoor*', a rare joke of Orfeo's. Drink and you'll see better.)

Nonno's wine always seemed to fly in the face of modern laws. It was an ancient juice produced by feet and hands and muscle, according to rules set out by the Romans. And yet it was so delicate and unstable it could not travel. This did not stop us trying, and at the end of the four-hour car journey back to Varese we had nothing but vinegar and memories. It was as though the wine had recognized our arrogance and self-destructed to spite us. As we drove I wondered how far it would allow itself to be taken before turning bad; to the *acquedotto*? To via dei Radici? To the region's border?

Nonno once told me a story about witches who would break into your *cantina* if you had crossed them. Their revenge was to piss in the wine, or to drink the wine and replace it with piss. This happened to a man he knew.

'How did he anger them?'

'By telling stories about them.'

'But you...'

And then, I don't remember; he probably stole my nose.

In another telling, the evil ones were enraged by self-absorbed peasants, who forgot about them and failed to leave them fresh water to drink. Thanks to the *roja*, Nonna said, we were safe on that count, at least.

155

Nonno was full of these stories, although to call them 'stories' is perhaps misleading. They were fragments, scraps of folklore and legend, lessons of indeterminate value and application.

He fancied himself an educator, I think. One Christmas, when I was about six, he took my sister and me out to the hutches and gifted us a rabbit named Nerone (because he was fat and black), who we talked about and tended to – more flower offerings – every day of our visit. We worried that it hurt Nerone when Nonno pulled him out and held him aloft by his ears, but neither of us wanted to be the one to say so. When we returned at Easter, we were served a stew so golden and delicious, and when Nonno pointed to it and told us the story of its making, he seemed genuinely astounded by our horrified reactions. We had grown up in a different land, had been raised in some strange, foreign style. I did not eat rabbit again until I was in my twenties.

His repertoire was his own, and he took it to the grave. There was the one about the cemetery, where flames leapt from the coffins of those who had not made amends (of course, he had seen this himself one night, cycling home from the bar); the one about the man who lived just down the way, who always left Mass before the rosary, until one night something terrifying happened to him and he never skipped it again and hardly spoke a word for the rest of his days; the one about the shepherd who grew lazy and left his sheep in the mountains too long, saying 'I'll move them to the plains next week... next week... next week,' and then the winter came and they all froze to death. And the one about the woman who fell asleep with her mouth open, and her soul, in the form of a fly or a mouse, depending on the telling, escaped to go and perform some good deed or other, but her husband, thinking it a pest, killed it, and so, killed her. Mortality was a theme, I realized years later. And the otherworldly.

I did not know then about the *benandanti*, a tribe of 'good-farers' believed to sink into deep death-like sleeps during which they would slip away from their bodies and travel miles across the Friulian plains, carrying fennel stalks as weapons, to fight ritual battles against witches and warlocks who threatened the harvest. The outcome of these jousts between good and evil determined whether the village would see abundance or famine. At other times the *benandanti* journeyed to gatherings where they danced and feasted and joined a procession of spirits, among them many animals, and were told the names of people who would soon die. A sleeping *benandante* must never be disturbed, or the spirit would not be able to return home to the body. Failure to return meant death.

Now, I mix my memories and Nonno's stories with what I learnt long after his death. I try to make it all flow, as if staging the conversation we might have had if only he were still here. I have read Carlo Ginzburg's *The Night Battles*, a study of Friulian witchcraft and agrarian cults, published in the 1960s. I have noted the consistency between Ginzburg's interest in covens, with their rituals, signs and incantations, and his mother Natalia's interest in families and the uttered and unuttered things that bind them. I have read, too, about the maleficent spirit with many names – *cialciùt, cialcìcula, çhalçhùt, vencul, pesarìn, pesarûl, smarva, orcul, fràcula* and *morà* – a presence made of darkness, in male or female form, that visited Friulians at night, breaking into their bedrooms to sit on their chests, so heavy they could hardly breathe. Some say the demon leached the sleepers' blood, others say it sucked the milk from new mothers' teats. To protect yourself you must leave a spindle of yarn in your bed, or a pomegranate, quince or blessed olive branch of the sort Nonna gifts us every year around Easter. Or you should piss in a jug and make a cross with your arms in front of your chest.

These primordial beliefs, composites of local, Germanic and Slavic lore, tempered by Christian persuasion, flourished in the aftermath of the Second World War. A series of conversations with people in Maniago and the surrounding area, recorded between 1946 and 1951 by the painter and folklorist Lea D'Orlandi, shows that experiences of the *cialciùt* were common almost to the point of banal. It's easy to laugh – if you didn't have a jug to piss in, apparently, a pumpkin would do just as well – but perhaps it helped people to make sense of the death and torment they had seen all around them in recent years, when people were found dead in their homes or by the side of the road, were attacked by foreign presences or mysteriously made pregnant, and when friends disappeared without a trace in the middle of the night.

I know the *cialciùt* well myself. I have been visited regularly since I was about six years old, sometimes several nights in a row. Lying in bed, I can see the room around me and sense – even see – the threat. A nebulous dark form, fear itself, climbing up the wall and approaching the bed, reaching out for my neck, squeezing until I gasp for air. But still I can't move, I am pinned to the bed. I try to shout out, to call for help, but my mouth won't work and my throat is closed. All I can manage is garbled noises, yowls, moans. Eventually, suddenly, something gives in my chest and I wake up sweating and compulsively making the sign of the cross. I do not believe in God, but it seems, when terror takes hold, part of me still does.

Apparently, in Newfoundland, the incubus is called the Old Hag, and in China, they speak of 'ghost oppression', because the sleeping person is especially vulnerable to self-serving spirits. Awake, in the early hours, I steady myself and call the demon by a different name: Sleep Paralysis, a condition linked to anxiety and post-traumatic stress disorder, in which, between waking and sleeping, the body cannot respond to the mind's instruction. It's as though the person has split in two and can't come back together. I read about it on my mobile phone, reassured by the screen's bright light. The NHS recommends avoiding big meals before bed, too much alcohol, sleeping on your back. It is believed to run in families.

*

About a year before Nonno died he instructed my dad to go into the *cantina*, to the old chest of drawers that sits next to the fridge. In the second drawer down, he would find a document, telling the story of his life.

What my dad found instead, among the stacks of papers was a single page: 'LA DISCENDENZA DEI LENARDUZZI', the Descent of the Lenarduzzis. (In fact, in his awkward Italian, Nonno misspelt 'descendance'.)

It tells of how two brothers set off from a small Friulian village called Pozzo (literally, 'Well'), with their wives, children and scant belongings piled high on a horse-drawn cart. The date is given as 11 November 1876, which seems unusually precise for this kind of story. The Lenarduzzis left behind in Pozzo were too many, and the field they shared too small to feed them all. The brothers reached Campagna – the countryside around Maniago – and began sharecropping a large plot of land belonging to the Conte D'Attimis, corn mostly but also wheat and barley.

What follows is a list of names, with births, deaths

and marriages added in between the lines, apparently in a different sitting. After the brothers Giuseppe and Leonardo (whose wives are not named), come Maria, Luigi, Guglielmo, Luigia, Giovanni and Candido. Then, another Giovanni ('Giovanin') and Amelia (who goes by 'Linda') and they have three children: Maria, Leonardo ('Leo') and Orfeo. We know where we are now. We recognize these people.

It continues, in its strange mixture of past and present tense:

> And Leonardo marries a girl from Maniago Libero called Dirce and their wedding day is 25-10-1947 and they have the joy of two sons, Manlio, born in Campagna 17-8-1948 [the date is incorrect] and JHON [he could, apparently, never spell my dad's name] born in Manchester 20-8-1953 and they hoped to have another son but unfortunately destiny did not favour it and the baby was born dead and so they decided to adopt a beautiful little girl just born and they gave her the name Lucia born 20-4-1969 and she marries a lad from Arba named Giuseppe born 5-6-1966 and they are residents of Campagna.

A final line throws us back to 1950: at the age of 20 months Manlio and his parents emigrate to England 'e la storia dei Lenarduzzi la potete continuare voi stessi'. 'And the story of the Lenarduzzis you can continue yourselves.'

But where is Nonno in all this? 'Manlio and his parents' – a strange act of self-erasure, as though the firstborn is the hero of this tale and his father Leo just a minor player, who exits the story in media res, hardly figuring at all. Leo is born, marries, has and doesn't have children, and disappears in 1950 as the family sets off for England. There is no mention of what he found, and made, when he got

160

there, of all the houses and the jobs and the challenges overcome. None of the stories that his wife tells me are here, only stories anchored in a deeper past, in the fields his great-grandfather first tended.

What does it mean when a couple, Leo and Dirce, experienced the sweetest, fullest chapters of their lives in different times and places? It's as if they're dancing together, holding each other tight as they always did, but their feet are moving to different tunes. I wonder if, in the end, Nonno simply thought that England, for all her opportunities to get on and make money, had not actually been so kind to him and his wife, with two heart attacks, a nervous breakdown and a dead son between them. And if he cannot deny England's deleterious effects on his family and its health, he can at least deny her importance in the story he records for posterity.

I am, it seems, back in the *cantina*, looking for traces of Nonno in the dark, catching him here and there, reflected and distorted in old glass bottles. Is this what Gaston Bachelard meant when he wrote that words are 'little houses', and 'to go upstairs in the word house is to withdraw step by step; while to go down to the cellar is to dream, it is losing oneself in the distant corridors of an obscure etymology, looking for treasures that cannot be found in words'?

On the afternoon of Nonno's funeral, my dad tells me, he went down to the *cantina*, to the big cupboard where Nonno kept his work clothes and everything else that didn't belong upstairs. He took two things for himself: a heavy iron plane for shaving wood and a long tape measure coiled around a wheel. It does not give the distance between two points in Italian centimetres and metres, but rather in British inches and yards.

*

I don't remember many conversations with Nonno. Perhaps this is because I didn't speak Friulano and he couldn't always be bothered with Italian. Perhaps it is because I was young and cripplingly shy, even with certain members of the family. Perhaps he was simply tired. Lord knows he slept a lot. But I do remember him showing me things. Ours was a language of pointing and looking and doing as he did.

His catchphrase: '*Ce ca l'è?*', pronounced something like 'che ka l'eh' in English, 'What is it?' 'What's going on?' My sister and I would be in hysterics because we thought it sounded like the chickens who followed him around the yard. *Ce ca l'è, ce ca l'è, ce ca l'è.*

His lessons: *This is how you strip the corn, watch. This is the poo of a fox, and the fox will eat the chickens. Pass me that wire. We fix it like this. Feel this wood, it's hard and dry, from a willow – perfect for making clogs.*

He had piles of wood, of varying lengths and quality, some for carving, others for building, others still for burning. He taught me that a knot marks the place where a branch once grew, before it withered and died or was swallowed up by the expanding trunk of the tree. Each knot in wood is a could-have-been; a phantom limb.

Put out your hand: this is good seed and this is bad, vedi? Squeeze it. See? Those clouds – no, look – he pokes at the sky and I can see the soil under his nail – *those ones – they are storm clouds.* Thunder and then lightning, as if he had summoned it himself. *Count the beats between them and you'll know how near or far it is.*

This grass – look – is pistic. Pinch it just here and pull, firm and slow.

Pistic. Now I also know it as *silene vulgaris*, from the

Greek Silenòs, a semi-divine figure, the jovial old god of winemaking and drunkenness, educator and protector of Dionysus. He embodied the spirit of the treading dance, when bare feet stomp the grapes. *Seiô*, 'to move back and forth' and *lênos*, 'wine-trough'. His large round belly is evoked by the plant's bulbous flower, which is, in fact, shaped like an upturned chalice. Silenòs was famed for his love of sleep.

You find it by the side of the road, free food for travellers, the poor man's spinach, Nonno said.

Pistic appears to take its name from the Latin *pisticus*, itself derived from a Greek word meaning 'faithful'. In the seventeenth century, *pistic* was the name for someone guided by faith rather than reason.

Most people don't even know they can eat it.

Silenòs was also an oracle, privy to the whole of the past and future. In the *Symposium*, Plato praised Socrates by likening him to Silenòs, the symbol of great wisdom housed in an unlikely, rustic body. In English, we call this plant bladder campion or maidenstears.

And now we must take it to Nonna, for the pot.

*

When Nonno died he was seventy-five and I was nearly thirteen. I told my dad recently that I could not remember the sound of Nonno's voice at all, and he dug out a home movie from 1997. I was surprised to hear him speak in Italian, albeit with that familiar rise and fall, the sing-song of Friulano. In the film, the whole family is seated around a long table, with a white cloth and two glasses each. We are in a restaurant, the one in Barcis, by the lake, which Nonna still chooses for special occasions. It is Nonno and Nonna's fiftieth wedding anniversary and Nonno is standing to make a speech, to thank us all for coming from England and from other parts of Italy. He is struggling for breath, and stands slightly bent over, with two fingers pressing on the table for support. He is moved. You can see tears in his eyes as he looks around blinking, counting us, taking stock, and saying each of our names in turn, like some incantation directed to a higher power.

*

It's 1971 and a green van turns off the main road by the *acquedotto*, onto the track. Orfeo, a good-looking twenty-seven-year-old, is standing with a bucket of cement in one hand thinking about what to do next, and he hears the wheels meet the rough ground before he sees the van and starts waving. He's happy – his older brother is finally home for good – but he can never seem to really let himself go. His is the shyness of a boy born long after his siblings and cousins have grown up and left for work in foreign places. But he smiles and there are hugs and kisses. He meets his niece Lucia for the first time, pinches her pink cheeks, steals her nose. She cries because it's the only language she has.

Orfeo has been working on this house for about eighteen months, following his brother and sister-in-law's designs as best he can. It's not finished, not even nearly. The floors aren't down and there's no glass in the windows, but the bones are there, and now Leo is back they'll do it together. And while they're working, he'll bring up his idea about building a house for himself right alongside, between here and the *roja*.

The family moves everything from the van into one room where they will eat and sleep until the next room is complete. And then they'll move into that room while they work on the next, and so on until the last green tile is laid.

'We had a whole system,' Nonna tells me.

'Like crop rotation?'

'Well, something like that...'

On the first morning the family woke up, they were three bodies entwined on a single mattress in the middle of a room filled with the stuff of their previous life. Leo was happy. (Nonna smiles now, thinking about his smile then. They could almost be facing each other across the table.) While Dirce dressed Lucia and prepared breakfast – a tin of baked beans brought over from Manchester, heated on a camp stove in the hallway, with bread supplied by Orfeo, and strong black coffee – Leo slipped out of the house and walked through the fields his great-grandparents had called home, taking in the same mountains they saw and the ripe smell of corn desperate for harvest. I imagine him tearing off a cob, peeling back the husk and sticking his thumbnail into a kernel – just as he showed me – to produce the milky sap that confirms ripeness. (You do it even when ripeness is beyond doubt; you do it simply because you enjoy the fact that you know this language.) I wonder if he felt the expansion in his chest that I feel when I'm there – the feeling of new, or forgotten, space opening up between the ribs, of oxygen reaching the very tips of the lungs' branches, budding almost. It starts in the mind, but something happens in the body.

Now he is in the vineyard. The vines had been planted before even the first brick was laid. Orfeo had sourced them from friends and acquaintances and plotted their rows carefully. There is *fragolino bianco* and *fragolino nero* and *clinto*. It would be about three years before they got their first proper crop. That's just how long it takes for vines to settle in.

165

After breakfast, while Dirce is tidying up and trying to keep Lucia entertained, Leo disappears again. This time, he goes further afield, to Dirce's old house in Maniago, to take cuttings from Angelo's vines. They have grown wild in the many years since Angelo's death but they are still good and strong. He takes some *sgaylard* and some *bacò*, other banned grapes, but he knows what he's doing, and they all know how good they taste. He has heard Dirce's story over and over again, about how she would escape her mother by hiding under the vines, where, into a hunk of bread stolen from the kitchen, she'd press grapes pulled from above her head so that the flesh burst and their juice soaked into the white crumb. He walks past the giant bush of lacrime d'Italia and tries not to look at it. No cuttings of that will be growing on his land. They have seen tears enough.

He will plant these old vines among the new ones, alongside the roses and the dandelions, and, in time, create a blend that belongs to this family alone – the taste of two families, in fact, with all their stories combined – nurtured by the soil and the air he knows they have always belonged in, really. He will wait, anxious but confident, for that first crop, the first expressions of this wild idea of his.

*

What am I looking for in this man that I have grown, cultivating stories like he did the land and animals, pruning and feeding and selecting?

About a year after Nonno's death, I found a faded photograph of him from 1943. He is lying on his side in a field, the grass tall around him, laughing open-mouthed and surrounded by friends. As merry a scene as you can imagine. Their bicycles are discarded in a heap behind them and there is bunting attached to their handlebars. Jovial bunting, adorned with the swastika.

The image threw me because of Nonna's stories about him hiding in the corn stacks when the SS or *Squadristi* came looking for young recruits, and the countless other stories and experiences that had made me see him as a man in charge, a brave man, strong and kind. I cried, concluding that he must have been a fascist after all.

'Ma, no, nina, non era fascista,' Nonna tried to reassure me. 'But you had to go along with it or there would be trouble. He didn't have a choice,' she said. And we left it at that.

Earlier this year, I mentioned the photograph to Nonna again.

'Do you remember how upset I was?' I asked.

'Si, si, nina... but you know he had to pretend, otherwise they would have come for him.'

When the Germans invaded Italy in 1943, Leo was moved from one factory making knives to another under Nazi control, making metal components for machinery. We do not know what sort. He went, said Nonna, because he could never have said no. 'What should he have done? They paid.'

I play around with the words 'metal' and 'mettle' and can't make them fit.

The occupiers also made other demands on Leo's time. He was signed up to a rota of night shifts, patrolling the factory walls to make sure no *partigiani* gained access, presumably to gain knowledge or sabotage production.

'Everyone knew the ragazzi had to do the patrol to be left in peace. You used not to say if you saw anything. And we knew who all the *partigiani* were – my cousin – Leo's friend – was one of the leaders.'

Most of the time, this is enough for me to keep piecing

together my version of Nonno.

'He had a tremendous sense of justice,' my uncle Manlio tells me on the phone one day. 'He was the proudest man I have ever known.'

'He was never a political man,' says my dad another time.

I struggle to make these details fit, too.

Nonna once told me that towards the end of the war, once *zio* Gioacchino had (hastily) moved back from Sheffield to Maniago, he began staying in after dark. Even by day, he never used public toilets.

'If he needed to wee while he was out, he didn't go to the bar – he came to my mother's house.'

'Did he feel vulnerable, do you think? Unsafe?'

Nonna looked at me blankly.

I clarified: 'Because he was – or had been – a fascist. To be caught with his trousers down...'

'Ah, no, nina, it wasn't that...'

I remember a scene from school, when I was about fifteen, a fight that broke out at the gates between the grandfathers of two boys in the Italian-language section. The first called the second a fascist and the second retaliated somehow, and it came to blows in front of us all. We whispered among ourselves that the first man must have been a *partigiano*, that the fascist had probably dobbed him in, had had him tortured maybe. That's what it was like during the war, we reasoned. The men must have been in their eighties now, and neither was in good shape, but suddenly they were in their twenties again and fiercely, unresolvably, divided. Things were that black and white, it seemed. Some days I think they still are.

*

Leo liked to build things. A house, hutches for rabbits, a wooden bed for my favourite doll, towering pyramids of corn-cobs to dry for the chickens, stable enough to crawl into. And a social and moral hierarchy in which Italians are invariably at the top. Manlio recalls how, when Leo worked at the terrazzo firm in Manchester in the 1950s and 60s, a pecking order was firmly established.

'The English did the general labour – the brute work, if you like – and the Scots pushed the heavy rollers and polisher across the floor. The Italians were the only ones with skills.' They were *terrazzieri*, renowned craftsmen, who designed, selected, cut, placed, levelled and finished to an unmatchable degree. Such mastery could not be learnt; it was passed down from generation to generation, in the blood, they said.

(But let's remember, a moment: 'The Home Office experience suggests that Italian immigrants do not, generally speaking, make any valuable contribution to the economy of the country.')

Leo did not mix with those he considered beneath him. He was, Manlio says, appalled by the lifestyles he saw around him, marked by gambling, stealing, womanizing and drinking of a heavier, more hopeless sort than he had ever known. It was not entirely foreign, of course; he knew how it happened, how it could creep up on a man. You had to be strong to stop it.

'He knew he didn't want to be like those men.'

And that was when and how he formed his unchanging view of British society.

'He never came to see *our* England,' says Manlio.

And I agree with him, although I am not sure that such a place exists. I know many Englands and am not sure which it is that we share.

Leo had, I think, a misplaced sense of control,

fashioned after the war, as a reaction to having had none at all. Such a sense of sovereignty would be misplaced in anyone in any circumstances, but not everyone exhibits it as overtly as Leo seems to have done. Not everyone builds a life on it. Having always been strong and healthy, he assumed he would stay that way; why should he not always lift two bags of cement? Though he went to Church most Sundays, he was not as devoted as his wife was – or as she encouraged him to be – and I do not think he believed, as she did, that his health and his future were always in the hands of the Lord. Or not yet, or not entirely. He saw himself as a maker, too, and a very skilled one at that. At work, if nowhere else, he was the master. He worked extremely hard and slept particularly soundly on the seventh day, when his family knew never to wake him.

His first heart attack at the age of forty-four shattered the illusion. Faced with his own mortality, the sleep from which he could never be roused, and the knowledge that death could pounce on him with no warning whatsoever, reach into his chest and crush his heart in its hand, his thoughts turned to Italy.

'He wanted to leave everything in England immediately,' says Nonna. 'He was scared he would die away from Italy.'

And so they went back. 'How could I not agree?', she asks, the question still live.

The control over him seemed, in that instance, hers alone. It was heavy to carry and painful to act on, because by giving him what he needed, by embarking on that particular story – the one in which Leo got to die in the land that had birthed him, in the plains his great-grandfather had ploughed – she was relinquishing another story. The one in which they stayed in England, where they *had* been happy, after all, and she died in the country where her

170

father was, and his father, and the son she had so recently placed in their care.

*

Campagna, 1992: Leo is on a ladder, smoothing over a crack that has appeared in the wall of the house. It appeared during the great earthquake of 1976, when about 1,000 people were killed and hundreds of thousands left homeless, but the crack seems recently to have grown wider, unsettled perhaps by the construction going on beside the house. Lucia and Giuseppe, engaged to be married, are building their home-to-be right on the side of his house. There will be a connecting door, leading off the living room, which they will all share. He imagines them sitting on the green three-piece suite that Dirce insisted on bringing back from Manchester. It's still (sort of) comfortable twenty-odd years later.

He dips the pointing trowel into a bucket of cement and applies it to the infelicity. The earthquake's epicentre had been in Gemona, about 50 kilometres away. They ran out of coffins. The Queen of England sent Italy a message of sympathy, and Dirce was as moved as if it had been addressed to her personally. The three of them – Lucia a seven-year-old fireball, wedged, kicking, between him and Dirce – slept outside in the cornfield for a week, waiting for aftershocks.

And then Leo falls. He lands on his side and is found winded by Giuseppe.

At the hospital they X-ray him, illuminating the infinite fine filaments of his lungs. No ribs are broken, but 'a dark mass is spreading across the left lung,' the doctor says. The presence we all dread. He did not say this to Leo, but rather to his wife and daughter, who having not

171

long graduated as a nurse, has ushered them out of the room to talk in private, leaving Leo resting in bed.

'We agreed we would not tell him,' Nonna told me.

'He never knew?'

'No, we didn't think he was strong enough – it would have broken his heart.'

He is operated on because they have told him a story, in which a small portion of tissue has been very badly bruised by the fall and he will feel much better once it's removed. He had demurred, saying it would heal on its own, but they insisted. Only they know the stakes and that they can't risk his going home now. A modest, routine procedure. Recovery will be straightforward, they say, plenty of sleep and he'll be dancing by Lucia's wedding day next spring. And then they take his left lung.

*

For the first six years of my life, Nonno was a softer version of the titan his sons had known, who measured a man's worth in bags of cement. I remember his preternatural strength put to other uses, how he could swing me on one flexed arm and my sister on the other and make it seem effortless. I thought he was on top of things – he had only to bang his fist on the table and lunch would miraculously appear – until I realized that he was not.

For the final six years I knew him, he was pale and broken. The animals disappeared and the empty farm buildings looked like an abandoned frontier town in a TV western. He rarely left the sofa apart from to go to bed. He watched the rosary on TV every day, without fail, and on Sundays, the Mass delivered live from the Vatican. He wheezed and coughed like I had never heard anyone cough before. More often than not he was hooked up to an oxygen canister, with the thin tubes wrapped around his ears and poking into his nose. And this I understood. My own asthma, acute at this stage, made me feel closer to him. I remember, one time, holding his hand as he sat on the sofa and neither of us said anything as we watched the Pope lift his palm to the crowds.

Nonno's was my first experience of death and yet I didn't really experience it at all. My sister and I did not go to the funeral, though had we been given the choice we would have. Why would we not want to be where the rest of the family was? How could that be 'too much' for us? Perhaps my parents worried we would try to wake him, but of course we had always known better than that.

I remember well the discussion afterwards, it must have been on our next visit through, over the choice of the photograph to place on the tomb. Nonna thought it should be the one of Nonno in Sunday best, serious and dignified, while everyone else lobbied for one taken before he was ill, after one of our lunches: it shows Leo askew, smiling, taking us all in, his shirt collar undone. Nonna won that battle. Of course she did. It was never in doubt. And so, we see the starched and sombre man every time we visit the cemetery. But back in Nonna's kitchen, to the right of the TV, propped on the old VHS machine (bought by my parents and never used), we find the Nonno we're all looking for, in a golden frame, with a red plastic rose and a wooden crucifix positioned behind it.

I have another photograph I would like to offer for the record, a personal favourite I keep in the drawer under my bed. I do not know who took it or when – the mid-1980s, I guess. Nonno is sitting back on the sofa in the corner of the kitchen, dressed in an old shirt and his navy-blue work coat. One arm is bent and propped on a bright red cushion, with his hand falling back over his snow-capped head. His chin points to the ceiling. He is fast asleep, mouth open: his soul, it seems to me, is exposed and free.

What would I tell him if he were to wake up?

Ce ca l'è?

I'm writing a book about the family.

I live in the countryside now. In England, yes. I know. But I like it here, I've met good people, and I have a dog that looks like a wolf.

I still don't speak Friulano – sorry – though I understand a little more than I did.

I would not tell him that his vines, now past fifty years old, are giving up, but then he would know it already. That's just their life expectancy. No crop goes on forever.

The bar at the end of your track, I'd say, by the *acquedotto*, sells English beer now (*t'immagini?*).

A couple of years ago I went to Africa. (No, I did not see lions).

And I've seen the *cialciùt*, too, and I think I know what it is, though I still haven't managed to control it. Have you?

Ce ca l'è?

'It is what it is,' his son John might say, beeping the horn as if to chase demons away.

VI.

It's mid-July 1965 and, because it's Stockport, it's raining and cool enough that Dirce is wearing a jacket that most people here would save for autumn. One of the ones she made in the hundreds (it felt like thousands) a couple of years earlier, of a wool so heavy she can still feel the strain in her left shoulder. It's double-breasted, which is a blessing because it means that, by misaligning the columns of buttons, she can just about do it up over her swollen belly. She doesn't mind the wet – always has an umbrella on her anyway just in case – and she made sure, as ever, to close all the windows before leaving the house, so all is in order there.

As she eases herself through the door of the hair salon, a bell announces her arrival and everyone turns automatically to stare at the newcomer. She is used to this – although she had thought it would be quiet at two o'clock on a Thursday. Apparently no one has anywhere else to be. She feels the women's attention drop to her middle and back up to her face, eager to catch her eye and smile knowingly. She is in the waddling phase, though she has lost a lot of weight in the past ten days. Can't digest a thing.

Having been ushered to a seat by one of the hairdressers, who holds the back of the chair firmly as Dirce lowers herself into place, she takes in her own reflection and exhales for what feels like the first time in ages.

She does not wait to be asked.

'A perm, please.'

The hairdresser, already fingering Dirce's coarse straight hair, looks at her, puzzled. It isn't advised, she explains, kindly, 'for the baby'.

Dirce, whose gaze has returned to her lap where she is

squeezing her palms together so tightly that her knuckles have gone the colour of butter, breathes in slowly.

She has imagined herself saying this for days.

'The baby is dead.'

It sounds like something that has happened elsewhere, to someone else.

A few hours later, she steps out into the rain, sure-footedly navigating a grey-brown puddle that has formed in the centre of a shattered paving stone. A scarf in brightly coloured rayon is arranged tightly over her curls, and everything is under control. The smell of the perming solution follows her for weeks, like the smoke of an electrical fire hidden in the walls of a house.

*

Summer 2019: We are sitting in Nonna's kitchen indulging in a ritual of ours. We have spent about an hour discussing the various tablets she takes, for her head, heart, blood, stomach, shoulder. The latter is particularly bad at the moment. 'I can't even reach down for dandelions anymore,' she says. 'And, as you know, they are a cure for me, a true, true cure...'

The old cures are always the best cures, she says, remembering the summer of 1960, a holiday – rare – in Puglia – rarer still to be anywhere other than Manchester or Maniago – at the house of cousin Angelino's new wife. Every day, she says, they would go to the beach and Leo, using the boys' small spade, a ridiculous sight, would dig deep into the sand. Incredible how beneath white powdery dunes that scorched the soles of your feet lay such dark, gritty dampness. Once Leo had scooped out enough to accommodate Dirce's entire body, she would lower herself in and the boys would busy themselves covering her over, patting her into place, burying her alive. They used the underside and edges of the spade to smooth the cement-like surface, just like their father had taught them. I have seen a photograph. Only her head emerges, tight curls framing her face like petals around a carpel.

The sand and the salt water worked miracles, she tells me, and though she does not specify what exactly they worked on, I do the maths and know that in the summer of 1960 she was nearing the end of her thirty-third year, by which point the family curse had made itself felt.

Today, she passes me box after box of medication, and I read the names aloud and indulge her with questions – *What does this one do? Does it help?* – and observations – *Ah, so many; one for every decade of life.* She likes to tell me how many milligrams of painkillers she takes: currently it is 3,000 mg of paracetamol per day – 'quello inglese' – the British stuff that she asks us to bring every time we visit, along with good, strong tea. She is convinced that British paracetamol is the best, no matter how many times her daughter the nurse tells her it is all exactly the same. On the kitchen table, there is always a half-full glass of water, at room temperature, with a faint semi-circular cloud around the rim, where Nonna's lips repeatedly kiss.

She runs through what she says is a recent conversation with the doctor, but I know I have heard it many times before.

Her: 'This medicine doesn't work, give me that other one I used to take before.'

Him (and here she puts on a certain air, puffing out her chest and lifting her chin): 'I've studied tens of years to be a doctor and you, *signora*, come and tell me what to prescribe to my patients?'

Her: 'Listen, you have your experiences and I have mine. Give me the medicine I had before.'

He protests a little more and, eventually, does what she asks.

The moral of the story, and a favourite line of Nonna's: 'Lui non capisce che noi siamo specialisti dei nostri propri corpi.' He doesn't understand that we're specialists of our own bodies.

Then, she asks after my lungs. 'Tutto sotto controllo,' I say. Everything's under control. Or, sometimes, 'tutto a posto,' everything in its place. And it's true, my asthma has been under control for years now; I have the right drugs for the right things, and I know exactly what my chest can handle. I tell her so all the time, but still she worries. She reminds me how I used to be set off by the corn, the cats, the rabbits, the dust on the old road – the list goes on – and how once I missed a cousin's wedding because I'd been rushed to Maniago hospital for oxygen, 'but made it back in time for lunch!' She recalls how impressed the doctors were that I didn't even flinch when they inserted the cannula, and that when it went wrong and they told me to look away, I kept my eyes fixed on the blood spurt. 'They said your blood-oxygen level was the lowest they'd seen.' I like how she turns my weakness into strength.

Next, invariably: 'You're too thin. Do you eat?'

'Yes, I eat. This is just how my body is,' I say.

But she is not listening as her eyes range over me.

'You need to fatten up,' she says. 'You need *ciccia*' – flesh – 'on that bony chest, to keep your lungs warm.'

I shake my head, laugh, mumble something about metabolism, running, yoga, age, maybe nerves.

'Your mum used to be like you,' she says. 'Like a little bird – *pip, pip, pip*.' She picks at imaginary crumbs on the tablecloth.

If I'm lucky she will be derailed by this memory of my

mother Irene as a young woman and tell me again about the summer when John first brought this new English girlfriend to Campagna and all the local women took bets on her being hideously scarred, or having pegs for legs, because she always wore flowing floor-length skirts. 'And always black, *everything black*.' (It is common knowledge that Nonna despises black clothes; they are the negation of the lively reds and pinks she surrounds herself with.) On the last day of Irene's visit, when she was hanging bed sheets out to dry, Nonna grabbed the hem of her skirt and pulled it all the way up to her waist – 'and there they were: two perfect skinny white legs!'

But if Nonna's mind has not been drawn by the warm glow of the 1970s, she will persist on the matter of *ciccia* a little longer, and lecture me on the importance of eating heartily, as much as the men even, 'because we work just as hard as them, if not harder'. Sometimes I think the whole conversation is a vehicle for her to talk about her own appetite and how her stomach was 'ruined' not once but twice: first by skipping meals when she was a child in mourning for her father; and then again, when she was thirty-three, when everything – decades of pain and anxiety, and the wrong drugs prescribed by doctors convinced they knew better – came home to roost. Now, everything is a poison to her – *un veleno* – whether because of the sugar or the salt or the lactose, or because it's too hot or too cold. (Ice cream, Lucia would point out, is a surprise exception to the rules.)

'And your foot?' she asks, recalling an old running injury.

'Better, you know, I'm still standing...'

'Eh, si tira avanti' – one pushes on (actually, pulls) – another classic line, delivered with a sigh and a smile and sometimes a bringing together of the hands, part clap, part prayer, a solemn signal that the exchange is ended. Amen. We have worked our way from our heads to our toes, acknowledged our pains, measured and accepted each as part of the lot we are to carry as we keep pulling ourselves, ineluctably, on.

We do this at least once every visit, talking about illness, scars, brushes with death, the way our bodies do, or mostly don't, work to our satisfaction. There is something quietly life-affirming in it, reminiscent of that line from *King Lear*: 'The worst is not / So long as we can say "This is the worst."' Not only do our pains confirm to us daily that we are still alive – maybe that's why we talk of medical 'conditions', each gripe being a caveat to existence – but talking about them is one of the ways in which Nonna and I bond. She is schooling me, I think, preparing me to cope with greater suffering to come, in age or by accident.

Tutto sotto controllo, everything under control: this state is, for Nonna, the ultimate objective. But it seems imbalanced as a concept, the sentence itself dangerously lopsided. That everything – *every* thing? – should be contained by an idea – control – so difficult to summon let alone sustain. I imagine a flimsy rope bridge stretching across white rapids, or the lid on my mum's ancient pressure cooker, with its terrifying scream.

*

Nonna will talk to me about everything. But she will not talk to me about her mother. Not really.

Novella is always there, in the background of almost every story, but there is a tacit agreement that I will not ask too many questions about her. The very thought of doing so fills me with dread. We both know that probing is likely to lead to harm. If ever Nonna lets anything slip, says something she had not intended to – and the more I needle the more likely this is – she instinctively follows it with 'ma non lo mettere questo'. 'But don't put this in' – in this book, she means, whose existence pleases her or troubles her, depending on the day and the topic, or depth, of our conversation.

Ma non lo mettere questo is a hand pulling back from a stove. Whatever Nonna has just told me is not to be touched, off the record – except it is there every time I press play on our interviews. I try to unhear it from the recordings, to skim over it in my notes, but I know it's there, scored into my thoughts. She knows it, too. A conundrum coalesces around the phrase: How am I to tell a story I am forbidden to know? How am I to conjure this woman whose existence is constantly diminished? Or, in fact, am I not to do so? Is it not my place at all?

Recently, when we spoke about Novella, I pushed too hard and Nonna fell back into the 1930s, to moments whose immediacy took us both by surprise. She addressed her mother as though she were right there in the room and then spoke Novella's part, too. I had never witnessed Nonna cry and to have done so now, down a tinny phone line with 1,000 miles between us and no recourse to hold her hand and chase away what I had summoned, was especially painful.

When I called back a few days later, with a brighter topic in mind – the story of how, when she was forty-three, she came to adopt the little girl she had always wanted – she told me she had hardly slept for two nights. 'I said too much, I was too negative.' Nonna sees the positive in everything and everyone: the glass is two-thirds full. But Novella is an exception. The glass cracks in her hand.

The previous night, Nonna said, she had had one of her dreams, and its meaning was crystal clear. She was in a field, surrounded by 'zingari', 'gypsies' – she uses the word she grew up with, ignorant of its power to wound – at one of their heady parties, where there was music and dancing. She could smell rich foods being prepared, bubbling away in immense blackened pots with steam suspended above them like spirits, and there was a palpable sense of excitement, of some important culmination: a birth or a wedding or a funeral. But all of a sudden there was trouble, an unknown person on the edge of the encampment, and she knew that no good could come of it. The 'zingari' drew in closer, reaching for her hands and tugging on her clothes. 'I felt then that I was their protector – although I was not one of them – and my purpose was to defend them against whatever was coming: "They're good people," I shouted, "they're good people." And then I woke up. You see?'

*

The words 'painkiller' and 'analgesic' (from the Greek for 'without' and 'pain') suggest that it is possible to vanquish suffering once and for all, to expel it from the body. Compare these with 'pain management' and 'pain control', both of which accept that without treating the primary cause the pain will remain, latent yet potent. The variation in tone, from managing to killing, suggests something like a sliding scale from polite bureaucracy, necessary if things are to function, to unabashed autocracy; from a measured approach to suppression at all costs.

At both extremes and in the in-between, is the open-ended, always-unpredictable negotiation between one way and another: 'Control.' A concept with material roots in the Latin *contrarotulus*, a counter roll, an alternative record against which the accuracy of accounts given by a primary source can be checked. There are two versions of the same thing running in tandem, so that one is understood in relation to the other. But, you have to ask, which is the more reliable? There is a tension between these records of reality; they are rivals for your attention and trust.

Centuries later, probably in France, the noun became a verb, *contreroller*, used to designate domination over something or someone. And to truly control someone, it might be necessary to kill their pain as well as your own.

*

Leather boots discarded by the front door, wrinkled by rain and dusty with scree. The laces are knotted at intervals where they have snapped and been tied back together. Pine needles everywhere.

*

In the story Nonna tells about her own life, Novella is less a person than the aftermath of a person, more atmosphere than flesh and blood. She is absence accumulated to form a presence. The safe distance between us and her, measured in terms of what can and what can't be admitted to the story, is forever re-assessed. Although Novella has been dead more than forty years, her power is undimmed.

'As long as we have the memory of a person, they will never truly leave us.' A platitude that cuts both ways. With none of my own memories of Novella, all I have are fragments from Nonna, which I string together like glass beads. No wonder I feared the old woman as a child; she is an unexorcizeable haunting. And sometimes in the mirror I think I see her moving under my own skin, in my

183

heavy-lidded eyes and flat cheeks. How much of her is in me? Does Nonna see it, too?

'Who *was* Novella?' I ask one day, emphasizing the past tense of the woman. Nonna reconfigures the question, pulls us back further still, and tells me instead about Novella's family, which was another 'high' one, albeit not as high as Angelo's. ('She was lucky to catch him when she did. His heart had just been broken by another woman, a great beauty...')

Do not, she interrupts herself, be misled by the family name, del M———, which is the most common in the area. 'And – while we're at it – do not write that we are from Maniago when we are not.' This has clearly been nagging her for some time. 'We are from Maniago Libero.'

Maniago Libero is the part of town that lies closer to the mountains, just beyond the confines of what was once the Conte d'Attimis's land. Until the twentieth century, she explains, Maniago and Maniago Libero were separate communities, the former belonging to the Conte, and the latter belonging to a small group of 'zingari', probably from Hungary, who had settled there.

'When was this?' I ask.

'Ah, *chissà*...' – who knows. 'Centuries and centuries.'

They called it 'Maniago Libero' because the land was free for the taking, *libero*; and they could live there differently, according to their own rules. 'They worked hard, built everything for themselves from scratch, and stuck together... That's why everyone has the same name,' she says.

Our family, then, has always travelled to find what it needs, gathering scraps here and there.

(A note for the counter roll: the most widely accepted explanation for the name Maniago Libero dates it to the first half of the 1300s, when a small order attached to

Millstatt Abbey, a Benedictine monastery in the south-ernmost Austrian state of Carinthia, established itself on the western edge of Maniago, which came under the patriarchy of Aquileia. The visiting monks were known by their all-black hooded tunics. 'Libero' is thought to be a mis-modernization of the old word 'livri', meaning 'fin-ish', so that Maniago livri means something like 'Maniago Ends' – which it does, right there in the last strip of land before the icy waters of the Cellina.)

Whether or not the land of Maniago Libero had ever been truly free, by the late 1800s, Novella's family owned pockets of it, of varying quality, which they rented out for money or a share of the crops. Some plots were in the fer-tile plains, some on the steep rocky mountainside, so, in a good year, the family would have had adequate supplies of wheat and corn, meat and dairy. Together, the rents must have added up to a moderate income, too.

Novella's father, another Pietro, was a bridge engineer, responsible for constructing one of the bridges that still straddles the Cellina. I can't help noting the irony of a man whose job it is to build bridges fathering a daughter infamous for burning them. I ask Nonna which bridge is Pietro's but she cannot recall, so I am free to imagine that it is the one that she and Nonno later first met on and that its stone and steel are imprinted with that moment that means everything to this family and nothing to anyone else. In that sense, everything is, and all of us are, because of Pietro's minute calculations that put people where they shouldn't rightly be, suspended in the air.

It is thought that the Etruscans, whose bridge-build-ing skills were considerable, believed that the crossings they constructed were in violation of Nature's plan, as conveyed in the direction of running water. So, in Latin, partly derived from the Etruscan alphabet, we have the

185

word *trans-gradi*, across-go; to transgress. (They did not know about gravity: that bridges stood because of Nature's laws, not in spite of them.) In some places, fragments of terracotta discovered at either end of these ancient bridges suggest that rituals may have been undertaken: prayers and tokens in exchange for the rite of passage and forgiveness of man's hubris.

As with most women of her time and place, Novella's mother Maria was eternally pregnant, a martyr to her own fecundity. That there were eventually eight children – five boys and three girls, with others lost along the way – is a testament to that once widespread combination of unqualified faith in God's plan and pragmatic realism. Line up as many as you can and increase your odds of having a good number left by the time He has played His hand. A modest attempt to influence that which is impervious to influence.

The sons in this family are all heroes, Nonna is quite insistent. Go to the monument outside the church near the house that was Pietro and Maria's, she says, and you'll find the names of these men. The oldest, Carlo, was injured in the First World War. Riccardo, the next in line, died in the Second. In the same conflict, their brother Giovanni was lost in action, never confirmed dead but never found alive. Until both his parents were deceased, the door to the house was left permanently unlocked in case he found his way back to them. Maria was what Nonna calls a *madrina del Italia* – a Godmother of Italy – because she had amassed the full set of war heroes: one dead, one injured, one lost. A proud *tricolore* of suffering.

(For the counter roll: from the First World War, the title of 'madrina del Italia' was conferred on women who, encouraged by the government, wrote letters to soldiers on the front, to boost morale and allow the men to tell stories

186

of strife and anguish that they could not tell their own families for fear of upsetting them. Not to mention the widespread illiteracy that meant most parents could never have read such letters, let alone written back. During the Second World War, the initiative was wholeheartedly adopted by the Fascist government, with a strong emphasis on the duty of the women – and, in fact, young girls, too, known as *figlie della lupa*, 'daughters of the she-wolf' – to extol the virtues of war, patriotism and sacrifice. I do not think Maria was a *madrina* in this official sense. As for the story of the unlocked door, of a household waiting with bated breath for the hero's return, we will never know if it is true or if it is what it sounds like: a plot from a romance novel. It is possible that Pietro and Maria borrowed the detail themselves, the surreal intensity of events having tipped them into a self-consciously dramatic mode.)

Novella's other brothers, Vito and Urbano, were too young to fight, and that's all I know about them. Whatever else they may have achieved in their lives apparently pales in comparison to the sacrifices of the older brothers. Although one of them, Nonna says, gave almost every penny he earned to the Church – 'everybody knew'. (I presume this was at least partly to smooth his passage into the next life.) She can't now remember whether it was Vito or Urbano, anonymity having finally caught up with charity. Perhaps this brother's name is written down somewhere, too, in the church accounts, in a box-file in a backroom.

Among the daughters, Italia came first, born in the 1890s and named for the young country that great men had been promising for decades would bring a better future for all. You could not ask for a more literal interpretation of the statesman Massimo d'Azeglio's plea to his countrymen and women to settle down and 'make Italians'. Italia, patriotism in person, joined the ranks of countless other Italias and Italios (and Italas and Italos and Italinas and Italinos...) up and down the land, to which fact we owe this immortal line from Nonna: 'C'erano tante Italie una volta.' 'There were many Italys once.' It is perhaps the truest statement in this whole book.

In the early 1900s came Novella, Clementina and a younger sister, Valentina, who died when she was seven, after pulling a cauldron of boiling water onto herself while playing hide and seek with her siblings. Much of what I hear from Nonna about the surviving sisters has them fighting each other and anyone else perceived to have slighted them or the family in some way. Theirs were long, flaming rows that often spilled out into the street and almost always ended in cuts and bruises and prolonged periods of stony silence.

'My mother had a strong arm,' Nonna says in a proud tone unusual in the context of Novella. 'She was really tough. They were all scared of her temper.' And into the silence that follows creep a hundred untold stories, like a tide rounding a sandbank. I imagine Novella punching some cousin or other for disrespecting her or talking about her behind her back or taking something from her without permission. I imagine a sister – perhaps the one who lost twins in twenty-four hours, who strung the first one up in a basket above the stove to wait for the death of the second – telling Novella to simmer down, to go home and count her blessings. 'What are you so angry about? You have two healthy children. What more do you want?'

Sometimes – 'But not often?'; 'Yes, yes, often, write *often*' – there was singing and dancing and embraces, with sisters and sisters-in-law and daughters and cousins all cooing over each other's dresses and plaiting each other's hair, and food and drink made and enjoyed together. They were always in and out of each other's houses, these women, and in and out of each other's business. All of them, it seems, could flip one way or the other in an instant: one moment they were best friends, the next enemies. The prevailing sense is of chaos, of emotional exhaustion and women on the edge, held back – just – by family ties.

'There was something in the blood, you know?' says Nonna.

'It sounds quite intense,' I venture, because it feels like she is waiting for some kind of appraisal, if only so she can correct it. Which she immediately does.

'*Era normale*,' she says. 'All the families were like that.'

We are on the phone but her shrug is almost audible.

It's as though, according to some Manichean rule, the exceptionalism Nonna values in other members of the family – in her father, most notably – depends on the sheer unremarkableness of her mother. Novella is the exception to the exceptionalism that Nonna believes defines her family. I note how 'it was normal', and variants such as 'it was fine', 'that's just the way it was' or, even, 'we did well', are just so many ways of saying *ma non lo mettere questo*, coded acts of censorship.

It's difficult to tell whether the brusque dismissal is born of self-delusion or self-preservation, but either way the result is a dulling of the feelings and a shaping of the narrative before I have even written it. Our case was not special, Nonna implies; our hardships were the same as everyone else's, or lesser, so there's really no point dwelling on them now. Novella herself Nonna describes as 'normale, normale, normale'.

So write about something else, Nonna urges; write about the good sons and the war memorial. Or write about Carlo's son Arduino, the *partigiano*, whose name isn't on the monument although he fought under the green flag of

189

the local *brigate* Osoppo and saw off the Fascists as well as the Wehrmacht. And then write about what the communist *brigate* Garibaldi, who fought under the red flag, did to the poor Catholic men of the Osoppo at the end of the war, how they slaughtered them at Porzûs. Gunned them down simply because they did not agree on the definition of freedom.

Nonna is appalled by my historical ignorance. 'How do you not know about the massacre at Porzûs? You have two degrees; what have you been studying all these years? The massacre – *that* is the story to tell. They don't know it in England.'

'I will,' I say, 'at some point,' although I know I probably never will. Others have told the story of this massacre and others like it, far better than I could. I ascertain that Arduino was not involved but that Pasolini lost his younger brother Guidalberto, who also fought with the Osoppo. But I want to talk about 'us', to know about the other family battles, I tell Nonna, the kind that do not cease with an armistice or have winners and losers. They go on daily, undignified and unresolved. The scars are real and enduring – 'you are proof of that' (I don't say) – but there are no medals or monuments to refer to. In fact, there's nothing written down at all.

*

A brittle yellow halo around the edge of the hot copper *paoiolo*. The crust left behind by polenta. A prize for brave and nimble fingers.

*

Last summer, I wrote some things about Novella in a

190

notebook while Nonna was talking and, seeing her eye on the page, I nervously asked if I could keep them. Permission was bemusedly granted. Apparently these details are of little value, like the crumbs she brushes off the table after breakfast. She doesn't know that, in my mind, some of them become whole mouthfuls, soaked in the juices of other stories. Maybe she does.

Novella was neither tall nor short and neither fat nor thin. *Normale*. Her hips were wide, her hair dark but not quite black, her lips fuller than ours. Her appetite, too, was *normale*. (She was not like her daughter, who, when she was young, could easily eat three bowls of *minestrone* and still be hungry.)

She preferred not to work. 'She was not lazy, but she was not like you and me.'

One day, sick of having to chop logs because Angelo's chest was playing up again, she threw the axe to the ground and said to him: 'Ma va' a reméngo!' – 'Get lost!' (A truer translation of this Venetian insult might be 'Go wandering'. And that, of course, is precisely what he did, first to England, and then to his grave.)

She was religious and went to confession, sometimes twice in the same week. But she did not pray as often as she should have. She was highly superstitious, alert to jinxes and omens, and frequently pointed out how in the months leading up to her wedding to Angelo, seven relatives died. *Seven!* The marriage should never have gone ahead, she said. How could they have allowed it when misery was written in the stars?

Novella bore misfortunes and grudges like no one else, and perhaps for this reason she was predisposed to seeing the worst in every situation and person. She wore calamities like rosettes and regularly presented them to her daughter one by one, each narrated with vivid feeling as though the events had just occurred. Except for one, the tenderest of all, which she kept mostly to herself: the story of the lost son, Manlio, born 'between you and your brother', and dead two weeks short of his first birthday of an illness that took him in the middle of the night. When it rained, she ached to go to the grave and shield it with an umbrella. He had not been weaned by the time he died. 'You drank that baby's milk,' she said. And then they never spoke of it again.

After her husband's death in 1935, Novella wore black. 'Black, always black, only black.'

In 1937, about a year after returning from England to the old house in Maniago Libero, Novella bought a heifer. But the cow turned out to be pregnant and her milk was scant and watery. Novella killed her – shot her in the head with a brother's rifle – and bought a second heifer, who milked for many, many years.

At intervals Novella was employed. Sometimes she weeded and preened the gardens of wealthier local women, sometimes she planted or chopped young pines on the mountainside for a man who knew her father. For a few summers, she left the children behind and went to be a live-in cleaner in her sister's house in Venice. These jobs did not pay well. She could have sold the few plots of land that her father had given as part of her dowry, most of which had, for various reasons, ceased to yield much in the way of rent or crops, but she preferred not to. It was a matter of pride. 'If you had land, you did not sell it, not ever.'

Novella was a good cook and the extended family called on her for baptisms and weddings. She was especially accomplished at *paste* – her gnocchi were famous – because she had cold, quick fingers. For celebrations, she wore a long black skirt with the finest of green trims.

During the early years of the Second World War, Novella let rooms in the house to soldiers of Mussolini's army. One day, one of the men said, 'If I didn't know that Dirce was your daughter, I'd say she wasn't.' Both mother and daughter took this as a compliment.

Novella hated cold water, the metallic taste of it. She could not bear to drink it for the splitting headaches it gave her.

When she was about five years into widowhood, in her late thirties, a local man, much older than her, proposed. Her brothers told her to accept, but she did not. The siblings fought for many months, and then moved on.

She had a soft voice, surprisingly high-pitched, and sometimes mother and daughter sang together while folding the sheets. 'Balocchi e Profumi', 'Toys and Perfumes', was a favourite song. The lyrics tell the story, from the perspective of a little girl, of a mother who spends money on herself. The daughter laments: 'For your little one / you never buy toys / Mamma, you only buy perfumes for yourself!' (Nonna sings me this over the phone one day, sorely out of key but word-perfect.) One day the girl falls ill and the mother, racked with guilt, buys her the toys she so coveted. When the girl sees them, her eyelids grow heavy and she dies.

(For the counter roll, where it will be written in the lightest of pencil, because there is little certainty to be had in these matters: The song, a popular interwar tango, is said to counsel against materialism, with both mother and daughter paying the highest prices for their misplaced priorities. There is no father figure to speak of, which, alongside descriptions of plump sinful lips and silk cushions, has led critics to conclude that the woman is a prostitute. But, after the First World War had claimed hundreds of thousands of Italian soldiers, is it not possible that she is a young widow? Perhaps one who married well only to lose, suddenly, the life promised to her? And now she is the sole guardian of children who depend on her entirely. Suffocated by reduced circumstances, she is desperate to taste just a little of the old freedoms, to feel like a woman again. And which of these – prostitute or self-centred mother – would, in the great court of public opinion, be considered the worst?)

I beg more information on Novella from her grandchildren, but the words soon seem to run out. There are no hugs or kisses in their accounts, but they recall her as a source of small amounts of pocket money and biscuits, or, in my father's case, having proudly embraced his role as cigarette-lighter-in-chief from the age of around ten, a lifelong nicotine addiction. (Her brand was Player's, whose slogan, 'Whatever the pleasure, Player's complete it', seems almost sardonic in the context.) And when, at the age of thirteen, he had his jaw broken in a fight and locked shut to heal, it was Novella who scooped out the flesh of a watermelon and mashed it in her hands, sifting out every last pip, so that he would not be deprived of its goodness. For Lucia, so much younger than her brothers, there was one time when her parents were out and she slept in Novella's bed and the warmth of the strange body surprised her. She also remembers Novella as having blue eyes, which she absolutely did not.

Moments of lightness, of presence and personality, are matches struck in a damp cellar. Narrative anaemia is a dominant trait among inheritors of this woman. 'I don't know', 'I couldn't say', 'I don't recall', 'I'm not sure' – these are the bones of Novella's legacy. So, ambiguity prevails, and this seems apt for a woman whose very name recalls a form that is neither one thing nor the other – short novel or long short story? – and much more besides; the sour-sweet irony of a woman whose name is Story, who can't, or won't, find her way to being told.

'It's like she was two different people,' says Manlio, Novella's oldest grandchild, who knew her for the first three decades of his life, sharing homes and even beds. 'I never could work her out, how she could be so attentive to me, but when it came to her relationship with Mum, all darkness and negativity.' It is easy to imagine, I say, that Novella felt a special connection with him because he had the name of the son she lost. 'Maybe, maybe... I don't know. Perhaps.'

When I make the same observation to Nonna, implying that it was a kind gesture to name her first child after her mother's dead son, she is dismissive and, I think, a little defensive. 'I did not name him for her; I named him for my little brother.' The dedication must have been unclear at the time, though. Who was it for? Whose life, whose suffering, was being commemorated in this child? I wonder if an explicit statement on the matter was ever made, but expect not. In its absence, mother and daughter would have been free to see it their own way, to tell the story that most soothed them.

Either way, it seems obvious that Novella would have cherished this boy and the man he became, seeing something more than her grandson when she looked at him and feeling something singular in her throat when she called his name, pleasure and pain balancing out in a syllable each. And if you speak this family's language of omens, you might appreciate some significance, too, in the fact that shortly before Manlio's thirty-third birthday, Novella died. It's as if the family curse passed over him and was, instead, satisfied with her.

Also, it is common knowledge that, as Manlio puts it, 'Novella was more inclined towards men than women'.

Her relationship with her son Pietro was close, which brought agitations all its own. There, it seems, the love was too intense, so that while her daughter was starved of affection, her son was lavished with it. No woman was ever good enough for him, and certainly not his wife Anna. The couple's happiness was forever undermined by Novella's jealous criticism. By the time I was old enough to read *Sons and Lovers* it was inevitable that Novella should be cast in the role of Mrs Morel.

Pietro received the love, and carried the expectations, that should have been distributed across two sons and a husband, and this made it all the more painful when Novella chose to abruptly deprive him of it. 'One day,' Nonna recalls, 'Pietro displeased her, I don't remember how, and she was sitting at the table playing cards, and when he went over and tried to kiss her cheek to apologise, she slapped him across the face and said, "Leave me alone – yours are the kisses of Judas." He was about seven years old. She left her mark in other ways, too: the turbulent del M––– temper coursed through Pietro's veins; 'he would go from light to dark in one beat'.

When Leo, Dirce and little Lucia left Manchester for Italy in 1971, Pietro and Anna and their three children went, too. Novella had no choice but to follow. Nonna can't tell the story without sighing heavily, nor without repeating, 'but I didn't want to come back', 'it was not my choice', 'I could not stop Leo' – and this, it turns out, is one of the few things that mother and daughter had in common. Neither had the upper hand. Novella tried to persuade them all to stay – their place was in England now, enough with the back and forth – but it quickly became clear that her son-in-law could not be swayed, and so she redoubled her efforts on Pietro, with whom, in spite of her constant grousing, she had lived for the past decade, ever since Dirce's time in hospital. And they had built a nice life together – *haven't we?* – mother and son. I imagine her remonstrating: 'You think things will be better back there? Don't be so foolish. There is nothing for us, only hay and cow shit.'

But her power had ebbed, and the young ones had heard all about *il boom, il miracolo economico*, that had happened in their absence. There were new opportunities back home, they said. Things were better there.

To leave Novella behind was, of course, out of the question. She could not have survived alone, nor would she have wanted to. In Nonna's telling, she does not appear to have had much of her own life in England – my enquiries about hobbies and friends lead to nothing, and the few jobs she had were short-term, mostly because she fell out with colleagues. Instead, she took liberally from the lives of others, namely her daughter and son. They belonged to her, so that everything they did was an extension of her. When they were little, she made decisions for them – *enough school; find work* – and when they were grown up, she continued to push them this way or that – *take on more work; stretch for the bigger house* – and usually got her way. She had her own room in houses they paid for, sat at their tables eating food they had bought; and why learn English when they could speak it for her? She was a matriarch. This was control.

Except the very substance of the word changed when she wasn't expecting it, and all the things that had once made her strong now made her vulnerable. In 1971, she had no income of her own. No house. No friends. She couldn't hold a conversation with the neighbours or work out the bus timetable. I picture her in her late sixties as a small, curved figure dressed head-to-toe in black, perched high on the mountainside above Maniago, looking down at the people and properties she owned – counting, measuring, slowly realizing that she has lost it all. She was now a woman to whom things happened, to whom things were done, for whom everything seemed under threat or already lost. Perhaps she had always been that woman.

For the final time, she returned to the old house in Maniago Libero, whose ownership she granted to her son in exchange for bed and board. She was a guest in her own house, where she saw out the last decade of her life, smoking the roll-ups she now professed to prefer, playing cards, and gazing out the window at the courtyard where she once chopped logs while Angelo fussed over his plants. And after her death, her children learnt that she had parcelled out between them the few plots that she had held on to: everything went to her son and, to her daughter, a scrap of stony soil on the far edge of town, which yielded nothing but problems.

*

A dusting of flour on the flagstones outlines the spot where a pair of clogged feet were planted. A bucket waits by the sink, full of emerald dandelion leaves, yet to be separated from their gold heads.

*

One of the things that Nonna does to pass the time, or to distract herself from aches that paracetamol can't reach, is to play cards. It's a coincidence that she keeps her cards in an old medicine box, the original Dal Negro box having disintegrated long ago. On these occasions, she does not play with other people – that would require more energy than she has to give, and friends are scarcer these days anyway – but rather alone. And the game she falls back on most readily is one she remembers her mother playing, sitting by the kitchen window for a quiet hour. She tells me this one day on the phone, when she needn't have brought Novella into the conversation. We had been talking about something else entirely: tomatoes, and how I have not inherited her skill in growing them.

The game does not, as far as either of us knows, have a name more specific than *solitario*.

'Maybe we should call it "Novella",' I suggest.

'Do not misunderstand,' Nonna says. 'She did not teach me – I would not even touch the deck – but I observed as I sat opposite doing the day's sewing or whatever it was.'

This game is different to the classic solitaire. For one thing it is not played with the French cards used in Britain but with *carte trevisane*, the traditional cards of the Friuli-Venezia-Giulia region. In Italy, the style of playing cards varies geographically, like the language, according to complicated histories of sovereignty and trade. Most of the north-western regions use cards that follow the French suits said to have been chosen in the Middle Ages to represent the four pillars of the economy: the clergy (hearts), the merchant class (diamonds), the military (spades, which began as swords) and the peasant class (clubs, in French *trèfle*, meaning clover, a weed; the weakest of the suits). Most southern regions play with *carte spagnole*, whose suits are swords (the military or nobility), cups (clergy), coins (merchants), and sticks, *bastoni*, actually more like cudgels (for the crude peasantry, of course). North-eastern regions, including the Friuli, play with *carte settentrionali*, meaning simply 'northern cards', whose suits are also swords (although curved like sabres), cups, coins and *bastoni*, which are more like sceptres, or, perhaps, elaborate walking sticks. Each deck is social conflict writ small and pressed into one dimension. Perhaps this is why dropping a pack of cards so that they flutter about and land all over the floor feels disproportionately catastrophic.

The suits – called *semi*, 'seeds' – can be traced back to the Mamluks, the Muslim warriors and former slaves who in the Middle Ages dominated most of north Africa. The Mamluks were the Venetians' most important trading partner, so it's not difficult to imagine that the cards might have found their way on board, slipped into a merchant's pocket to take home for the family. They are the perfect traveller's game – portable, versatile, charged with countless dramatic scenarios. As with other decks, aces can be high or low, depending on the game, but here each ace is inscribed with an aphorism or warning. *Non ti fidar di me se il cuor ti manca,* says the ace of swords; 'Don't place your trust in me if you are lacking a heart.' *Se ti perdi, tuo danno,* says the ace of *bastoni*; 'If you get lost, your fault.' Each blessing bestowed, the cards teach, can easily become a curse.

You hold all of this in your hands as you shuffle and deal. As with most Italian variants, *carte trevisane* consist of forty cards, rather than the French deck's fifty-two, with three figures in each suit: knave, knight (replaced by a queen in French-derived decks, such as the Milanese), and king. The cards are unusually slim, and the monochrome depiction of the Doge's Palace that adorns their backs renders the colourful designs on the facing side all the more vivid. There is no queen in our deck. 'She is at home stirring the polenta,' says Nonna.

To play the game which I now secretly think of as Novella's, you set all the cards face down on the table, in four horizontal rows of ten cards each. To begin, you pluck the final card from a row chosen at random (let's say it's the seven of cups), and place it in the corresponding spot in one of the other rows: so seven cards along, from the left. That row is now the row of cups. The card turned over to make room for the seven of cups – let's imagine it's the ace of coins – now needs to be laid to rest in its own place, and so you designate another row to be the row of coins, and lay the ace in first position, far left. And so on and so forth, until everything is in order, with all the cards ranked correctly in their respective suits. The challenge is to pull this off before all four kings have been uncovered, otherwise you have failed. Sometimes – it's rare but it happens – you might reveal the final king when there are just a few cards left face down, and you turn those over one by one to discover that they are all, miraculously, in their rightful place. *Tutto a posto*.

'Challenge' implies that if only you're up to it, you can win. The neatly ordered rows, the free choice over which card to begin with and which row to designate as which suit, these things give the player an illusion of control – it's as if you are overseeing the smooth operation of a system, when in fact, absolutely everything comes down to chance. There is no skill whatsoever involved, although you tend to concentrate as if there were. If you win, you claim the credit personally. If you lose, it is the fault of the cards, the fates, God, if you like. One can live a whole life like this.

I must have been about eleven when Nonna taught me the game, shouting through from the kitchen to explain the simple rules. I remember that Nonno was sitting on the sofa behind me, bent over between two buckets, plucking pistic leaves to drop into one and tossing the stalks and pale bell-flowers into the other.

It was just us three. I had wanted to stay longer at Nonna's on this visit – the idea had struck me a few days earlier that I could have her all to myself – and it was agreed that she would accompany me home by train five days later. So, when my parents and sister set off early in the morning to head home to Varese, I rolled over and went back to sleep, feeling special, excited at the prospect of independence. I remember my dad leaning over me to give me a goodbye kiss: 'Are you sure you won't get bored?'

As I padded through to the kitchen an hour or so later, the house was eerily quiet. The whole place was strange, as if I had slept through an earthquake or a revolution. And then it came on suddenly and forcefully: a melancholy I had never experienced. Everything seemed heavy and slow, muffled, and though for most of the days that followed I was on the verge of tears, I felt numb at the same time. Although I did not recognize it then, this was, I think, my first experience of homesickness. I imagined my family moving around our house without me, my empty bedroom with the shutters closed and all my things inanimate in the dark. And there was another sensation, which I am still reluctant to face, to admit to myself: the impression that I didn't really belong there with Nonna, in Campagna; that when she said, as she often does, 'Questa è anche casa tua', 'This is your home, too', it wasn't really true.

I moped about the house and traipsed through the fields, down to via dei Radici and back again, running my fingers through the tall grasses like I'd seen people do in films, looking up to the sky defiantly, willing it to fall (I still just about believed in God). I wallowed in an inflated sense of detachment, of difference, of being alone in the presence of others, and weaved around myself a narrative of abandonment or exile, as if it hadn't been my decision to stay here all along. These feelings felt important and adult. I wrote a poem – terrible, obviously – about being torn in two opposite directions. I must have been unbearable company, so when Nonna taught me to play cards alone it was probably as much a gift to herself as to me. For the remaining days, the game became a compulsion, although the habit left me almost as soon as we boarded the train back home – *home* home, where I would be back in my place.

*

A grey-yellow stain on a pale cloth, left by hands too hastily washed and dried.

*

It's 1936, and the days are short and frigid. It's late and Novella is alone with no idea where she is. All of the houses look exactly the same: small and square with no space between them and bricks the colour of raw meat. She has been walking for what feels like hours and her feet feel as dead as firewood. When she spots a policeman – such curiously tall helmets – she is both relieved and frightened. She approaches him and unleashes her panic. He looks at her, baffled by a torrent of sounds that are surely words although not ones he recognizes. Whether he guesses or she, at some point, says something that sounds like 'Italian', we'll never know, but before long he has ushered her down the road some way, his hand patting her shoulder gently every now and then to make sure she keeps moving, to a house where a woman he knows called Carla lives. Carla speaks Italian, indeed she is Italian, Roman to be precise, although she married an Englishman years ago and considers Manchester home now. It probably isn't the first time he has called on her for help with her compatriots. And so this is how Novella met Carla.

No matter how many times I have heard this story, it remains unclear whether or not Novella knew her own address. *Ma certo!* – 'of course!' – says Nonna. But there are different ways of knowing and they are not equal. It's possible that, English street names meaning nothing to Novella, her sense of place was purely visual – left past the large oak tree, straight on after the bright red post-box, and left again just after the house with the gate that hangs off its hinge. She would probably have known to say *Ciii–Tam*, or the name of the church, and been able to find her way from there. But it's also possible that, on this occasion, in the weeks after her husband's sudden death, Novella was lost in a far deeper way.

Somehow, though, with Carla and the policeman's help, Novella got back to Cheetham and the house where her daughter and son were anxiously waiting. The nine-year-old Dirce would probably have made minestrone for dinner, while little Pietro clattered about with the train set his father had bought him the day the fever set in.

Nonna remembers that a stranger came into the house with her mother, pulled Novella's coat from her and hung it by the door before ushering her to a chair at the kitch-en table, without either woman saying a thing, as though they had performed the routine hundreds of times be-fore. The stranger – who was older than Dirce's *mamma* but younger than Nonna Maria – sat there smiling and asking Dirce questions about her day.

'She was kind and warm and she immediately loved me,' says Nonna. 'She told me how pretty I was, how nice my dress, and how clever that I already knew how to cook.'

'And what was Novella doing?'

'Ah, non mi ricordo,' she says. 'Sitting there, poor thing.'

And then, as if rushing to the conversation's conclusion, or borrowing lines from a different conversation altogether, she adds: 'Si lasciava guidare, mia mamma, sempre'; 'My mother always allowed herself to be driven.'

That night, Carla stayed maybe an hour or so, until she could see that everything was in order again, on the surface at least, before letting herself out, with a promise to stop by again soon. And this she did, becoming over weeks and months a fixture in Dirce's life. Every few days she would appear and ask Novella if she needed anything, or if they would all like to come over for tea and cake or a particularly good cut of meat, or if she could take the children out of Novella's hair for a while. She had no children of her own and the house was so quiet, with her husband at work all day.

'And she knew that my mother was not kind to me.' So, one day there was an errand at the Post Office that Dirce might help with, and another day a sewing task of some sort (because 'she had noticed how neat my hems were'). Increasingly, she wanted to be read to in Italian and gave Dirce the choice of the books on her shelf. *Cuore* was there, alongside many other titles Dirce recognized from her father's trunk. Carla liked to have letters read to her, too, from friends and relatives in Italy, and often dictated replies while she was busy in the kitchen, with some sweet eggy mixture all over her hands. She was full of compliments for Dirce's handwriting, the kind of praise the girl had assumed she would never hear again.

Other times, there were no tasks at all, only impromptu gifts – a pen or a hairclip with a small pink star – and hours spent playing English cards. Pairs was their usual game, also known as Memory, which Carla always lost because hers was no longer sharp. Sometimes they sat side by side and tried to build a castle, leaning the edges of cards together, scaling up cautiously and giggling when, inevitably, the whole thing collapsed.

A close bond formed, so that soon Dirce spent as much time as she could with Carla. And one day, Nonna tells me breathlessly, the following conversation occurred across the kitchen table in Carla's house:

Carla: 'Oh Novella, you mustn't take her back to Italy, a child as bright as her can do great things here, you mustn't leave!'

Novella: 'I can't stay, I need to go back, it's too difficult here.'

Carla: 'Then you must consider leaving Dirce with me, please, I adore her and will adopt her! I have always wanted a daughter just like her!'

Novella: 'No, no, she is my daughter. *My* daughter and you cannot have her.'

It seems unlikely that Dirce would have been party to such a conversation, though it's possible that, out of the child's earshot, a version of it happened, suffused with the kind of calculated warmth that women can do so well.

'Would you have stayed with Carla if Novella had agreed?' I ask Nonna when she has finished her story.

'No, never, it would have been wrong,' she says, flatly. 'My mother needed me, and I was her daughter and certain things you cannot choose or change.'

Need is not the same as love, although one can become the other. I do not point this out; it is not necessary.

'My mother loved me. She was not always good to me, but she loved me.'

I try to think of the right thing to say, knowing that anything I come up with will be an irrelevance at this stage in their relationship.

'She called me nina, even!' Nonna adds, astonished by the memory.

And it's true that, among the impressions I have of Novella, it's hard to imagine a scenario in which this term of endearment figures at all. *Nina*, the nickname Nonna spreads liberally among the women and girls she cherishes. How strange that it should have been learnt from the mother she says despised her.

'Did you ever use to imagine, afterwards, what your life would have been like with Carla, in England?'

'No, never.'

It always feels uncomfortable, like some kind of betrayal, to say that I do not believe her.

After Nonna and I have hung up the phone, I find myself wondering whether Carla might even have offered Novella money in exchange for the child. It seems possible. Such informal arrangements were common in Britain at the time. Adoption had only been granted basic legal recognition in 1926, and remained in many cases a casual, secretive, often impermanent solution to undesirable circumstances. And Novella's circumstances were far from desirable. Would money have complicated the decision? Was there a corner of her mind that had entertained the offer? And whose future was she imagining when she said no?

I circle back to that line that Nonna feeds me almost every time I try to scratch the surface of Novella, to discover her character and motivations. 'Si lasciava guidare.' She allowed herself to be driven. Which is to say: she was not in control of her own life. A failure of the grossest order. Here, though, the criticism is dipped in pity. *Poor thing*, that's just the way she was, going back and forth between Italy and England on the back of her husband, and then her daughter and son. *She just sat there.*

The image doesn't seem quite right anymore.

Now I see Novella in the stable again, a rifle swinging by her side, standing over the steaming body of a cow.

I imagine her shouting out of an upstairs window, 'I don't need anyone!', or words to that effect, at her brother's broad back as he walks away.

'Most of us come to an accommodation between the "Mother" in our heads and the woman who reared us,' Anne Enright wrote in her memoir of parenthood, *Making Babies*. I have scribbled that line in my notebook beside the story of Carla, Novella and Dirce. Enright does not say 'come to terms' or 'make our peace', but 'come to an accommodation': temporary lodgings, sometimes, when lucky, a home-from-home, but never *home* home. Perhaps we save that final point of arrival for our deathbeds. Until then, the process is cyclical rather than linear. It involves going over familiar ground, stumbling on stone-like memories, sometimes crumbling them in your hand or throwing them to one side, but more often finding in them confirmation of what you already know, or think you do. You look again, from a different angle and a safer distance. And then, maybe after a gap of forty or so years, you do it all again, this time, for the benefit of someone else, who keeps asking questions, unsettling settled matters.

The story of Dirce's young life at a junction between England with one woman and Italy with another comes up again and again when we talk about Novella, and I think that's because it trips Nonna up. It won't sit neatly in the story she has spent a lifetime patting into place, in which her mother is a cruel but ultimately powerless figure, inconsequential in the grander scheme, unable to impede her daughter's happiness. Here, in the story of an adoption that might have been, is a scenario in which Novella's word was law, her control absolute and game-changing: the ace of swords when you were holding your breath for the seven of sticks.

*

Flecks of dried blood on a wall. A black eye. Later, when the girl looks in the mirror, she sees blue and purple, red, yellow and green.

*

I had almost forgotten about *solitario* by the time, more than a decade after learning it, I was living in Paris, studying for a year at the Sorbonne. There, side by side in neat booths, students learnt through headsets to enunciate like the Parisians, to skip certain letters and elide syllables, to make the right sounds in the right places, in ways that only natives know to do.

No matter how well I spoke the language, this place did not feel remotely like home. This was not helped by the fact that I was not allowed to be living in the apartment where I was, that my bedroom was (ironically) a living room, sneakily converted by my flatmates, with an old tablecloth to cover the door's etched-glass panels. Any post was to be addressed 'c/o'. 'And try not to let the *guardienne* see you!' So, in a way, I was never really living in Paris at all.

I called my parents in Italy daily, emailed friends in England, and wrote letters to Nonna, when I was supposed to be doing grammar exercises. One day, lying on my stomach in the park around the corner from the apartment, I plucked a dandelion and pressed it between the pages of my letter. 'At least I know you won't go hungry,' Nonna wrote back, forgetting the 'c/o' so that the letter languished on the guardienne's table unclaimed for weeks, until I persuaded my flatmate to go down and pretend it was hers.

I found myself playing *solitario* regularly, sitting cross-legged on the wooden floor, often into the early hours, delaying sleep when I knew that, more often than not, the *cialciùt* would come. I played with a familiar absent-minded concentration that seemed to float me on a plane somewhere above the present. As I had done years before, I ignored that these circumstances were ones I had chosen, not an enforced exile but a blessed opportunity. It suited me to tell the story that way. I sank into myself. At night, I went to my room early, if not to play cards, then to read, almost exclusively English classics, or to stream old television shows. The crackly recordings of 1980s Sherlock Holmes, with Jeremy Brett's over-powdered face and the predictable-unpredictable endings, were especially consoling. And by day, as I walked from the south-western edge of the city, where I lived, to the central Latin Quarter, where I learnt, I listened to Italian pop music from the 60s and 70s – Mina, Domenico Modugno, Fabrizio de André, Lucio Battisti – mouthing the words to myself, wringing out every last feeling. I took great pains to learn whole songs line by line, to get the timings just right, and listened on loop twenty or thirty times, until the music receded into the background, its rhythms as much a part of me as my own pulse.

I did not watch these shows or listen to this music when I was growing up, though if anyone had asked me I probably would have said, half believing it myself, that I had, that they were an essential part of who I was and where I came from. They were cues to others as much as to myself, badges of belonging, like posters on a teenager's bedroom wall. I wanted to own these things, to preserve them in a personal archive to be mined whenever I felt unsure about my place in the world. That these shows and songs tended to predate my birth by decades is probably no coincidence: knowing them seemed to strengthen my grip on the cultures I considered mine and feared losing; rather like with family trees, where the further into the past we can stretch a line, the more authentic and valuable seems the present.

By revising my attachments to England and Italy, I was performing a dual belonging which I did not confidently feel. There had always been a subtext of insufficiency, even fraudulence, about this hyphenated identity I had inherited – that I was not English enough to call myself English but not Italian enough to call myself Italian – and, in Paris, this intensified. To reach firmer ground, I pushed back against this other culture that now surrounded me. (I have written and deleted 'infiltrated' too many times now to ignore.) At least, that's how I make sense of it now: I was building bridges to Italy and to England. The irony is that the betwixt and betweenness of being in a country that sat almost exactly halfway between these two places I call home was a fairly accurate reflection of the stuff of me.

Deprived of people and places I craved, I orchestrated a system of privation to match and more or less stopped eating. At the start, I told myself that it was a canny way to save money to then spend on train or plane tickets home. When I took these trips, I staggered under the weight of the foods I carried with me to enjoy with friends and family. Whether or not I ever truly believed my own reasoning I don't know, but soon, it became a question of eating just enough – small servings of plain, flavourless things – to ease the hunger pangs, but not so much that the new pain came, the duller ache of a full stomach, stretched beyond capacity. Not to mention the sense of failure if my brain relinquished control to my body by admitting unsanctioned foods. I repeated silent vows and if I betrayed them, because of visitors, say, I would restrict food for days afterwards until order was restored and appetite silenced. I was devoted. A negotiation played out ceaselessly in my head, with a tally of individual items and ingredients – if an egg, not the pasta; if bread now, none later – running alongside the list of things I would say I had eaten if anyone asked, a calorific fantasy reel of chocolate éclairs and creamy omelettes I could almost taste. After a while, I hardly knew which version of the day was real. I was disappearing.

Not eating was, I think, what is popularly called a 'coping mechanism', a term introduced in the 1960s alongside 'coping strategies' and 'coping skills', all terms to be held at arm's length. You could say that I developed skills, that I had a tight strategy, but it would suggest an agency I never had; 'mechanism' at least seems to deal in the subconscious, where the trouble began. To see me it would have been clear that I was not coping at all; or perhaps, that some part of me was calling the shots at the bewildered expense of the rest. I have not since experienced the same mixture of power and powerlessness.

This is how I see it now: if homesickness is a feeling of hollowness, a figurative ache for the absence of the things that sustain a person, I made it real. Homesickness took on a material life in me, manifesting in taut skin and bones. Longing became physical and my stomach growled for people and places. This did not stop when, at the end of the year, I returned to England. I put the playing cards away in a drawer and forgot about them again, but the rules of the new game stuck. It would take several years until I won that one, or, let's say, until I came to an accommodation with it.

*

Straw dragged in from the stable. The broom left out, its instruction implicit, leaning against the wall in a way that seems almost calculated to make it fall just before you reach it.

*

We used to bicker, my sister and I, over who would assist Nonna in making gnocchi. There was never any doubt as to the supreme importance of the task; it was – and still is – an essential part of every visit to Campagna, the meal looked forward to by all of us and excitedly discussed from the moment of arrival.

We would hover at her elbows like altar girls as she cracked the eggs into a well of potato and flour and lightly fingered the edges in towards the bright orange centre, as if healing a volcano. Once the pale yellow dough was bound and dusted in a large round, she would cut it into four portions, rolling each into a long *salame* about the width of her finger. Then, she would pick up the pace and with machine-like precision, run a knife the length of the dough, with a steady *toc-toc-toc* as it touched the table. We bit our lips as the blade chased the guiding fingers of her other hand up the line, leaving two-centimetre nuggets of dough in its wake. Finally: Nonna's index finger would skip from one *gnocco* to the next and, with a flick of the wrist, leave a dimple in each one, where the *ragù* would later pool.

213

As Nonna ran off the gnocchi, my sister and I tidied them into neat rows – *svelta-svelta-svelta*, quick-quick-quick – on a muslin cloth spread across the far end of the table. The aim was to touch them as little as possible while spacing them equally, to allow the passing air to form a light crust on the pasta. We tried to outpace each other, to impress Nonna with the speed and dexterity of our work, and the table was soon full of row after row of gnocchi, each nugget firmly stamped with the digit of its maker and brushed with the invisible touches of her wards. Later, she would bring a battered tin pan full of salted water to the boil – 'as salty as the sea at Grado' – and drop them in in batches. We'd watch as they sank into the cloudy depths and minutes later somersaulted back to the surface; bloated, sheened versions of their former selves.

The name gnocchi, with its singular *gnocco*, is said to come from the word *nocchio*, a knot in wood, although another theory has it coming from *nocca*, meaning knuckle. And they do look a little like pale, swollen knuckles whose skin is pulled taut across them so you can make out the bone and its dimple. Nonna once told me that Novella used her knuckle rather than her fingertip to shape the pasta, as if knocking tentatively but insistently on someone's door. Trialling it myself one time, I found the technique preferable, the smooth stump being less liable to pierce the dough than a fingertip with its nail.

Recently, when I mentioned this to Nonna, she said she had never heard of such a thing. In fact, she denied having learnt to make gnocchi from Novella, claiming instead to have picked up the recipe while working in a restaurant in Maniago, not long after returning from Manchester for the final time with Leo. I pressed her on the matter only lightly because she was clearly in a digressive, or evasive, mood and I soon found myself being lectured to on the importance of faith, because *that* can get you through anything.

This happens more often these days: one minute you can be talking about the weather or the price of potatoes and the next you will feel the full force of the gospel. If I didn't know better, I might have joked to her that gnocchi could get *me* through anything, but Nonna's belief is no laughing matter. The best approach is to lay low and wait for it to pass, like an electrical storm, and before long the conversation will move back to the safer territory of aches and pains and the many small things that are sent to test us. *Tutto sotto controllo, si tira avanti, amen.*

Latterly, conversations about ailments have tended to take a new direction, or rather, the inevitable one, previously deferred: the worst. The family tomb, which sounds far grander than a glorified filing cabinet near our distant cousin's dairy farm, has been weighing on Nonna's mind. It was built by Nonno, and with only six spaces in total, and two of them already taken, she has started to worry about who will go where, when and for what reason.

On visits to the cemetery, which we make like clockwork after Mass, we stand in front of the tomb – LENARDUZZI written in gold lettering across the top – and take in the three rows by two that may be allocated to whichever of us asks for shelter. Each grave, or grave-in-waiting, is designated by a square of pinkish marble, set against the grey of the broader structure, like a three-storey house beneath an apex roof. In the top left lies Nonno, with that photograph of him in his crisp white shirt, and beneath him his cantankerous sister, who for complicated and contentious reasons ended up here, away from her own husband and children, visited indirectly by us alone. The neatness of these arrangements in death seem only to emphasize the chaos of the lives lived and of ours still in process.

These days Nonna doesn't stand before the tomb of the Lenarduzzis as long as she used to. Plastic flowers have long replaced fresh, so there is less demand for time to stop, tease out the dead stems and replace the water. I used to see her lips move in prayer, but now, if they do, the prayer seems shorter. To look at her, she might be doing a sum in her head, like a long division – divide by two, carry the remainder... – and it's difficult to tell if her eyes are fixed on Leo's stone or on the one to its right, which we all know will be hers. I wonder if the sense of order, this idea of tidying people into their right place, reminds Nonna of the sheer impossibility of the project; of her grandfather, father and son on a hillside in Sheffield and her mother in a tomb up the road in Maniago Libero, all unvisited for decades, for different reasons. Not to mention the rest of us, scattered here and there, at various stages in our lives and with new family ties and traditions to consider.

It is telling that I had never been – never been taken – to the small cemetery where Novella lies until last summer, when, under the name of 'research', my dad, sister and I made the journey, barely ten minutes from the house by car. In truth, even then, it was something of an afterthought, a detour en route to the supermarket on our way back from a visit to the church in Maniago Libero. We had gone to see the place where Nonna and Nonno were married, outside of which stands the war memorial that Nonna insisted on our seeing. (*Mettilo questo*. Put this in.)

We brought no flowers, only our phones to take photographs, twenty-first-century grave rubbings. The tomb is much larger than the Lenarduzzis' and more austere, its pale stone stained with rusty trails from the iron lettering of the family name, del M–––, set beneath a black

216

iron crucifix. At the centre is a shrine to the Virgin Mary, to the left of which are Novella and several others whose names are faintly familiar from walk-on parts in Nonna's tales: the sister Clementina and brother Urbano; the son of one of the other brothers (or is it the cousin?), the one who was a lawyer (or was it a vet?).

Above them is a square whose markings have faded almost to the point of invisibility. You can just about make out the curved shape of an angel, swooping down to fold a small body into its own. Novella's baby Manlio lies behind this stone flag, presiding over countless stories we will never hear about people whom even he never got to know. I take a photograph, surreptitiously, to take home, to remember how it was there. It can't capture how even on a hot day the coolness of the stone reaches my cheeks, the relief of crunching gravel underfoot because there is no other sound, the tightness in my stomach. How strange to be so intimately connected to all these people, to owe them everything and give them nothing. It starts to rain, and as we head for the gate I think of Novella with her long skirts and a big, black umbrella.

Later that day, over coffee and ginger nuts in Nonna's kitchen, I am scrolling through the photographs, absent-mindedly. There are more than I remember taking of the tomb and the war memorial, tens of quick-fire photos taken dispassionately as references for potential future research, further branches to explore (but probably not). One of the photographs taken just inside the entrance to the church shows a Bible open on a lectern, an invitation to curious pilgrims. I did not stop to read it then, though I remember thinking it might be good to have some record of it to consult later, by zooming in, as I do now, to read the text at my leisure, scanning for some kind of meaningful detail. I guess I went to church with the opposite of an offering in mind.

The book is bound in sage-green leather, with creamy pages and bold black lettering interrupted by occasional headings in red. It is open to the Book of Consolation, to the bit where God, Lord of the Israelites, orders Jeremiah to start a book: 'Write thee all the words that I have spoken unto thee,' He says. And so, Jeremiah records the horror of the situation, of a time in which a whole people has lost its way, becoming mired in sin and condemned to exile. 'Thy bruise is incurable, and thy wound is grievous. There is none to plead thy cause, that thou mayest be bound up: thou hast no healing medicines.'

The language and context are mostly foreign to me, memories of Bible classes as obscure as the belief itself. I call Nonna over from the stove where she is stirring the polenta, to ask her if she can tell me, briefly, the story of Jeremiah and his book and of these wounds that won't be healed. There is hope – isn't there? – in later passages? Isn't that the whole point? The consolation promised in the title, a city rebuilt, a home regained? Will the church warden turn the page tomorrow? Or will he skip backwards or forwards to another story to reveal by fragment alone? (Are *we* allowed to turn the pages? I think about going back.) 'What is the meaning of it?' I ask her.

She stands over me and squints at the phone screen, wiping her hands on her apron. After a minute or so she says: 'The important thing is to pray. Don't bother with the stories. It doesn't matter if you remember who did what and when. Just pray.'

*

A black cat – *la gatta nera* – scored into the corner of a thirty-third birthday card from a friend. An interpreter of omens translated into the language itself. Mother and daughter both believe that they speak this language fluently: the black cat, bad luck on four legs – do not let her cross your path! But I'm told that in Japan the meaning is exactly the opposite.

*

There is, scientists think, a particular region of the brain where psychological imprinting happens, a specific quarter in which vital lessons about how to engage with the world are stored for life. This imprinting is the first process, occurring in most species immediately after birth, through which every animal learns by mimicry how it should be. In humans, the imprinting period lasts from the age of three to eleven – this, in other words, is when we are at our most impressionable. A child hears her mother talking, is subconsciously struck by the act – she is, you could say, impressed – and so she emulates, just as a bird hearing its mother sing knows to do the same. When researchers deadened or removed a particular portion of birds' brains, the imprinting ceased. Of course, in humans, learning continues until death – through teaching and storytelling and experience and countless more subtle forms of knowledge gathering and conditioning – but all that belongs in a different category to imprinting. It's a bit like the difference between etching and painting; the one cuts into the surface while the other adds layers. The first of these is far more difficult to undo.

*

Every year at the start of Lent, Novella gave her daughter a length of thread in which were tied, at roughly two-centimetre intervals, forty knots, one for every day Jesus had fasted in the desert. Dirce was to loop this around her chest and tie it in a bow, so that she had it on her always, beneath her blouse. At the end of every day, she was to undo the bow, light a match and burn a single knot while picturing the thing she had chosen to give up. Because every day of Lent is a gamble and nobody knows who will gain the upper hand, God or the Devil. Both of them are in you.

'The day was done,' Nonna explains, 'the temptation resisted, and only – you'd count the knots – however many more days to go.'

Eventually, the thread was short enough to tie around her wrist, and then to keep in her pocket. And when the last knot was gone, there was only the memory.

I ask Nonna if she can remember any of the things that she used to give up. It's not as though she was surrounded by riches and pleasures.

'Ah, non mi ricordo... You know, something like chocolate or sweets or silly games.'

Novella and the children went to Church more often than was strictly required. On Sundays, they attended the earliest Mass so that sleeping in was never an option, in spite of the long week's work. This meant Dirce, whose dresses had grown shabby, did not need to sit alongside the better-dressed girls she once went to school with, and this, at least, was a mercy. She did not want to be reminded of what she was missing.

Before confession, Novella, eternally in black, would kneel in a pew with her head in her hands muttering for what seemed like hours. And then she would head for the confessional box with her eyes on the ground. Her daughter observed and did the same.

Perhaps Novella was asking forgiveness for not saying

her prayers daily, for only praying when she had to, in full view of others, or when she needed something. Or for being superstitious, in spite of knowing the Commandments off by heart. *You shall have no other Gods before me.* Perhaps she was laying out the rough fabric of her life and character for the priest to scrutinize in all its complexity, as she asked him repeatedly – scarcely letting him speak – whether she had not made the right decisions given the circumstances, and whether she might not be forgiven considering the way she had been tested and everything she had lost or sacrificed.

And maybe the priest would patiently count everything up, weigh this against that, and prescribe the right prayers in the right number, for the poor woman's condition. Seven Hail Marys to ease the pain that gathered around her temples. Twenty turns of the Act of Contrition for the tangle that sat somewhere between her stomach and her heart. Did she say these prayers? Did they help her? Three Our Fathers for your doubts.

Or perhaps Novella was just telling stories about herself, working her way through those well-fingered rosettes of suffering, relishing the centre-stage, grateful for the captive audience, because being listened to is a tonic as old and powerful as time itself.

*

An open window, the lace curtain beckoned by the breeze and brilliant white against the darkness inside. The sound of a woman singing drifts into the street. *For your little one you never buy toys Mamma, you only buy perfumes for yourself...* A second voice, straining, off-key, joins in and for the briefest of moments there is harmony, accidental, and so, impossible to recreate.

221

VII.

Nonna was sitting on the back seat of my parents' car, dressed as if for Mass, except smarter still – the pale mushroom-grey skirt-suit seemed closer to wedding attire. My dad was in the driver's seat in a sheepskin coat I remember from childhood, with my mum beside him in a long black gown. 'If we don't leave now it'll be too hot to travel,' my mum said matter-of-factly. Everyone was dressed for different seasons and occasions. The engine was idling as Nonna reached to pull the door shut. With the other hand she held the seat belt at a slight remove from her chest in the way she always does, to stop it creasing her blouse. This was in Campagna – I could see the corn beyond the car, tall and blue; though I had recognized the place before then, by the light. I could hear the car's wheels begin to turn and press into the gravel. They had been waiting for me but I'd taken too long and so they were leaving: my parents were driving Nonna to Sheffield, to the cemetery to see Angelo, Old Pietro and baby Anthony. I took in all this from the house, through the window of the bedroom that used to have Novella's bed in it before it was relegated to the *cantina*. The bed was there though. My dad's eyes were on the road and Nonna's were on me, and I was shouting at her not to go yet: I had questions, I needed to get some things down. Just wait a minute, *ti prego*.

I woke up with no air in my lungs and skin pricked with sweat, my fingers moving instinctively to my forehead and then to my chest, lightly tapping, like an atheist initiate catching herself halfway through the old habit. The gesture acknowledged that a fever had passed through in the night; I had been hot but now was cool again. And I had those dream words in my throat: *Ti prego*, please, 'I

223

pray of you'. Italian dispenses with the preposition, so it's more like 'I pray you', which in the context seemed somehow profoundly true. Dreams and prayers bubble up from the same place, don't they? Expressions of desires, hopes, anxieties. I dream you, I pray you, don't leave me. It took several minutes before I could shake the sense of panic, of time running out and of failure, and to feel sure that the scene was not memory. It was the grey suit that finally did it. Nonna would never wear anything so drab.

But by this point I was already thinking in symbols. That the corn was ready for harvest. That my mother was dressed for a funeral. That Nonna was smiling – at peace? – as she closed the door on me.

When I telephoned over breakfast I didn't tell Nonna about the dream. Her fluency in omens would have led her down the same paths as me. I did mention that I hadn't slept at all well, that I'd had a fever, now passed. But anyway, how was *she*, I wanted to know, 'Tutto a posto?'

'Yes, well, *si tira avanti* – but tell me, how long is it since you were last here?'

'Almost a year,' I said, hardly believing it myself.

'When we were in England, we used to come back once every two years and you could almost bet that in the middle year someone would get ill, without fail, fevers like you wouldn't believe, Leo's heart attacks, tonsilitis, otitis, Manlio's peritonitis...' – she was on a roll now – 'And my own problems.'

'Extreme versions of homesickness, you think?' I fed her the line.

'Well, there's something,' she said, 'something that... happens, maybe.'

I told her she might be right, and that Italians strike me as particularly susceptible to homesickness. I base this on my own feeling, and how whenever I meet another Italian abroad, within minutes we are competing over how much we miss the place. It makes sense because the Italian diaspora is diffuse, the result of a history of political and economic unrest and the personal desperation that rises to meet it. She knows that; I know that. Angelo and Old Pietro knew it, too.

'But then,' I ventured, 'aren't we homesick even when we're home? It's like a mirage we convince each other really exists, this idea of an Italy in which things are always better... You know?' I asked, hoping that she would return my thoughts to me, tidied and corroborated.

A pause. I thought about quoting to her that line about the long road to Ithaka, 'better it lasts for years', from the Greek poet C. P. Cavafy, who spent his childhood in England, but I didn't know how to introduce it and felt too self-conscious anyway.

'England always felt like home to me,' she said. 'From when I was nine. But Italy was home, too. Always both.'

'So, then, one way or another, you've never *not* been homesick?'

'I suppose not.'

I ploughed on – pity poor Nonna – because I'd been doing lots of reading. Beginning with Hippocrates, I said, a long strand of physicians diagnosed homesickness, or its relation, nostalgia, in displaced populations unable to get back to the land of their birth. Symptoms were said to include fever, nightmares, despondency. It could, they thought, be fatal. In the seventeenth century, the Swiss doctor Johann Jakob Scheuchzer said that mountain people were particularly susceptible because extreme barometric changes wreaked havoc on the body's pressure levels – any air would be oppressive compared to the light air they had been raised on. He prescribed a return to the homeland – 'obviously' – or, failing that, a cure of bright, young wine. ('I could have told you that,' Nonna deadpanned.) A recent study I found online, conducted by the clinical psychologist Ad Vingerhoets, suggests that a course of paracetamol might alleviate 'expat blues'. I laughed; Nonna didn't.

That day, for a while after Nonna had brought our conversation to an abrupt close – 'the *rosario* is about to start...', the volume of the television rocketed – I thought about my family's famous fevers. Old Pietro, builder of houses, overcome with fever after great physical exertion; Angelo, too, gone in a matter of days, not long after the upheaval of moving the family to England; his son, the first baby Manlio, burnt up and extinguished within twenty-four hours. The twins. Baby Lucia, who, as soon as they arrived in Italy, this time for good, broke out in a sweat that lasted four days and four nights and they thought she would die. And I drifted back through my own fevers, which seemed to come and go so suddenly, beginning in childhood: half-cast memories of delirium, experiences of dissolution, the feeling of something – life, I suppose – sloshing in and out, like water.

We make no distinction in Italian between having a temperature and having a fever. There is only *febbre*, and we are eternally on guard against it. An open window, eating too quickly, drinking too-cold water; little provocation is needed. We seem almost to fetishize *febbre*. In my family, we don't feel for it on each other's brows with our palms but rather with our lips, in long, gauging kisses.

When I was seven, my appendix was removed and Nonna came to stay while I recovered at home, so my parents could go to work. At some stage I remember her holding a thermometer up to the light, squinting and leaning over me to kiss my forehead for confirmation. The rest is fragments. There were blankets, much bustling, sockless feet suspended in night air, orange streetlights through the car window, the cold white walls of the hospital ward. I was writhing and pulling at the bed sheets and a nurse was holding me down. I saw my dad in the doorway looking concerned, still holding his briefcase, the usual green-blue trench coat folded over his arm. Only a few years ago, when it came up in conversation, did he tell me he was never there – he had been in France for work for the whole month. I'd dreamed him into place. Perhaps, while he was away, I was feeling homesick on his behalf.

The irony in Nonna and my theory of homesickness is that the reason I can't get home now is illness itself. Since early last year, the world has been overrun with a *febbre* that spreads and recurs and kills. For almost eighteen months, every day ends with a tally of the infected and the dead. We run the Italian figures against the English, as though they were just another set of accounts, incomings and outgoings, to record and understand. The process is one of reconciliation: first, the two countries with each other; then us with the figures.

We're invested in these shifting abstractions and strain to understand the language. As it is with all foreign vocabulary, we cling to the basics: up/down, here/there, us/them, good/bad. Until the numbers come down, and until vaccine levels go up, we can't go from here to there. We attempt to explain the figures to ourselves and then to each other. We run through different scenarios. We dismiss them. We do it all again. *Si tira avanti.*

Every day is the same but much is different. The easy movement between England and Italy I had always taken for granted disappeared almost overnight. Were I to travel from England to Italy now, I would be doubly undesired, made to undertake quarantine on arrival in Italy – especially since, at the moment, 86 per cent of new Italian infections are with the 'English variant' – and then again on return to England, where the rate of infection is, for now, considerably lower than in Italy. I would be viewed with suspicion, criticized, penalized for failure to comply. I understand the reasons and condone the restrictions, but it does not lessen the feeling of bereavement for a privileged way of life lost. Is this, I wonder, something like what Angelo felt as European relations grew hostile and he was forced to concentrate his family in one place, to choose one home over another and commit absolutely? And is this not a version of what all migrants feel? Bodies moving across borders are observed, evaluated, controlled, only many people, whole generations, have been allowed to forget it.

In the early days of the pandemic, the Italian government introduced a law that confined people to within 200 metres of the home. Citizens were allowed out to go to the supermarket or the pharmacy. Sales of paracetamol soared. Stocks dwindled. *La Repubblica* reported that sixty per cent of the world's paracetamol was produced in China and India, and this *vulnerabilità* could be *un problema*. To stay fit, and to distract themselves, my aunt and uncle retraced my childhood loop through the beech trees, down towards via dei Radici and back through the vines, four times daily.

For a while the churches remained open. When the government demanded their closure, Campagna's priest went from house to house with the Eucharist and his paraphernalia. When that, too, had to come to an end, Nonna joined millions of Italians in watching the Mass on television. Religious services have been televised on Italy's national network since the 1950s, when television sets first began to appear in homes and bars, but the pandemic has considerably lifted viewing figures – a positive rise, we are told, amid all the negative ones. A sign of unity and hope. People who didn't use to practise faith now do. But I do not think that Italy has become more Christian in the casual approving sense of 'charitable', which we tend to attach to the word. Rather, it feels like a relapse. Or muscle memory kicking in.

We are plague people, prone to fevers, false lucidity and amnesia. Italians are not alone in this, but a history of rampant recurrent disease appears to have imprinted the national consciousness and conditioned the population to think always in terms of threat, contagion, eradication and return. And barriers. Natural ones: a mountain range, seventh-century plague doctors thought, would protect Florence from the worst of it; islands were a gift; soil, if the pit was deep enough, would protect the living from the mass of infected dead. And man-made ones: walls; doors; policed borders. And *lazzaretti*, quarantine centres built of stone and mortar – geometry set against chaos – or ships at anchor, a safe distance from the shore; strange temporary homes for people deemed dangerous. It took a new pandemic to remind the world that the Italians – or, rather, the Venetians – gave us the word 'quarantine', from *quarantena*, denoting a forty-day isolation period considered, for reasons steeped in Christian belief, to be sufficient for the purification of the body.

Through history, prayers, penitence and trinkets of devotion have been the first line of defence. During the plagues that ravaged the peninsula from the mid-1300s to the final major outbreak, the Great Plague of Milan, which lasted three years from 1629, the churches organized frequent processions that wound through crowded towns and cities, doing the disease's job for it. Early on, the Black Death saw a resurgence in flagellantism, whereby sins were atoned for through public acts of self-inflicted pain.

Cities regularly saw their populations halved. The fever struck, followed by aches that began in the head and reached the entire body. Then came chills, rashes, the relief of death. In the late 1470s, the Republic of Venice lost some 300,000 people. If the private prayers of the survivors had been spoken aloud, the cumulative sound would have been deafening. But still bodies piled up in the streets, every death the will of God. (And yet – people said – *someone* must have brought it in?)

Grocers, apothecarists and resourceful cooks, marrying faith and ancient learning, tried to alleviate the physical symptoms of a disease otherwise out of human control. Pomanders, pungent fumigants, pills, tinctures and syrups proliferated. Theriacs, advocated by Galen and revered as cures for snakebites and other poisons, were considered the most powerful, with lists of ingredients often running into the hundreds. Each item was weighed and blended carefully: rose water, sage, ground snake flesh, rapeseed, balsam, saffron, black pepper, cinnamon, parsley. Some recipes recommended soaking the mixture in wine for a time, before finally incorporating honey, which would allow the paste to stick to the patient like a second skin. It was most effective, physicians advised, when concentrated on the chest, close to the heart.

Before long, the pastes were being imported into Britain. They were known as Venice Treacle. But strict regulation of foreign goods fuelled domestic production, too. An advertisement placed in a London newspaper in 1670, touted a 'Famous and Effectual MEDICINE TO CURE THE PLAGUE': a powder was to be mixed with liquid for the patient 'to drink freely in their sweat', a posset 'with Sage, or Sorrel, and Dandilion'.

*

In early March 2020, my parents were on a cruise off the coast of Brazil and following news from home closely. The whole of Lombardy was in 'lockdown' – use of this English loan word is now widespread, the Accademia della Crusca notes – as were provinces in the Veneto and other northern regions. The world was watching Italy struggle and fail to contain the virus. And soon my parents started to notice that people onboard, with whom they had previously been friendly, were now politely, persistently avoiding them. If they struck up a conversation with anyone new, the moment they mentioned that they had come from Italy the atmosphere changed. Excuses were made and my parents found themselves alone. After a while, they started to tell people they were from England, and that helped, for a time.

When just a handful of infections had been confirmed in Italy, the attacks on people of East Asian descent began. Newspapers reported a case in Bologna, where a Chinese-Italian teenager was beaten up by a group of four men. 'What are you doing in Italy?' they shouted, 'You're bringing us diseases? Get lost, you and your virus.' The scene was witnessed by a man, sitting on a nearby bench, who stepped in to help the boy. A report on *Bologna Today* says he was a Moroccan, and this reminds me that until recently 'marocchino' was a catch-all term for any dark-skinned immigrant, a label akin to *vu cumprà*, whose mock pidgin Italian – 'you buy?' – was intended to conjure desperate and untrustworthy street hawkers, pests.

There were other attacks. Chinese businesses were boycotted. The Chinese embassy expressed serious concern. A national poster campaign was deemed necessary: 'The virus is the enemy, not the Chinese people.' In Naples, *La Repubblica* reported, a bus driver departing from Piazza Garibaldi saw a man with a suitcase – 'un uomo orientale', an 'oriental' man – waiting to board and accelerated away from the bus stop. A passenger is quoted as saying, 'He did the right thing, we don't want the virus here.' Calls for a ban on all travel from China were soon followed by calls for a ban on all boats coming from Africa, where no cases of the virus had been reported. As one virus spread around the world, it awoke this old one, too.

Perhaps this is also muscle memory. We have always grafted diseases onto select groups of people. During the fourteenth century, the Italians were gripped by the idea that certain people might be intentionally spreading plague. They accused local Jewish communities, which had, they reasoned, always wanted to eradicate Christianity. Men, women and children were burnt alive. In the fifteenth century, syphilis, meanwhile, was, for the Germans, the 'French Disease'; for the French, it was carried by Neapolitans (who said it was French). In Turkey, it was the 'Christian disease'. In the nineteenth century, British colonists considered cholera to be inherently Indian, a product of an uncivilized way of life. Around the same time, the Americans were blaming it on the Irish and the Italians – destitute, filthy migrants who clambered off ships into crowded harbours looking for work. Their clothes were said to be saturated with sickness. In 1916, Italian immigrants were accused of causing an outbreak of polio in New York and on much of the East Coast, and two years later, along with Jews, they were shunned as bringers of influenza. We have forgotten what it is to be blamed, to be the scapegoat of a society's ills.

'When I was a girl it was malaria everyone was scared of,' Nonna told me one day, when I had called to update her on my parents' predicament.

'It was very common,' she said, 'and very dangerous.

You would get a fever and twenty-four hours later you were dead.'

I asked if it was malaria that took the first baby Manlio or the twins, but she didn't know. 'It's possible. You prayed it wouldn't happen but there were cases. The marshes were not far from here.'

Malaria, a sickness in the blood, is ancient but with us still – a historical constant, like the famous mosquito preserved in amber. Though it was eradicated across Europe decades ago, it is rife in Africa. Medicine has not yet found a solution; vaccines work, for a time, and then they don't.

In the early 1970s, the Chinese scientist Tu Youyou discovered artemisinin, a powerful anti-malarial compound, in the plant *artemisia annua*, sweet wormwood, which belongs to the same family as the daisy and the dandelion. She had been inspired, she said, by traditional Chinese medicine, which prescribed a drink of hot water and artemisia – *qing hao*, 'blue-green herb' – to cure intermittent fever. Artemisinin became the core ingredient in a new generation of anti-malarial drug. But resistance was already noted by the time Tu Youyou was awarded a Nobel Prize in 2015.

This shapeshifter has gone by many names: camp fever, ague, intermittent-, swamp- or marsh-fever. Until the turn of the twentieth century, when the female Anopheles mosquito was identified as the cause of infection, the marsh air itself – heavy with the smell of stagnant water and rotting vegetation – was assumed to be poisonous. *Mala aria*, bad air. *Paludismo*, swampism, or, I suppose, swampitis. The beggars and brigands who hid out in these inhospitable water-lands, whose hair and rags were thought to be impregnated with the 'seeds' of contagion, were viewed with fear and revulsion. Like

Caliban, they could summon 'all the infections that the sun sucks up from bogs, fens, flats'. Their touch was the kiss of death.

Since Roman times, the plan had been to drain the swamps, to render them inhabitable and agriculturally useful. But successes were few and short-lived. Some say the fall of the Roman Empire can be linked to a particularly bad outbreak of malaria, or 'Roman Fever', as it was then known. (I write this a few months after the Italian government collapsed in disagreement over how to handle our own pandemic; the country is now on its sixty-ninth government since the end of the Second World War.)

The Sisyphean struggle against the waters continued for centuries, but the Fascist era into which Nonna was born brought an intensification. The aftermath of the First World War had seen a steep rise in cases of malaria, especially in the Veneto and the Friuli, where fighting had made it impossible to carry out routine maintenance of dredged lands. Quinine tablets were widely distributed, at great cost to the administration. In 1923, a year into his reign, Mussolini put his characteristic spin on an edict from the late 1800s and declared war on the putrid waters. I wonder if he didn't feel a particular outrage because malaria was a disease that contaminated good Italian blood.

The *bonifica delle paludi* – the reclamation of the swamps – was the propogandists' dream come true. It was, they said, Italy's panacea: once these wastelands were rendered fertile and buildable, people would no longer need to emigrate in search of a better life. Because, in a sense, the loss of thousands of fine, strong Italians had, for at least half a century, been the nation's most debilitating illness. Not only was the constant population drain a source of embarrassment for the government

– not to mention concern: Italians abroad were Italians out of control – but all too often the migrants themselves suffered great indignities. So, a promise was made: Italy's total liveable, farmable land would be increased by a third.

Returning to land south of Rome partly drained by Augustus centuries earlier, a workforce of former soldiers put in place a system of levees and pumps, and, in 1932, on the soil that emerged, Mussolini's architects built Littoria, whose pale stone architecture, simple but ostentatious, with a tall clocktower at its heart, shone like a beacon of cleanliness and renewal. A few years later, Pontinia was erected nearby, and people, primarily from the Veneto and the Friuli, flocked to the area to make their homes afresh. Strange that this proud Christian nation should forget so readily God's admonishment against building on soft ground.

'That was a good thing he did, you know?' Nonna said. 'People don't like to admit it, but it's true.'

I say nothing when Nonna says such things. *He was let down by those around him. He lost control of the generals. He was misled, people forget.* These lines, residua of her formal education, I think, don't seem to fit with the other things I know about her, so mostly, I let them wash over me and try to forget. I can't bring myself to engage because, I confess, I'm frightened of what else might come out. Sometimes I think of *zio* Gioacchino and imagine him showing Dirce and Leo around his garden in Sheffield, not long after the end of the war, once everything that happened had happened, with heaps of bodies across Europe to prove it. And those photographs of Mussolini and the others bloated and hanging upside down from the roof of the petrol station in *piazzale* Loreto. Was there talk of good things then, or is it the passage of time that has allowed

235

such expressions to emerge, like gaudy winter blooms?

Ma Mussolini ha fatto anche cose buone, 'But Mussolini also did good things': a common phrase in Italy, increasingly so as distrust in democracy grows and social media creates fertile ground for historical revisionism. Spend enough time in the country and you will hear the words spoken, sometimes by the person you least expect. A good, kind person. Imagine it being slipped into conversation casually, muttered wistfully, like the refrain of a half-remembered hymn. Think of it bobbing up to the surface like a cork in water, or a body – it startles you that way – and consider the heft of that opening 'but', and all that lies bound and weighted below.

There's a book with precisely that phrase as its title, in which Francesco Filippi, a historian of mentality, unpicks the most (let's say) misremembered claims made in favour of the Fascist regime. I bought a copy a couple of summers ago, while I was staying at Nonna's, in the old bookshop in Maniago's main *piazza*. Its black spine punctuated a row of pastel-coloured romance novels near the shop's till, where someone must have discarded it at the last minute, and the familiarity of its title – as intended – struck me. I took it home, half thinking it would be good to have some quick statistics to hand should Nonna and I end up having *that conversation*. The other half of me knows we never will.

I carried the book around the house with me, meaning – I think – to read it between meals, chats and games of *briscola*. I left it lying about – a lazy, inchoate provocation, perhaps. And as usual, I scribbled notes in the margins and underlined more of the text than not, especially sentences that state the blatantly obvious, as if in preparation for an exam. For example:

> The foundation of a possible totalitarian future also relies on the rehabilitation of the totalitarian past. To show the reality of that past is a first step in preventing that past from becoming future.

And:

> In the following pages you will drown in 'facts', reconstructed with unassailable and almost maniacal precision, even if it must be said that yes, of course, Fascism also did 'good things' ... It would be science fiction if, in twenty years, it hadn't, right? Even a broken clock, wise men say, tells the right time twice a day.

Double-underlining denotes loud agreement or, I suppose, relish. I mark up books like other people write diaries: performatively, with future readers in mind.

The *bonifica delle paludi*, I read, was not a success. Of the millions of hectares promised, only a fraction was delivered. There was not enough viable land for everyone, and what there was tended to be physically and economically exhausting to maintain. During the Second World War, channels were neglected again. Some, especially in the north, were a gift to retreating Weimar soldiers, who flooded them on purpose, surrounding the *partigiani* with filthy, malaria-infested waters. Much of the work of reclaiming the land then fell to future administrations or was abandoned altogether.

Pontinia and Littoria, renamed Latina after the war, are still standing, though. Hundreds of thousands of people live there now, among an extraordinary number of non-indigenous eucalyptus trees, planted to absorb the soil's excessive moisture. One of Italy's tallest skyscrapers, the Torre Pontina, was erected in Latina in 2007.

Residents go about their daily lives, travel to and from work, pick up the children, drop them at their grandparents', and forget how this place came to be built. They forget that where they stand was once water; they forget about the deadly swamps. But the soil remembers and the stones of some of the buildings, too. Metal surfaces are acutely susceptible to red rashes. The canals and dikes require constant attention. And in the centre of the town, the pale clocktower ticks, marking time until the waters return, and their war ends, properly this time.

Il Duce did not eradicate malaria, either. (I dog-ear this page at the top and bottom and run a thick wavy pencil-line the length of the text.) It took the Marshall Plan and vast quantities of American DDT before the World Health Organization could declare the country free of the Anopheles mosquito and, so, of the disease, in 1970. The ecosystem was devastated for decades.

The spectre of malaria won't be dispelled so easily, though. I read about a case a few years ago, when a four-year-old girl died in a hospital in Lombardy. Some worried that the death signalled the return of an old problem. The girl had not been abroad, only to the Venetian coast for a brief holiday. The infection's provenance was a mystery. Some Italians thought they knew how this had happened: African migrants, coming off boats, had brought malaria with them and passed it on to the child. The day after the death, the conservative daily *Il Tempo* ran the frontpage headline: *Ecco la malaria degli immigrati*. 'Here is the malaria of immigrants'. In fact, while it's true that two children from Burkina Faso were being treated for malaria on the same ward, it was human error – the reuse of an infected needle – that was responsible for transmission. But that's a detail, a different story even, and not everyone is interested in hearing it.

*

In late April 1981 a tall man approaching thirty is walking along Lombard Street, in the City of London. He's rushing for the train home, as he does every evening, even though he knows there's plenty of time – he's punctual, has worked out all the shortcuts, built in margins of error, and yet everyone else is rushing, so. He's wearing a navy suit which blends into a mass of dark blues and greys rippling in one direction, like the nearby Thames. His hair is short, straight, almost unbelievably black, and his skin is dark. That makes him stand out a bit, I suppose. He's white, though. He really is like all these other men. He's still got the suits his mother made him – and two beautiful waistcoats, one in maroon, the other in a bright blue verging on turquoise – but he would never wear them to the office.

He buys his suits from Burtons now and lives in a maisonette in the suburbs. When he dresses in the morning he sometimes thinks of that Greek guy on his accountancy course – who was sent home by one of the company partners for wearing too pale a jacket and with mismatched trousers.

He is walking – quick-quick-quick – and thinking. Not about how, in the sixteenth century, northern Italians laid the foundations of the banking system we still live by today, nor about how Jewish moneylenders once favoured, indeed, protected by the Crown, had to be expelled before that could happen. (He'll read a book about these things many years later and recommend it to anyone interested in history and immigration 'and that sort of thing'.) But now, no, he's not thinking deep thoughts about how tides can turn and fortunes change. In truth, we don't know what he's thinking.

239

Maybe he's remembering Easter, a few weeks back, when, after a long lunch, he and his wife and *mamma* sank into their chairs and said very little, smiling as they drank bright red wine like it was water and gazed at the mountains. (Had they always been so blue?) Maybe he is remembering how much – what? – healthier? warmer? more present? – all these things – his father had seemed as he plonked an unlabelled bottle of grappa on the table, winked and left for his *pisolino*, nap. Maybe he is thinking about his boss's reaction, just now, when he told him he was handing in his notice because he's accepted a job offer back home. ('What, you're moving back to Manchester?'; 'No, Italy.'; 'Blimey, are you sure?') Maybe he's thinking about how soon he won't be 'a Mancunian with a funny surname', as his boss had put it, but rather, an Italian with a funny first name. And accent.

Or maybe he's just thinking about what there'll be for dinner when he gets home. A mental scan of the fridge loops back to *mamma* and the faded Wall's ice-cream box full of gorgonzola and light, nutty Montasio, which she snuck into his hold-all before they set off for the airport. (The cab driver back in England was fuming about it – the stench! Foreign food always stinks. He made them put the windows down even though the rain was horizontal.)

A few miles away, a woman nearing thirty is watching the clock on the far side of the room, which seems to be stuck at five to six. She looks around and the office is deserted so she tidies away the pages spread across her desk. So many things she almost convinced herself she cared about: building regulations, soil analyses, subsidence solutions ('mass pour vs beam-and-base'). Much of the south-east of England is built on clay, she now knows, which can contract and expand 'dramatically' depending on the weather. The liability when it comes to fixing

240

things once they start to sink isn't always clear-cut. That's what she was hired for.

Marginally more interesting is the company's other specialism, which is to move important buildings – Tudor manors, medieval churches, the birthplaces of great men – from one place to another to make room for a motorway or housing estate, or to a site that can accommodate a visitors' centre. The buildings must be brick-for-brick the same, only there rather than here. Like Captain Cook's cottage, transplanted from North Yorkshire to Melbourne in the 1930s. Yorkshire stone surrounded by an English country garden, surrounded by... Australia.

It's more difficult to say what she is wearing, but it's probably long and black. Her colleagues are always wondering whether she might like to wear something a little less 'serious'? (Is that the word they used?) They all wear dark suits, of course. Serious suits. A curious logic. One of them likes it to be known that his suits are Italian, bought while consulting on plans to stop the leaning tower of Pisa from leaning. So, presumably, it would just be the plain old tower of Pisa again (ha ha). She particularly enjoyed telling him that she was leaving and moving abroad – 'to Italy, in fact'.

It's also more difficult to imagine what she's thinking about, beyond the contents of the fridge and what's for dinner. Because she doesn't have a job lined up in Italy like her husband does. He'll be checking a company's accounts, making sure everything is above board, much like he has done over here for the past few years. 'While I...' – the sentence stalls every time she tries it; she can't even imagine what kind of room she'll be sitting in. And 'of course' that's part of the appeal. 'Of course' it's all very exciting, the infinite possibility. But 'I'll find something' was a terrific statement of confidence one day and of near total dejection the next. She is of the age when, for a woman, choices that don't really feel like choices start to impinge. She will never forget how when they called to tell her parents in Liverpool that they 'had some news', her mother shrieked and called her father in from the living room. 'We're moving to Italy for two years, to see what it's like' was not in their script.

When the man and woman meet an hour or so later, in the golden glow of the fridge, they don't know that within six months they will be living in converted stables in the grounds of the grand Raimondi-Odescalchi estate. Their landlord – because these stables have long been sold off to private owners; the villa itself has changed hands a few times – will be a Mr Bergman, a notary and a rare Italian Jew, who will point to the chapel opposite the front door and say that General Garibaldi married his second wife right there. 'You feel the history of this place every day.' And, as if on cue, they will see the ancient *contessa* walking around the grounds with her parasol, dressed in black, like someone from another era. (Later, they will be invited to use her swimming pool, but the hours and rules specified will be prohibitively complicated.)

One day, early on, while her husband is at work in Milan, the woman will get back home laden with food shopping and the key to the front door will snap off in the lock. She will see it as a 'marvellous opportunity to learn a few key words' (ha ha) and go off in search of Pierino, the man who fixes things about the place. He will smile and listen patiently as this pale, blonde woman tries to explain what has happened – 'um, *porta... e*, um, key, key? *Clé?*... snap!' – when to simply show him the stub of the key would have saved them both time and effort.

The woman will get bored sometimes, with her husband working long hours, 'While *I...*' She will keep herself busy organizing get-togethers with other expats, at which she'll mostly speak English, the common language among this group of international arrivals. And, like most of the other expats, a few days a week she'll give lessons at a language school in Milan, teaching English to Italian businessmen. The locked-out episode will become a stock scenario in her teaching, 'because it will happen to everyone at some point', and words like 'in', 'out' and 'help' are pretty important.

Life will trundle on, and as the end of their two-year experiment approaches, they will decide to stay (another shriek). She still hasn't found work, but his money is enough, and she is pregnant now, so that's something. And life is good. Three years after the first daughter comes a second. And three years after that, just when she is beginning to despair at ever 'resurrecting' her career, there will be a fortuitous meeting with an American on a train, who, seeing English words in the book she is reading, will ask her if it is 'fact or fiction?' (It is *Middlemarch*.) After various interviews and documents, translations, certificates and elaborate stamps, a job will transpire, which will lead to another job, and then another, and forty years after the key snapped off in the lock the couple will still be in Italy. Except on the inside now, and they will call it home.

Theirs is a story of ease and excited discovery – of a young couple that thought 'Oh, shall we live somewhere else?' and did. Everything will go well, really. They will earn a good living and find satisfaction in their work. They will go on two-week holidays to villas in the south of Italy, which will feel like another time and place entirely. They will eat well and become increasingly interested in wine. At the age of thirty-three, this man will not die suddenly, as his grandfather did, nor will he have a nervous breakdown as his mother did at that same age. Instead, he'll look at one daughter dancing around and babbling bilingually, and then at the new arrival, whose hair is as black as can be. And he'll think 'Well, this is the best of both worlds, isn't it?' There will be no antagonists here, only a strange and not unpleasant sense of detachment, of being in and out at the same time.

And one day all these future things will be past things, memories shared with me, their now adult younger daughter, over the phone. And I will trouble those nice images and busy myself with the gaps.

'But weren't you a bit worried about all the bombings?'

'That was pretty much over by the early 1980s.'

'Er, no, it really wasn't.'

'Oh, no, true, the *strage di Bologna*' – i.e. the worst terrorist attack Italy has known – 'was about twelve months before we arrived.'

'How can you *forget* the terrorism, the daily threat of being blown up?'

'Well, it wasn't daily... and we had the IRA in England...'

But, 'now that you say it', my dad remembers the bullet marks in the walls of his office block, left by the radical left-wing Brigate Rosse, the Red Brigades, when they stormed the place in search of someone high-ranking to kidnap. And my mum remembers how, going to meet him there, she was met by heavily armed guards at the double-door entrance to the reception and not allowed inside, even with a baby in the pram and a toddler in tow. Now we are on a darker footing.

'It can't have been easy to make friends,' I say, 'or to, you know, socialize, because, Mà, you didn't speak Italian, and, Pà, you spoke Veneto rather than Italian...' I say this knowing that, in Italy, if you're not from the region in which you are living, you may be considered almost as foreign as someone from another country.

A number of stories force their way through this particular chink, including how, early on, after an important meeting, my dad was pulled to one side by a colleague and told: 'We do not use *il voi*; we use *il lei*.' That is, the polite second-person address enforced by Mussolini, was no longer in use in the 1980s. My dad had learnt *voi* from his parents, who had carried it with them when they left the country in 1950, like a linguistic fossil.

This was the same meeting in which my dad got all the professional labels wrong, calling the *avvocato*, *dottore*, the *dottore*, *ingeniere*, and the *commendatore*, *avvocato*. These labels, representative of the diplomas one has earned, are more important than people's names. Another time, my dad, eager to explain some aspect of a project he had been working on, and confident he was getting into the swing of things, addressed an associate as *dottore* – 'if you'll allow me, *dottore...*' – and received the lecture of a lifetime. Because the man was not a *dottore* and – indeed – prided himself on having got to where he was without the easy ticket of this or that extra qualification, which everyone knew money and contacts could buy.

They did make friends, though, my parents. Mostly expats. Except for Angela, a *milanese*, who my mum met at the language school, and her husband Gigi. My parents were witnesses at their wedding.

'They're probably the only Italians who really let us into their family,' my mum says now. I'm watching her on my phone screen; her jaw clenches and her lips tighten.

'In Italy, it's harder to make friends,' my dad adds. 'Acquaintances, sure, we had lots of those, people to meet for *aperitivo*, but not close friends. There's a reluctance to invite new people into the family, I think. Or that's how it felt.'

I'm reminded of an article I read about the uneasy

relationship between James Joyce and Italo Svevo in Trieste. Joyce, who was teaching Svevo English at the time, and who was used to seeing his adult students as friends, was frustrated by a persistent barrier when it came to Svevo, in spite of all they had in common and the often deeply personal conversations they had. In a letter to his brother Stanislaus, Joyce bristled at never having been invited to the house 'except as a paid teacher'. Was he not Svevo's friend and equal? (Do those categories necessarily coincide?) Must he always be an outsider here?

'It would probably have been easier to make friends with George Clooney,' says my mum. 'He lived just down the way, in Laglio.'

'But he wasn't there yet,' I point out.

'He *was*. A friend in the expat group said he was a really nice guy, played basketball with the local kids, built them a new court...'

'Mà, he wasn't famous yet – *E.R.* didn't even start till 1994...'

She won't be persuaded, and so we move on.

'Did you ever think, Pà, how neat it was that, when you came to Italy, you were pretty much doing the job – looking after the accounts – that Angelo was doing when he left for England? Sort of.'

'Not really.'

'And, Mà, isn't it funny that you were working for a company that specialized in transplanting homes?'

I see her shoulders rise and fall. 'It was just a job.'

For me, nothing is 'just', at least not in the sense of 'merely'. And how is it that this word, bound up with justice, rectitude, became so belittled as to mean 'no more than'? An online dictionary of etymology puts it ponderously: 'the sense decayed, as it often does...', but the root

246

is clear: the Latin *iustus*, meaning righteous, true and perfect, from where we also get *ius* – 'legal right', inviolable, upstanding.

The entry also points to another 'just', a relic of the original sense that speaks approvingly of neatness, of an exactness born of someone's authoritative influence. To make something *just so*, to be *just right*. I feel like this dictionary is talking to me. Neatness is my concern, my motivation. I think of my childhood bedroom, my books, stuffed animals and carefully selected ornaments (more animals), lined up on shelves, facing out or each other, to an exact degree. Every night before bed, I would police them, carefully scrutinizing, nudging, putting everything in its rightful place. Otherwise, I couldn't sleep. I seek such order in all things; I impose it.

Without my attentions, I think, this family story of ours is just – there it is again – a space (I imagine a tundra) through which this person passed and that happened, and then this person and that, with no overarching pattern or structure; no links between us, no communion. So, I start by sorting through what there is and then establishing sympathies between these apparently disparate elements, much as I did in my bedroom, where the small ceramic frog and the Kenyan elephant had always to be gazing into each other's eyes. I consider this work akin to building cairns, gathering mismatched elements into crude monuments of recognition that stand for decades, symbols that say, 'I am now, in my own way, where you once were and where another of us may one day be.' The affinity has only to been found; there are connections, if you place things side by side, just so, look hard enough, squint, maybe close one eye. My mind is, I think, in a constant kind of sleep state, sifting, ordering, preparing.

Then, you have only to point out the sympathy to

others – if they don't already see it for themselves – to speak it aloud, to evangelize. Communion has always to be articulated and ritualized in some way, like when the priest crumbles and eats the Eucharist and remembers a completely different supper that happened 2,000 years ago, different but the same. Pattern, repetition, symbolism – why else do I still remember the exact order of things on my bedroom shelves; the names and stories of so many people I have never met; and all my prayers, so long after I stopped believing in their power?

*

Most of us at some point experience a moment in which – looking across the table at our parents, or closing the door on a dozing grandparent, exhausted by questions – it settles in us that we are (touch wood, *tocca ferro*) going to be the last one standing. And that we are, then, charged with passing things on, telling the stories, ingraining the memory and memories of those who went before. Often the realization comes too late. The older relative dies, without having passed on the past. (Is that where the word 'past' comes from?) Or the chain might be broken some other way: an accidental untruth, a wilful misinterpretation, the custodian of the story dies prematurely and there is no one after.

I have been thinking about this as the pandemic spreads, a disease which targets the lungs and steals the breath from young, otherwise healthy, people like me. I have read too many times a friend's account of having the virus and imagined the feeling she describes of 'a palm pushing down on my chest', of 'lungs like tar, like stone, like dead roots'. I put myself in her place. The *cialciùt* comes about once a week these days.

At the peak of her illness my friend thought there was someone in the room with her, too, a shadow figure from the past maybe – but not a threat – and her most urgent thought was to write messages to her children, about who they were and where they came from, to bridge the gaps between the past, present and future, just in case. I am aware now, differently than before, of my own childlessness.

When I tell my parents' story of moving from England to Italy, to others or to myself, I'm more likely than they are to point out the friction, anxieties and loneliness – to finger the pit marks in the wall. I look for darkness where my parents present me with light. They tell me about successful careers and happy families, and I ask if they weren't scared of commuting to work, worried about taking me and my sister on the *metro*, lonely being so far from their friends in England. It's a question of character and disposition, sure, but also of choice, maybe mostly unconscious, about what is significant in a tale, what makes it worth preserving. It's a question of admittance: what you will allow in.

Ma non lo mettere questo. Perhaps it's something to do with proximity to the life being recorded, this urge to self-edit, to eradicate the stuff that unsettles you and the story you want to tell about yourself. (Or is it the story you think people want to hear? Are those the same thing?) It's an act of self-preservation: the 'I' can seem so vulnerable, lanky, teeteringly rootless, so we try to create some structure in which to house it. This is easier when we talk of ourselves in the past because of the distance it brings – it's as if we were a different person, really more 'him' or 'her' than 'I', and, no doubt, more fiction than fact. In the present tense it's safer to hide the 'I' away, rather than to attempt to tidy it in real-time, with the ground constantly shifting and people waiting. Every time I start a sentence with 'I', there's the will to rip it out before anyone else does. There's nothing of interest in it, nothing has really happened. Not like other people's lives, in the past, with all those events – the wars, the bombs, the imposing arcs of full lives nearing death.

And when I think of my own past, of, now, thirty-odd years split between two countries, I do as my parents do and fish out the bitter things. I always omit, for example, the times I have met a cantankerous Italian border controller, who has asked me why, if I'm Italian, as my birthplace and surname suggest, I'm travelling on a British passport. 'It's illegal, you could get into a lot of trouble,' one of them once told me, and of course I believed him, because he was wearing a military uniform with gold buttons and badges and I was ten and travelling alone. I knew my mum was waiting for me through the frosted sliding doors at the end of the arrivals hall, but she seemed desperately out of reach.

I think about that moment every time I approach a border. It reminds me how porous is the line between curiosity and suspicion, and how deep the gulf between '*Amazing!* But how do you sound so English/Italian?' and 'So what gives you the right to be here?' It makes me look differently at the passport I hold in my hands as I stand in line, index finger parting the pages for inspection, ready to show the officer exactly what he needs to see – because I want this to be as smooth an exchange as possible.

After that incident with the border official, I used to rehearse my story in the queue, getting it down to as simple a construction as possible, knowing that if I got flustered, I'd struggle to get the words out at all. 'I was born and raised here. My father is Italian. My mother is English. I have both nationalities. My documents are in order.' Jaw clenching and unclenching; trembling bottom lip. *Può anche controllare*. 'You' – in the polite form, of course – 'can even check.' The neuroses of a child. Now I know they would never have checked because of the story they had already read on my skin, clothes, in the way I carried myself. The drama I was rehearsing happens to other people, at this border and others.

I have always travelled on a British passport – in fact, I never bothered to get an Italian one; there didn't seem to be much point until recently, when new borders – new to me – were imposed between my two homes. I have an Italian ID card, too. It is a legal requirement that this document be carried on the person at all times, the government website explains, 'so that they can be identified'. Mine allows travel within Europe and, at the time of writing, it is still accepted at the British border. To apply for this document, one must have lived on Italian soil for ten uninterrupted years or have an Italian parent. I am entitled not because I was born in Italy, but because my father – who was not born in Italy – is Italian by blood. *Jus sanguinis*, blood right. Just blood. But without this blood, I would have been an outsider, with an ID card with a stamp on the back declaring in bold capital letters: *NON VALIDA PER L'ESPATRIO*, 'not valid for expatriation'. Which seems to mean something along the lines of, 'We won't vouch for you, you're not our responsibility'.

I used to carry that invalidating card. When I was about thirteen, my sister and I were called to the city hall to be registered as foreigners living in Italy. There had been some confusion regarding our status, connected to some legal change, the kind of technicality in which Italy excels. My father, it turned out, had not ordered his own papers correctly. He had failed to claim his Italian nationality for reasons too complicated to divulge here, and so his Italianness was not extended to us.

We queued outside the *Municipio* for what felt like hours, in a line of people that snaked around the back of the building. I remember the awareness that we were the only white people present and the sense of indignation I felt. I was born in Italy. I had only ever lived in Italy. I was Italian. I was different to the other people in line who were, I presumed, looking at them, not Italian. The ignorance of that youthful impression is what makes me want to skip over the memory now; shame is a ruthless editor, but she leaves her cuttings all over the floor.

After a while, my mother, in a rush to get back to the office, made a phone call to someone who knew someone and eventually a woman in a neat skirt-suit walked down the white stone steps, brushed past a group of armed policemen chatting and drinking vending-machine coffee, and scanned the line. She spotted us instantly, although we had never met her, and beckoned us forward. We bypassed the line and were ushered inside. I remember sobbing at the woman who stuck down the passport photographs we had provided and asked us to confirm our names, ages and addresses before rolling a stamp across the back, folding it and putting it in a laminated sleeve, with the dexterity of someone who had done it hundreds of thousands of times. 'But I'm Italian; I was born here.' No one indulged my melodrama, as I recall. We emerged soon after with ID cards that labelled us 'British', branded on the back *NON VALIDA PER L'ESPATRIO*. For years I stashed passport photos of friends and small votive cards given to me by Nonna in the space between that back page and the plastic sleeve, to hide the stamp.

These days I travel on my Italian ID, a version updated since my father corrected the 'error' and I reached legal maturity and got my own papers in order. The photograph in it is exactly the same as in my British passport; both documents give my full name, date of birth, and place of birth (Erba, a town called 'grass'), except one says I'm a British citizen and the other, Italian. It seems odd that the documents don't mention each other, as though neither wants to admit to only partial jurisdiction, to publicize the neither-this-nor-that-ness of their subject. The Italian one is the more detailed, listing my profession (*Editore*), height (1,75 cm), hair and eye colour (both *castani*; 'chestnut', more poetic than 'brown'). *Segni particolari*, distinguishing features: '= = = ='.

By choosing to travel on this document, I'm signalling something to someone, possibly only to myself, and testing an idea: the present viability of being an insider-outsider. At the Italian border, the ID card guarantees the utmost smoothness and a sense of belonging ('*Ben tornata*', 'Welcome back'). But at the UK border – I wonder – do I mean it as a provocation? Am I asking for that self-centred drama all over again as I shuffle up the line, clutching my story? To have to justify myself in public, I who hate confrontation? I don't know, and I've never been challenged.

These pieces of paper matter because they dictate not only who comes in but also on what terms: how the person will be received, what opportunities they will be afforded, whether the path will be rough or smooth. My English grandmother was adamant that I should have a British passport. 'It opens doors all around the world,' she said, because she was born at a time when that was true. These documents determine whether a place will feel like home, immediately or ever. Each is the foundation of a country, an idea unique to every individual, in which she will try to build a life.

As Nonna said, there are 'tante Italie', many Italys, and

mine is different to hers which is different to my mother's which is different to my father's, and so on down the queue. And now we are back at the root of a matter that has stalked the country since its birth. Because after the question, 'Which Italy is this in which I find myself?' come two more: 'Which Italy do I want it to be?' and, inevitably, 'What am I prepared to do about it?'

*

While my parents were falling in love with Italy in the summer of 1981, it was being blown apart by people with conflicting ideas about which Italy this was and which it should be. If indeed Italy as a country should *be* at all, because that was by no means a settled matter. These were the *anni di piombo* – the years of lead, named for the volume of bullets fired – when factions of students and workers proliferated, forming countless iterations of Communism, neo-fascism and anarchism. Ordine Nuovo, Ordine Nero, Avanguardia Nazionale, Nuclei Armati Rivoluzionari (Nar), Prima Linea, Brigate Rosse (BR).

In the two decades from 12 December 1969, when neo-fascists announced the beginning of a new war by detonating a bomb in Piazza Fontana in central Milan, 370 people were killed and about 1,000 injured. Among the victims were magistrates, politicians, company bosses, police officers and journalists, including Carlo Casalegno, who wrote a weekly column in *La Stampa* called 'Il nostro stato' ('Our state'). He was murdered by the BR in 1977. Civilian deaths account for 270 of the total – people hurrying to or from jobs, having a *panino*, waiting for a train. And, as the number of victims rose, people of a certain age sensed that they had been here before, that some people would live and die by the green flag, and others by the red. Or by the black. And that there were infinite shades of each. To them, the *piombo* was also the leaden feeling, the weight of history that pulled them back to a country they thought they had left behind.

The BR, the group famous for the kidnap and murder in 1978 of Aldo Moro, leader of the Christian Democrats and responsible for an historic 'alliance' with the Communist Party, evoked that violent past in the name they chose for themselves: a nod to the Communist *partigiani* who, wearing red neckerchiefs, had fought under the name of Garibaldi. And who, in February 1945, at Porzûs in the foothills of the eastern Alps, had massacred the mostly Christian men of the *brigate* Osoppo because they failed to toe the line and fight alongside Josip Broz Tito's Yugoslav partisans. The Osoppo's homely – or isolationist? – Friulian motto, *Pai nestris fogolârs*, 'For our hearths', was at odds with Communism's borderless vision. Side by side, the two *brigate* had defeated the Wehrmacht and the Fascists, only to turn on each other over the question of which Italy it was, exactly, that they were fighting for. Some years before the BR killed him, Casalegno had referred to this period of existential conflict as a second Risorgimento.

In 1992, one of the founders of the BR, Alberto Franceschini, was released after almost two decades in prison for a string of bombings and kidnappings. The group had disbanded acrimoniously four years earlier because of schisms, stings, mass arrests and people singing like birds. But we would never be without the BR, Franceschini now said, because there had never been 'a funeral'. No reckoning, no wake; the body was still warm, in fact, breathing, and there were countless stories still to tell.

Shortly after 8 a.m. on 20 May 1999, in a nondescript Roman street, a group called the Nuove Brigate Rosse, the New Red Brigades, announced its presence with the murder of Massimo D'Antona, a scholar and consultant working with the Ministry of Labour on national reforms to the workforce. They shot him at point-blank range, nine times. Or, as the group put it in the missive that followed: a decisive blow was levelled at a 'central knot' in the 'neo-corporate political project'; the *brigate* are back to challenge the 'imperialism' of the central powers and bring about the 'dictatorship of the proletariat'. The language was borrowed from another time, familiar to some, but new and exciting to others.

A handful of incidents followed. In March 2002, the labour lawyer Marco Biagi was gunned down in central Bologna, a stone's throw from the shop on via Zamboni, where Angelo spent the summer of 1917. A year later came a deadly shoot-out between the police and members of the group, on a train travelling from Rome to Florence. Soon after were arrests, the usual telling of tales, high-profile court cases; finally, long sentences. And then an uneasy silence, like the instinctive holding of breath while feeling for someone's pulse.

The past doesn't stay in the past; the fever has broken, but it may not have left us entirely. Temporary recovery is not recovery proper, and without something as neat as death to round off the story, we can't know which one it is. In the meantime, it might look as though people have forgotten what they were like, those years of fear, tragedy and waste, but it's bound and weighted inside them. They simply aren't remembering daily. How could they?

'Do you remember all that? How it was to be in Italy, then?' I ask Nonna one day, during our *appuntamento*.

'Eh, si, come no?' ('Of course' – or, literally, 'How

not?', an infinitely more complicated question.)

'Tell me?' (Where would she even begin?)

'You can imagine.' (I can't.)

The conversation ends.

Part of the problem is that there is no collective memory of the *anni di piombo* – no one can be quite sure what to remember, nor who or what is to blame. Who fought the good fight and who the bad. No official historical account exists; there has been no process of truth and reconciliation. Theories and counter-theories abound. Judicial processes are tortuous, liable to fall apart, marred by civic mistrust. The state maintains the right to preserve in secrecy any item whose dissemination risks undermining the integrity of Italian democracy, so the actions – whether honourable or nefarious – of those in power during the *anni di piombo* are protected from the scrutinizing eyes of historians, the media and regular citizens. In late 2020, as the pandemic raged and the administration faltered, the confidentiality afforded to certain documents considered central to the story was extended until 2029. Secrecy breeds uncertainty, so whatever truths arise in the meantime can only appear naive and fragile, like towers built on sand.

The older people mostly fall silent; prefer to talk of other things. And the younger ones hear snatches of stories now and again, catch the tail end of a trial that started years before we were born, and scour the internet for accounts that resonate with how we see things, and how we feel. We have to link things together again somehow because the generational chain corrodes easily; it turns to powder and washes away.

*

In August 2015, a square was named for Aldo Moro and a monument erected in his honour in Terracina, just south of Latina, Moro's habitual holiday destination. Residents remember him strolling along the seafront, ducking into a nearby church to say a prayer and light a candle, while his security detail hung back to allow him a little freedom. Almost forty years after his murder by the BR, an imposing block of smooth metal, the colour, fittingly, of lead, was placed along the promenade. The surface was stamped with the statesman's words in silver, like a tombstone wide enough for an extended family:

Questo Paese non si salverà, la stagione dei diritti e delle libertà si rivelerà effimera, se in Italia non nascerà un nuovo senso del dovere.

'This country will not save itself, the season of rights and freedoms will prove ephemeral, if a new sense of duty is not born in Italy.'

Within weeks, the monument had started to rust. Red rubbed off on your fingers. Some residents began to complain about this eyesore. The case was not helped by orthographical errors – the 'p' of 'Paese' and the 'i' of 'Italia' were erroneously, insultingly, lowercased. A petition for the memorial's removal circulated with signatories citing, on the one hand, a missed opportunity – 'a grave offence to the memory of one of the greatest Italian men' – and, on the other, a resistance to remembering Moro at all ('Of all the many names we could have given to the square, did they really have to choose Aldo Moro? Why not Piazzale Galilei?'); for others still, it smacked of heavy-handed outside intervention in local affairs: 'Piazzale Lido is in front of the Lido, so let's call it what everyone calls it.'

The monument was telling its own story now.

A few years later, another monument to Moro, tombstone-like again, was erected in Rome on the site of his abduction. On its light sandy stone Moro's name is joined by those of the five members of his police escort killed in the attempt to protect him. A hearth-like semi-circular area in front is divided into six triangles – like pizza slices, I can't help but think – each supposedly representing one of the lives here remembered. Bollards are placed around the edge, protecting, pre-empting.

At the grand unveiling, President Sergio Mattarrella, whose father Bernardo, an anti-fascist, co-founded the Christian Democratic party in 1943, stepped forward alone to face the monument. He reached out, as if instinctively, to touch the *tricolore* draped across it, like a parent fastidiously smoothing a child's collar. A few days later, sometime after midnight, the letters 'BR' were daubed in bright red on the pale stone.

*

A story on the radio the other day: a species of bird in Australia, the regent honeyeater, is threatened with extinction because its numbers have dropped so low that it neither recognizes nor knows how to sing its own song. It simply doesn't hear it often enough; there's no opportunity to learn. Instead, it copies the calls of other more populous birds, but none of these are suitable mates. The situation is desperate. A project has been launched. Regent honeyeaters in captivity are played recordings of the song, in a language school of sorts. 'This species,' the radio presenter said, has 'forgotten it's song.' But as individuals, they never knew it in the first place.

*

On the morning of 2 August 1980, Bologna's central

train station, one of the country's biggest interchanges, was heaving with people. It was the first weekend of the summer holidays and the exodus towards the coast had begun. More people than usual were packed into the waiting room, grateful for the air conditioning, when a bomb was detonated with such force that much of the west wing of the building was reduced to rubble in an instant. The façade rippled down to the ground like a velvet curtain. Eighty-five people were killed, and at least 200 injured. (My parents must have read about it in the British newspapers, although they have no memory of this.)

The city's courts had just indicted a group of neo-fascists, members of the Ordine Nero, for a deadly attack six years earlier on the Italicus Express train between Florence and Bologna. The same group was almost immediately blamed for this latest attack. It seemed a clear act of retribution, or, as the prime minister Francesco Cossiga put it far more broadly, in a statement he later retracted: evidence of a ruthless 'right-wing matrix'. The full story of the *strage di Bologna* is still struggling towards the light, forty years later – a most Italian tale of intrigue, misdirection, corruption and violence, apparently involving Nar operatives, the Italian secret service, Palestinian terrorists, fixers, financiers and the infamous P2, a rogue masonic lodge. Ill-equipped as I am, I will leave this story to the brave researchers, journalists and activists driving at the truth.

The story I want to tell instead is that of a clock, which protrudes from the wall outside Bologna's station. Its story is well known, but also not really. On 2 August, this clock was frozen at 10.25, the moment in which the explosion tore through the building. The clockface cracked and shards came loose, wedging themselves behind the minute hand and jamming the mechanism. Photographs and news footage taken in the hours that followed, while bodies were being extracted from the detritus, laid out, placed in bags and organized on buses to be taken away, all capture that clock: its black hands, at 10 and 25, cleaving the white face in two, unblinking above the scene – an instant symbol.

The clock remained motionless, apparently forever more, until, in 2001, around the time of the anniversary of the massacre, Ferrovie dello Stato Italiane, the state-owned group responsible for rail infrastructure and services, carried out 'routine maintenance'. Just like that, some unnamed employee nudged the clock's hands back into play – imagine a hollow clunk as the minute hand lurches forwards for the first time in decades – thus 'discarding it as a symbol', the journalist Michele Serra wrote in *La Repubblica*, 'and remaking it a clock'.

There was outrage, from members of the public, relatives of those killed or maimed by this bomb and others, and the local press. Bologna mourned the loss of its monument to the *anni di piombo*. As Serra pointed out – sensitively, insistently – people didn't know the full story. They thought they did, they were convinced of it, even; but memory had taken on a life of its own.

In 1980, in the days after the blast, Serra said, when the site was being cleared, the clock had been fixed and returned to the time of the living. Of course it had; this was a working station, one of the busiest in Italy, and life went on. But 'In the collective and personal memories of the citizens of Bologna,' he said, 'that clock had never restarted since the day of the massacre.' An 'artefact of memory' had been created, an ammonite of feeling.

This process by which something-that-was-not became something-that-was – because people had *seen* it with their own eyes – was aided by images taken in the immediate aftermath of the attack, photograph after photograph compounding the clock's stillness, images reproduced innumerable times the world over. And, later, by the fact that the hands were stopped and repositioned at 10.25 every year on 2 August, while a commemorative service took place. More images were added on a yearly basis, like photographs of photographs, memories of memories, small stones piled on top of each other with a cumulative weight that renders the whole thing immovable.

Only at some point in the mid-1990s, when the clock came to a halt for some unknown reason, was the clock frozen intentionally, following the suggestion of the victims' families that it would make a suitable memorial. Some commuters complained and tourists missed their connections, but this was now Bologna's monument, a monument whose proud presence, it seems, had been assumed all along. In 2001, then, the people of Bologna were confronted with a false floor in their minds.

Next came the question of how to move forward, because things could not be exactly as they had been – not now that people knew. It was decided that someone, a man – who knows who apart from he? – should snip the cable, or pull the plug, so that time stood still again, giving us back the story we wanted. But the symbol had to be different somehow, so it was self-consciously explained: a glass plate was positioned beside the clock, declaring: 'This clock marks 10.25 on 2 August 1980. The time of the *strage di Bologna*. So as not to forget.' In the very act of remembering, people could now forget the stop-start story of a great forgetting. The intricacies of the past will be tidied to tell a better tale. The clock is memory itself, writ small.

A clock that doesn't tell the time inevitably recedes into

the background. People rush past without so much as a glance. The ghostly face exists on a separate plain now, suspended above the buzz of day-to-day life. Although it tells the right time twice a day, it is apparently useless except, perhaps, as a place for people to come together. Travellers can find each other beneath its blank expression, on a spot poised between the chaos of the main station concourse and the medieval maze of the city.

This clock tells you nothing, really, unless you make a leap – leaving the safety of your mother tongue behind for a somnambulant language of symbols – and admit that, like the white orb of the dandelion blown apart by your breath, it's not the time you're looking for, but something else. The opposite in fact: to dissolve the borders between past, present and future entirely, for a brief moment. To find a point of communion between then and now, them and us. Like when blowing a dandelion – once, twice, considering the thing and throwing it to the ground, obliquely satisfied – we feel ourselves taking part in an experience shared down the ages, unchanged.

And, so, then you look again, and Bologna's clock becomes the soft white sphere of a mature dandelion, or the mouth of a tunnel of light that drops you through time. Or an enigmatic form of punctuation, like an asterisk suspended – * – poised between rows of neatly ordered words, brightly signalling an omission or an explanation or appending some incidental detail from another story, which relates, somehow: a silent explosion – a Violet Gibson, a Liala, a Giuseppina Raimondi, a Novella – that might blast the structure to pieces.

VIII.

I have been here before, scouring the overgrown grass, as I am now, stopping at regular intervals, bending, squinting and moving on. Last time, fifteen years ago, I couldn't find what I was looking for. Then, it was winter and the light was fading, which made it harder, as did the tears I allowed to cloud my vision. An indulgence. Now, it's spring and I'm focused, methodical. I walk left to right, then top to bottom. I have enlisted the help of my husband and we're both bobbing and weaving between tombstones, searching, occasionally calling out to each other. 'This one's Italian! (But it's not him)'; 'Look for two cement urns and a plant pot in a terrazzo-y style (Nonno made them)'; 'I've done that corner three times, don't bother'; 'Irish here! And a Pole!' The only other sounds are a distant strimmer and a blackbird I can't see, though I know she's close. There is nobody else around. We have a rough map and a new sense of urgency: I can't leave until I've found Angelo, in the grave he shares with Old Pietro and Anthony, the grandson he never met. I've promised Nonna, and myself. I'm carrying a plastic bag full of flowers.

For weeks we've jokingly referred to this trip to Sheffield as a pilgrimage, but, in all seriousness, I don't know what other word would do. I am travelling into lands unknown, a foreigner in search of who knows what precisely. I've been anxious, worried that I won't be up to the task. I've checked and checked again the grave's reference number, printed off a copy of the map, marked in red pen the route from the main gate to the plot, and placed it in a plastic sleeve. And I've been secretly hoping for some kind of return on this investment – a modest revelation, a sign of divine approval, some sense of welcome, at least.

Ah, you're here at last – come, let us show you why you've both-ered to think of us all this time.

What I eventually find is a collection of stones, black-ened and in disarray, the scattered shards of various vessels, completely rusted, with moss in shades of blue, yellow, green and orange clumping around the pieces as if about to swallow them. It looks like the bottom of the sea.

I walked past several times without seeing it. I had been expecting something upright, that the tombstone would face me and immediately offer its vitals: name, date of birth, date of death. I had been reading the tombstones like words in a sentence and not contemplating the gaps that punctuated them, the deep green silences between. But that's where Angelo lies. His tombstone is flat on its back, tickled by tall grasses, staring up at the clouds. I crane over it, overlaying his body with mine, to read the inscription. I'm surprised to find myself mouthing Italian words.

S--UTTO, PIETRO
N. 13 DICEMBRE 1864, M. 1 OTTOBRE 1931
RIPOSA, O PADRE, NELLA PACE DELL SIGNORE
PURE,
IL FIGLIO ANGELO,
N. 2 APRILE 1902, M. 19 DICEMBRE 1935
R. I. P.

On the left-hand side in small lettering is written 'I FIGLI POSERO' ('placed by the children') and on the right, 'MOGLIE & FIGLI POSERO' ('placed by wife and children'). Old Pietro, aged sixty-six (not so old), put here first; followed four years later by Angelo, thirty-three, the son who had buried him. 'R.I.P.', a rare moment when the Italian, 'Riposa In Pace', coincides exactly with the

English, 'Rest In Peace'. I bend down and press my palm flat against the coarse mottled stone, which feels warm, even though it's a sunless day in one of the coldest British springs on record.

I translate 'posero' literally, awkwardly, as 'placed', where a proper translation would be 'laid'. I like how 'placed' suggests some kind of process by which a person becomes a distinct location, a patch of earth with qualities all its own – the body dissolves, I guess, suffusing the soil and the air all around. A microclimate of feeling, something like *terroir*. It seems less ridiculous than the idea of flesh and blood becoming bread and wine.

Angelo has been placed, then: this place, where I am now standing, is him. He is a destination. I breathe him in and start to cry.

*

'And the book?'

'*Si, si*, it's coming along...'

'Who knows if I'll be here to read it when it arrives.'

'Don't be silly, of course you will.' (*Tocca ferro*, touch wood.)

These days, every conversation between us contains this exchange, a central knot in which Nonna's slow acceptance wraps around my determined denial. It dawned on me the other day the extent to which my writing has been hers, part of a great unburdening, the spring clean of a lifetime; that whatever amassing I have done has been possible only because she has willingly relinquished her memories, like so many old clothes, which she no longer has need for. And if she gets lighter and lighter, what happens? The thought makes me want to call the whole thing off, to give it all back and keep her weighted, exactly where she is.

'You'll find me much shorter', Nonna said the other day, when I suggested that a trip to see her might by possible (*tocca ferro*, touch wood) by late summer. 'I'm shrinking!'

And yet to me she seems larger every day.

It's odd that the elderly grow smaller (a perfect oxymoron), as if they are receding into the distance without moving an inch. A trick of perspective, that hints at the truth: that Nonna has one foot on the bridge already but hasn't quite done with this world yet.

She's made similar crossings before – four times, in the back and forth between Italy and England, where each arrival marked a life after life, a self undone and with hope remade. Each time, looking out of the bedroom window at red terraced houses or row on row of green husks, she acknowledged that this place, with these people, was and wasn't where she was supposed to be. Maybe this accounts for her calm demeanour, the casualness with which she refers to 'l'ultimo viaggio', the final trip. The others were rehearsals.

Her name fits her better than I thought: Dirce, 'cleft' and 'dual', the space in between as well as the divided poles themselves; neither and both; absence and emphatic presence.

*

In my childhood bedroom, there was a shelf above my bed, in quite a strange position, I now realize – exactly halfway along the length of the bed and too high to be reached without kneeling up on the mattress. This shelf was where I put my most treasured possessions: a collection of small plastic dogs of various breeds, a peacock feather from an English country house, my tape player, a long-legged brass horse I considered the definition of elegance. After Nonno's death, I added a framed photograph of him in his work shirt, a poor-quality reprint of the one Nonna has in her kitchen. Not long after that, I added a plastic statuette of the Virgin Mary, which Nonna bought for me when she visited Lourdes with the Church. Mary glowed in the dark and if you unscrewed her bright blue crown, you could tip out the Holy Water that filled her body. This I did only on special occasions, the night before school exams, or if I was especially scared of demons in the middle of the night.

Special occasions included the birthdays and death days of relatives, when my usual prayer repertoire – the Lord's Prayer followed by a Hail Mary and then a free-wheeling monologue directed at departed loved ones ('Aunty Joan, I thought of you today because a woman on the bus had the same hair as you') – were extended into special editions in which I would focus on that one person, enumerating the things I missed about them and the occasions I remembered most fondly. Prayers were delivered kneeling up on the bed, facing my eclectic shrine, the mattress springs niggling my kneecaps, and rounded off by crossing myself with dabs of holy water.

By the time Nonno died, when I was nearly thirteen, I was beginning to doubt God's existence. Nothing had happened, there was no sense of betrayal or great disillusionment. I knew my sister didn't believe in God anymore because she said so loudly, refusing to come to Church with the rest of us, and I remember a vague, creeping embarrassment about protesting that, *actually*, God *is* real. The prayers became sporadic, one night on, a few nights off, to satisfy the warring sides of me (and hedge my bets). The guilt was constant – of course – which implies that I never really stopped thinking He was there, shaking

His head, watching me waver, feeling disappointed (or, Disappointed).

The threat of eternal damnation leaves quite a strong impression, but it was always more the Devil's intrusion into *this* life that frightened me into prayer, the thought of the sinister army of ghosts I believed he commanded, rising through my bedroom floor to get me. Hence the need for a counter offensive of angels. Long after the Lord's Prayer and the Hail Marys ceased, I kept talking to my dead – I cut God out and went direct, appealing to them for protection, summoning a benign entourage of familiars.

The list grew longer – not so much because people kept dying as because I started to collect relatives I had never met but only heard about from others, notably Nonna and my English grandparents, who knew so many dead people between them. Angelo was swiftly recruited, as was Julia, my maternal great-grandmother, who everyone agreed was an especially kind sort. By this time, my dad had admitted, after various inquisitions, that, no, he did not pray or think about our dead especially regularly, so I knew it was up to me to keep the good ghosts interested in us. ('Good' they undoubtedly were because they were family.)

Over the years the exigency dwindled and almost disappeared. I don't speak to dead relatives anymore. But if I can't sleep or if demons are circling, when others might count sheep I run through my list of names and, one by one, try to imagine faces, to see clearly the texture of their skin and the colour of their eyes. Old Pietro has started to feature only recently, with his impressive moustache. And Novella, sometimes, with her eyes the colour of space.

The religious trinkets and votive cards, meanwhile,

which Nonna continues to disseminate – miniature laminated portraits of Padre Pio, Our Lady of Lourdes in her grotto, St Anthony clutching white lilies – no longer sit in prominence on a bedroom shelf, but rather secrete themselves in handbags, purses and the car's glove compartment, fragments of faith that follow me everywhere. Their original significance has long been displaced. Now they mean purely because of all that Nonna means.

*

In 2009, the skeleton of a sixteenth-century woman was discovered on Lazzaretto, a small island in Venice Lagoon where plague sufferers were once quarantined. Her jaw was open unnaturally wide, to accommodate a brick. This was to stop her rising again to exhale pestilence and fill her filthy lungs with the life of those around her. She was, her buriers thought, the plague personified: a vampire.

Some years later, on the border between Umbria and Lazio, a ten-year-old child was unearthed, from the fifth century, when the area was marshy and mephitic. A tooth abscess suggests malaria as the cause of death; the rock wedged posthumously down his throat was intended to prevent him returning to contaminate the living. Scattered all about him were ritual remains – toad bones, the talons of large birds, and broken vessels spilling the ashes of sacrificial dogs.

Countless bodies have been uncovered in a similar state, with limbs bound and weighted with rocks, or with the sharp curve of a sickle blade pressed against the neck, or with the head removed and placed between the legs – so many signs of the determination of the living to guard against the transgression of the dead. Those who return

270

haunt, curse and plague. They are uncontained and, perhaps, uncontainable. Matter out of place. They want something from us and will torment us for it. At what point did this fear of marauding vampires overwhelm our desire for angels, for good spirit-travellers at our side?

Few are the cultures that warmly welcome the dead among the living, that request the presence of lost relatives by, say, setting a place for them at the dinner table. These revenants are defined by what they bring to the gathering, rather than what they might take. Carlo Ginzburg, in his writing on the *benandanti*, quotes Anna la Rossa, a sixteenth-century Friulian woman, who told neighbours that she conversed with the dead. 'On Fridays and Saturdays,' Anna explained, 'beds had to be made early, because on those days the dead would return exhausted' – exhausted, that is, from warring with the malign forces – 'and throw themselves on the beds in their own houses.' The living were grateful. Meals were prepared to fortify the wanderers; plenty of rest was needed before the next battle.

We see echoes of this, Ginzburg says, on 2 November, All Souls' Day, when great processions wend through towns, as the living remember their dead and embody their journeying souls. 'The deceased pass through the town in long processions, carrying candles, and re-enter their former homes where the charity of the living has placed food, drink and clean beds at their disposal.' The matter-of-factness thrills me – 'The deceased pass through the town' – the readiness with which the historian slips from the figurative to the real.

*

When it became clear that Nonna and I would spend

271

another Easter apart, I dug out an old shoebox and filled it with the things I would have taken but now had to post. Good British paracetamol, loose leaf tea, ginger nuts, hot cross buns. I wrote a card telling everyone how much I missed them, that I'd be there as soon as I was allowed, and that they would have to put some of Nonna's *tiramisù* in the freezer till then. I plucked the only sign of spring I could find in the garden – a slightly battered crocus – and pressed it into the card.

Easter is our Christmas, the time of year when the family comes together, and every year is different and yet the same. On the Sunday, *zia* Lucia, who does the main share of the festive cooking these days, impresses everyone with a selection of delicate starters inspired by a glossy magazine; then, there's the perfunctory lamb, sometimes pink and succulent, other times in some thick, golden *sugo* that creeps across the plate like lava. Various side dishes do the rounds. Everyone talks at once, about the food foremost, and later, as the wine takes effect, work, politics, plans and projects, and shares stories we've all heard hundreds of times.

Once the plates have been cleared by *i ragazzi*, the 'kids' (anyone below fifty), a respectful lull is punctuated by the miraculous return of the lamb, with his gangly legs tucked up to one side and his face serene. Ready to go again. His flesh is of pale yellow, his skin slightly crisped by the oven. His eyes are blank almonds. He is cake. He is symbol. We cut him into slices to be passed around the table and ignored while various *grappe* are introduced, lined up like eager volunteers and neatly poured into miniature tumblers. A rallying sip, before the final excesses.

The next day's meal will be a far simpler affair: reheated *rimasugli*, assorted leftovers, supplemented by fresh steaming polenta and a large bowl of wilted dandelions, glistening in salty oil, followed by *tiramisù*, the region's most famous desert of whipped, eggy mascarpone and *Savoiardi* biscuits, steeped in coffee and marsala wine. Nonna will have mentioned it several times during the meal, to make sure we all leave room for its soupy layers.

Tiramisù, the trifle's Italian cousin, stalwart of Italian restaurants the world over. The name – 'tira mi sù' – pull- or pick-me-up – is a statement of intent. As long as *si tira avanti* there will be *tiramisù*. As children we adored it, but the measure of marsala increased steadily as we grew, and I have never told Nonna that I don't like it anymore. I can't contemplate a world in which she no longer makes it. The ritual is indispensable; the symbolic value has eclipsed the thing itself. I crave the repetition, the knowledge that every year something in each of us will be reawakened as Nonna stands and scoops it onto her ancient saucers. As her spoon cuts through layers of space and time, we become children again, our memories as soft and heady as the booze-soaked sponge. We reach a higher plain: we are archetypes. A *nonna*, totem-like, surrounded by her devoted *ragazzi*.

(All this over, quite literally, a trifle – but how else do most of us experience history if not in the presence or absence of small things? A shortage of pasta and toilet roll, or the disappearance of Spanish lemons and cucumbers.)

The *nonna* is imbued with time-travelling powers. She is a passport to foreign centuries. She collapses eras. The word itself, Latin, mimics a baby's first attempts at speech, and, because there is no alternative word – no sentiment-free equivalent, as *madre* is to *mamma* – whether you're one or 100, you can only ever refer to this woman as 'nonna'. One word and you slip back into your childhood self, a previous you, assumed dead and buried under the weight of adulthood. The word – inflexible, primordial – is forcefully rejuvenating. (Which is good: pre-made sauces, soups and cakes trade on the idea, affixing *della nonna* as a byword for timeless purity, authenticity, things as they once were.) These grey-haired ladies, the mothers of our mothers and fathers, are workers of minor miracles. Resurrection is all around them, almost to the point of banality. ('Every morning for me is a resurrection,' Nonna once joked, in a rare moment of sacrilege.) In early medieval times, *nonna* became a respectful way of referring to pious women, which is where we get the English word 'nun': a wise woman who bridges the gap between Earth and the Celestial Realm.

It's hardly surprising that I should have placed Nonna at the centre of my ramshackle secular cosmos. When I go with her to Mass, I go purely to sit beside her in a perfect circle of gladness: she is glad to think I have welcomed God back in (He will be Glad, she thinks); I am glad that she is glad. I feel cleansed, refreshed. An hour in her presence, drifting in and out of her chatter, tasting her food, squeezing her huge soft hands, looking at whatever family relic she has excavated to show me – a wedding ring, a single clog, a peeling photograph, the hair of a lost brother – reassures me more than any other thing or person can. 'This is the place,' I think, as I sit in reverie.

The older I get and the longer I am away from her, from Italy, the more intense my need, the more I idealize her. The more aware I am of all I stand to lose: an opening into the ineffable. This last year, when I have been unable to sleep, I have sometimes crept downstairs to the sofa and curled up around my laptop, to listen to recordings of our conversations. I see the scene as if from outside: a dark room, my face alone glowing in the white of the screen, my eyes growing heavier. A study in tenebrism. And when she calls me *nina*, I fall back and sail through

274

the night, enchanted.

I have made of this ninety-five-year-old woman a repository for so much that I can't fathom let alone articulate. In her kitchen, I have built a vast and comical store of memories and hopes, expressions and feelings, which sit cheek by jowl with inchoate ideas about who I am and where I come from, about what it means to be from here (and from her). Like her TV cupboard full of votive candles, British paracetamol and stale biscuits, there is a logic, but it won't bear outside scrutiny. I try not to examine it too closely in case it brings everything tumbling down around me. I worry about where I'll put it all when she leaves. Or will she be taking most of it with her? And will I be able to call her back, to find it again?

*

The word 'homecoming' has always perplexed me. In Italian we have only 'ritornando', 'returning', as though nothing has changed – neither place nor person – in the interim. 'Returning' is wishful thinking, a romance in which every character has one true and rightful place. 'Homecoming' is accurate precisely because it doesn't quite land. Why isn't it home*going*? 'Home*coming*' suggests, to me, that you, the traveller, are being watched from that longed-for point of arrival, that there is someone already there, who has, perhaps, been there all along, willing you back. It is them you are coming for. Would that make them – the person already at home – the narrator of your journey? The perspective splits between two points; someone else is invested in the passage.

Or perhaps both of them are you, and you are, in fact, in the two places simultaneously: away, but coming back to yourself; one you seeking the other you, like the soul of the *benandante* slipping in through the mouth of its sleeping body. And then, you hope, life begins again, only more harmonious than before.

*

'I have been thinking a lot about the grave,' I tell Nonna on the phone. (I have called to let her know the flights are booked; I'll be coming in August.) I tell her I found it very moving to be where Pietro, Angelo and the baby are.

'Mio *papà* morirà quando muoio io,' she says, abruptly. 'My father will die when I die.' She seems almost possessive.

'I'm trying to keep him alive!' I say, feeling – what? – wounded?

'Then' – soft again, generous – 'you'll be the only person who remembers him.'

And yet I never knew him.

'When I see you in August, I'll tell you all these stories that have come back to me,' she says. 'My memory seems to be flourishing again in these weeks, I don't know why. I'll tell you them all. You can keep them when I'm gone.'

But I have not called to talk about Angelo today.

'I've been thinking about the grave, about all that blank space,' I say, 'where your baby's name should be.'

I see it clearly in my mind:

S--UTTO, PIETRO
N. 13 DICEMBRE 1864, M. 1 OTTOBRE 1931
RIPOSA, O PADRE, NELLA PACE DELL SIGNORE
PURE,
IL FIGLIO ANGELO,
N. 2 APRILE 1902, M. 19 DICEMBRE 1935
R. I. P.

– and all that emptiness beneath, room enough for another soul to be cut authoritatively into the stone. Instead, there is uncertainty: Where is everyone else? Why aren't the wives buried here? Where are the children? It's as though the family ended in 1935 – ran out, or stopped running.

'Did you not feel angry...'

'No...'

'... or disappointed...'

'No, no...'

'... that your religion...'

'No, no ...'

'... was so cruel that...'

'No, nina, ascolta –' Listen.

I give up trying to ask the question I want to ask and let her answer the question she imagines instead.

'When my baby was born he was... they have a word in England ... *Il mio bimbo era... era...*'

I wait while she searches her personal dictionary.

'...*era un* "stillborn". That is the word they use.'

I know this, of course. As I know that Italian has only the verbal phrase 'è nato morto' – 'he was born dead' – and that it's English that provides us with a noun – 'è un stillborn' – that make him a thing, not a baby who was born dead, but a different category altogether. How strange it must feel to be carrying something inside you that has been so othered, while, to you, he is an extension of your very being.

'When I was in labour, I was so scared to see him,' Nonna says, 'because I thought he would be black like bad liver, deformed – you have these ideas – and the nurses said – because a few times, just after, I thought I should see him – "oh, no, it's a terrible thing, to see a stillborn" and so, in the end I said I didn't want to.' And so she never did.

That night she was overcome by 'una febbre tremenda', a tremendous fever, when – she was told, because she has no memory of those hours – she shook the bed and screamed 'basta, basta', and they thought she was calling the baby a bastard.

The next morning, the parish priest, appeared at her bedside.

'What did he say? What did you talk about?' I ask.

'He was very kind – he knew me well – and he said he would take care of things, that he would take the baby to *papà* – that he would do this for us.'

When the priest left, he took the baby with him, and the next day, while Nonna was in hospital, a small service was held at St Robert's on Hamilton Road – just Leo and *i ragazzi* (the boys), Novella, a few of Nonna's closest friends. The baby was blessed – 'una cosa rara', a rare thing – and then driven to Sheffield to be placed with Angelo. 'And the priest didn't accept any money for it.' *Una cosa rara.*

'*Perché quei bambini lì*' – because those babies there – 'were not allowed to be buried in sacred ground, you know. They used to bury them outside the cemetery walls, or, even, the hospital would bury them, somewhere.'

I know this, too. 'That's my point,' I say. 'Didn't it, I don't know, pain you, that your faith didn't technically allow...'

'No, no, nina, ascolta: I knew he was dead before I gave birth to him and I knew that this was Il Signore's challenge to me, so I prayed and I prayed – because I wanted to save my other children, *capisci*? – and I knew that Il Signore had taken my baby to test me.'

The narrative makes no sense to me, but I think about how similar are the words 'sacred', 'scared' and 'scarred'.

'And I always knew that it was *mio padre* who had

taken my baby, and that he held him in his arms because he wanted a piece of me, and then he brought me Lucia, a gift.' And Lucia, too, is 'una cosa rara', her magic far stronger than that of flesh and blood. 'Capisci?'

It's difficult by now to make out whether she is talking about her padre or *the* Padre, her father or the Father. It doesn't seem to matter.

After the burial, Leo came back to the hospital and gave Nonna the order of service, along with the under-taker's receipt for the small white coffin, some flowers and a few other things. She kept these scraps of paper for decades.

'They were all I had of my baby, the only proof of him I had.'

'And now, where are they?'

'I burnt them some years back. I was getting old and, I thought, these aren't things to leave lying around the house.'

'But so, if I said to you now, "Let's inscribe the tomb with his name..."'

'Perché?' Why?

'Because then you'd have proof that Anthony was here...'

This whole time we have not used his name.

'Perché?'

'Because he deserves to be noted, to be registered, *o no*?' Or not? As if a tombstone were some kind of receipt given by God to the living, a record of services rendered, and payments made.

'Ma a cosa serve scriverlo?' What's the point in writing it. 'Cosa farebbe?' What would it do. 'Sono solo parole.' They are only words.

'Ma Nonna, everything is just words – every romanzo you've ever read is just words, this book I'm writing is just words – but words matter, *o no*?' I hear my own desperation. 'They make us feel... better.'

'Si, OK, but I know he is there, I know he is in the arms of mio papà, I feel it, I always have.'

There is a divide here between two different forms of knowledge, two different ways of recording events and experiences, and the one is almost incomprehensible to the other. Their values are incomparable. One exists inside a person, like the knots and rings of a tree; the other is made of words, placed outside for others to see.

On the tombstone, between Old Pietro's name and dates and those of Angelo, there is an extra word. It has been there all along, hiding in plain sight: 'PURE', Italian for 'also'. It is only one word, but it's a good one. It lives in both languages, albeit differently. Let's lend it to Anthony. A secret compromise.

*

A home truth is a fact that you have ignored or concealed from yourself. Sometimes someone confronts you with it and sometimes you admit it to yourself. Generally, there is something difficult and unsettling about this truth. In that respect, home truths are, perhaps, related to personal demons. The idea is that, in spite of the bitterness, the truth will make you stronger in the long term. Like facing up to those demons.

When I began this book, on the first page of a new notebook, I wrote, in my neatest italic hand:

'The growing good of the world is partly dependent on unhistoric acts; and that things are not so ill with you and me as they might have been, is half owing to the number who lived faithfully a hidden life, and rest in unvisited tombs.' — *George Eliot*

It is an embarrassing cliché, but it captured something

of the spirit I thought, then, was animating me: a desire to bear witness to relatives who had left no apparent marks on the world, whose fragile lives were carried aloft and deposited here or there, in this country or that, by events mostly beyond their control. I wanted to show them (in a manner of speaking) what came of it all and that we are still going back and forth between Italy and England, because of them, and that things were, in many ways, for this family at least, less ill. *Better*. I thought, in short, that my dead needed me to remember them and tell their stories, to try to work out who they were and what challenges they faced. Really, it is I who need them.

An inversion has occurred: a living person is haunting the dead, clinging to them, calling them back and asking them to stay a little longer, to explain themselves and to be a part of this story she is trying to figure out. Because without them it can't be told or doesn't seem worth it. Without them, the bridges she is crossing, losing some things and finding others, make little sense. The abutments subside and the arches cave in and are washed away, leaving only feelings and questions. Like, what does it mean to miss a country? A whole country! Is it even possible? And to miss the sound of a language around you and the feel of it in your mouth? And to note the way your posture changes as you reach the other side and feel like a different person. And, if you rarely speak your language, what part of you is being silenced and, maybe, lost? And, what does it mean to nourish one culture over another: what does that do to you? How easy is it to undo that choice, to flick the switch the other way? And does your claim on a country – your right to love it and to hate it, and to say so – corrode the longer you make your life elsewhere (because it seemed easier)? How is it that a person who has never lived in the Friuli, who cannot speak that region's language, can say – moved by a few too many *grappe* – that she feels 'friulana, nel midollo', in her very marrow?

Our word 'haunt' migrated from the French 'hanter', bringing with it the idea of frequency, of ritual returning to a particular place. It is unclear at what point it came to be the habit of ghosts, let alone sinister ones. Associations with obsession and indulgent cultivation seem to have got lost somewhere in the crossing, as did a much earlier Germanic link, which binds the word to 'home'. It makes sense to me, this earlier idea of haunting, of compulsive homecoming: a circling back to people and places, tending to them like rare seedlings.

*

Beyond the wall of Sheffield's City Road Cemetery is a house whose top floor – the bedrooms, I guess – overlooks the plot were Old Pietro, Angelo and Anthony lie. I wonder if the people who live there have ever come inside to see who, in a manner of speaking, lives here.

They might wonder at the foreign language on the tombstone, at the expanse of unclaimed space. What were these men, Pietro and Angelo, doing here? (Would they gather that they are father and son?) How did they lose their lives, so far from home? (They probably would not imagine that this place, too, was home.) About Anthony, they would have no idea at all.

It seems unlikely that they would come here, though. Every day when they draw their curtains, they see this grey grave – one among so many that look pretty much the same from a distance – and don't register its meaning. How could they acknowledge daily that for every marker of stone and soil there was once body and character and feeling. And that we, the family, who do not see the grave,

282

think of it often, this patch of nondescript ground on the other side of their wall, and feel its presence hundreds of miles away.

As my husband and I walked towards the cemetery gates, I texted a few photographs of the grave to *zia* Lucia, to show Nonna. ('Send photos!!! ☺' Lucia had said.) I had been careful to tidy up the place before taking them, in the way one does the house before company. I didn't want Nonna to see how shabby it had become, with no one to watch over it. The headstone was too heavy to lift even between the two of us, but we managed to straighten it out a little, to kick the corners of the border back into position and sit Nonno's cement urns upright again. It looked better.

Between the headstone and the mossy flat of the grave, I wedged the stems of the flowers, tightly, in case of wind. They are a bunch of red and white chrysanthemums, with wide green leaves, and smaller flowers of orange and pink poking through. I chose them for their colours and because chrysanthemums are a symbol of longevity. They are gaudy and made of plastic, cloth and wire. 'Don't take fresh flowers,' said Nonna, 'they'll be dead within a week.' These chrysanthemums will probably outlast us all.

I paused at the gate to look back, to commit the scene to memory. The groundskeeper with his strimmer had appeared and was working his way through our section now, buzzing through the tall grass, spraying the air green. Tens of moony dandelions were meeting their maker, casting their ghost-seeds to the breeze. And along the edges of the graves, where the metal blades couldn't quite reach, some sunny ones stood firm. They will die and resurrect in their own time, whether or not anyone is around to bear witness.

***

Fitzcarraldo Editions
8-12 Creekside
London, SE8 3DX
United Kingdom

ISBN 978-1-913097-97-4

Design by Ray O'Meara
Typeset in Fitzcarraldo
Printed and bound by TJ Books

fitzcarraldoeditions.com

Fitzcarraldo Editions